MAKING SENSE OF CITIZENSHIP

A Continuing Professional Development Handbook

Edited by Ted Huddleston and David Kerr

This Handbook has been developed by the Citizenship Foundation and the Association for Citizenship Teaching in association with the DfES, QCA, OFSTED, Citized and LSDA. It was written by Ted Huddleston, David Kerr and Don Rowe with contributions and expert advice from Tony Breslin, Peter Brett, Hilary Claire, Liz Craft, Julie Easy, Bo Emecheta, Terry Fiehn, Scott Harrison, Roy Honeybone, Lee Jerome, Bernadette Joslin, John Lloyd, Sarah Maclean, Jan Newton, Tony Thorpe and Chris Waller.

It was made possible by funding from the Department for Education and Skills.

The Publishers would like to thank the following for permission to reproduce copyright material:
Photo credits: Ablestock.com: 1; 3; 14; 15; 25; 47; 52; 63; 71; 75; 80; 86; 92; 103; 113; 116; 125; 129; 130; 134; 137; 138; 140; 141; 143; 146; 151; 157; 159; 167; 170; 175; 180-181; 184-185; 195; 201; 204; 205; 211; 215; 216. **DfES:** 11; 29; 38; 91; 104; 152. **iStockphoto.com:** 5; 13; 17; 23; 31; 37; 39; 42; 43; 45; 59; 69; 72; 76; 77; 89; 93; 95; 96-97; 101; 102; 107; 115; 121; 135; 174; 191; 202. **Nomad:** 54; 79; 81; 85. **Photo Alto:** 183. **Photodisc:** 110; 149; 155; 164; 187; 188; 189.
Front Cover: © Jacky Chapman/Photofusion **Back Cover:** Ablestock.com & iStockphoto.com
Acknowledgements: see page 230.
Every effort has been made to trace all copyright holders, but if any have been inadvertently overlooked the Publishers will be pleased to make the necessary arrangements at the first opportunity.

Although every effort has been made to ensure that website addresses are correct at time of going to press, Hodder Murray cannot be held responsible for the content of any website mentioned in this book. It is sometimes possible to find a relocated web page by typing in the address of the home page for a website in the URL window of your browser.

Hodder Headline's policy is to use papers that are natural, renewable and recyclable products and made from wood grown in sustainable forests. The logging and manufacturing processes are expected to conform to the environmental regulations of the country of origin.

Orders: please contact Bookpoint Ltd, 130 Milton Park, Abingdon, Oxon OX14 4SB. Telephone: (44) 01235 827720. Fax: (44) 01235 400454. Lines are open 9.00 -- 6.00, Monday to Saturday, with a 24-hour message answering service. Visit our website at www.hoddereducation.co.uk

© The Citizenship Foundation 2006
First published in 2006 by Hodder Murray, an imprint of Hodder Education, a member of the Hodder Headline Group
338 Euston Road, London NW1 3BH

Impression number   10 9 8 7 6 5 4 3 2 1
Year   2010   2009   2008   2007   2006

Cover photo © Jacky Chapman/Photofusion
Typeset in FormataBQ-Light by Nomad Graphique
Printed in Spain.

A catalogue record for this title is available from the British Library.
ISBN-10: 0340 926 813
ISBN-13: 978 0340 926 819

MAKING SENSE OF CITIZENSHIP

A Continuing Professional Development Handbook

Edited by Ted Huddleston and David Kerr

"We aim at no less than a change in the political culture of this country both nationally and locally: for people to think of themselves as active citizens, willing, able and equipped to have an influence in public life."

The Crick Report, Professor Sir Bernard Crick, 1998

MAKING SENSE OF CITIZENSHIP

Contents

MAKING SENSE OF CITIZENSHIP

Introduction: Using the Handbook

Making Sense of Citizenship is a practical handbook designed to encourage and support continuing professional development in citizenship education.

Why is it needed?

Citizenship education is now recognised as an essential element in the education of all children and young people.

It has been a statutory subject in secondary schools in England since 2002, and is an important dimension of work in primary schools and in post-16 education and training. It is central to the *Every Child Matters* agenda and plays a significant part in the youth work curriculum and in lifelong learning.

For many involved in education and training, citizenship education is very much a new area, one about which they feel uncertain and for which they are not adequately prepared. Its aims, objectives and characteristics are not always well understood and its implications for policy and practice still only partially recognised.

There is an urgent need, therefore, to build on the best emerging practice to develop a more consistent and unified approach to citizenship education – one that will promote high-quality learning and teaching, raise standards and guarantee effective provision across the different phases of education.

What does it aim to do?

The Handbook aims to explain what citizenship education is and what it means in different settings, from schools and colleges to youth and community work and work-based training. It sets out essential information and offers clear guidance on key areas such as:
- aims and objectives
- essential elements
- meeting statutory requirements
- curriculum and whole-school/college planning
- learning and teaching
- co-ordination and management
- assessment, recording and reporting
- continuity and progression
- monitoring and evaluation
- self-review and inspection
- staff training and development.

Who is it for?

The Handbook is for anyone involved in teaching, leading or promoting citizenship education – headteachers and principals, co-ordinators and subject leaders, teachers and lecturers, Advanced Skills Teachers (ASTs) and advisers, teacher educators and trainee teachers, governors and managers, youth workers and voluntary agencies, training providers and employers – in fact, anyone with an interest in citizenship education.

While the emphasis of the Handbook is clearly on secondary schools, on account of the statutory nature of citizenship education in this phase of education, specific attention is also paid to the needs of primary and nursery schools, post-16 education and training and youth and community work.

What is different about it?

The Handbook differs from other publications in the field in seeking to:
- offer a coherent and continuous overview of citizenship education for 3 to19 year-olds
- synthesise the key elements in official guidance documents in language and a style that is simple and accessible
- offer practical advice on how the guidance can be implemented effectively in a range of settings, based on latest developments
- encourage reflection on practice through specially designed questions and training exercises that seek to improve that practice.

How is it organised?

The Handbook is divided into six sections. Sections 1, 5 and 6 deal with issues that apply across all phases of education, such as the aims and purposes of citizenship education, continuity and progression, resources and training methods. Sections 2, 3 and 4 focus on issues more relevant to the specific phases – that is to say:
- Section 2: primary and nursery schools
- Section 3: secondary schools
- Section 4: post-16 education and training.

The six sections are subdivided into chapters. Chapters are organised into a number of two-page spreads, each of which deals with a separate topic using an easy-to-follow, question-and-answer format. The questions have been carefully chosen to draw attention to the issues of most immediate concern in relation to the topic dealt with. The answers are illustrated with practical examples, brief case studies, and suggestions and/or advice from those with experience in the field.

In every two-page spread there is an '**Improving practice**' feature which contains tasks and exercises designed to stimulate reflection on issues raised in that topic. In addition, there are a number of longer training exercises at the end of selected chapters. These tasks and exercises are intended as an aid to professional development and may be used in CPD training or for self-study.

Further information – including extracts from official documents, other resources for CPD training and development, and details of helpful organisations – is contained in a series of appendices at the end of the Handbook.

How should it be used?

It is not intended that the Handbook be read from beginning to end as a continuous narrative, but rather that particular topics should be selected for consideration as and when appropriate.

They can be read by individuals simply for their own information or advice, or photocopied and used as stimulus material to support initial or continuing professional development – the 'Improving practice' features contain examples of the kinds of discussion question and reflective exercise that might be offered in training sessions or workshops of this kind.

Wherever possible, topics from the Handbook should be considered alongside the relevant sections from other training and development resources, such as *The School Self-Evaluation Tool for Citizenship Education*; *Introducing Citizenship,* a handbook and training video for primary schools; *Raising the Standard,* a handbook and training video for secondary schools; and *Play your part: post-16 citizenship*. Helpful advice will also be found in *The Citizenship Co-ordinator's Handbook*. Details of these and other useful publications can be found in Appendix 9 on page 229.

Is it the final word?

Making Sense of Citizenship does not pretend to be the final word on citizenship education. Rather, its contribution is to represent the 'state of the art' as it appears at the time of writing. In due course, there will be new debates to be had, new ideas to be refined and new policies and practices to consider. The intention is that the Handbook will be updated to take these into account as and when necessary.

We hope that this Handbook provides a stimulus to continuing professional development in citizenship education and promotes a culture of reflection and discussion aimed at improving practice and raising the standard of provision.

Ted Huddleston
David Kerr
Don Rowe

Section 1:
What Is Citizenship?

Chapter 1:
Spelling It Out

Introduction

> Citizenship is more than a subject. If taught well and
> tailored to local needs, its skills and values will enhance
> democratic life for all of us, both rights and responsibilities,
> beginning in school and radiating out.

Bernard Crick, **National Curriculum Citizenship, 1999**

What you understand by citizenship education will determine the attitude you take towards it
and how you try to incorporate it into your professional practice. It is important from the
very beginning, therefore, to develop a clear understanding of what citizenship education is –
both as an individual and at an institutional level – and how it impacts on young people.

The aim of this first chapter is to help you to clarify and answer some of the generic
questions that apply to citizenship education, wherever it takes place.

It is relevant to anyone involved in teaching, leading or promoting citizenship education,
whether in the formal or informal education sector.

Contents include:
   What is citizenship?
   Why is citizenship important?
   Where does citizenship occur?
   What is citizenship for?
   How is citizenship learned?
   What makes citizenship distinctive?
   What citizenship education is and is not

Issues raised here are looked at in more detail in subsequent sections of the Handbook.

What is citizenship?

How you understand citizenship affects your attitude towards it and the relevance it has for your everyday professional practice. It is important at the outset, therefore, to have a clear understanding of what is meant by terms like 'citizen' and 'citizenship', and how they are used in education.

What does it mean to be a citizen?

A citizen is a member of a political community or state. How you become a citizen depends upon different factors, for example place of birth, family ties or period of residence in a country.

What is citizenship?

The term 'citizenship' has several different meanings:

- **A legal and political status**
  In its simplest meaning, 'citizenship' is used to refer to the status of being a **citizen** – that is, to being a member of a particular political community or state. Citizenship in this sense brings with it certain rights and responsibilities that are defined in law, such as the right to vote, the responsibility to pay tax and so on. It is sometimes referred to as nationality, and is what is meant when someone talks about 'applying for', 'getting', or being 'refused' citizenship.

- **Involvement in public life and affairs**
  The term 'citizenship' is also used to refer to involvement in public life and affairs – that is, to the behaviour and actions of a citizen. It is sometimes known as **active citizenship**. Citizenship in this sense is applied to a wide range of activities – from voting in elections and standing for political office to taking an interest in politics and current affairs. It refers not only to rights and responsibilities laid down in the law, but also to general forms of behaviour – social and moral – which societies expect of their citizens. What these rights, responsibilities and forms of behaviour should be is an area of on-going public debate, with people holding a range of views.

- **An educational activity**
  Finally, 'citizenship' is used to refer to an educational activity – that is, to the process of helping people learn how to become active, informed and responsible citizens. Citizenship in this sense is also known as **citizenship education** or education for citizenship. It encompasses all forms of education, from informal education in the home or through youth work to more formal types of education provided in schools, colleges, universities, training organisations and the workplace. At the formal end of the spectrum, it gives its name both to a distinct subject in the National Curriculum for 11 to 16 year-olds and to a general area of study leading to an academic qualification – both of which, confusingly, are sometimes spelled with a small and sometimes a capital 'C'!

In this Handbook we are primarily concerned with citizenship as an educational process. Following common practice, we use the term 'citizenship' interchangeably with 'citizenship education' and 'education for citizenship'.

IMPROVING PRACTICE

1   What does it mean to you to be a citizen? What has influenced your understanding of citizenship? To what extent has your understanding been affected by your educational experience?

2   How do the rights and responsibilities a person has as a citizen differ from those that come with being, say, a family member or a friend? Think of some examples.

3   What forms of behaviour should we expect of someone who is a citizen of this country in addition to those laid down in the law? Is it fair to ask schools to encourage these forms of behaviour? If so, what can they do to encourage them?

Why is citizenship important?

Why teach citizenship?

The principal justification for citizenship education derives from the nature of **democracy**.

Democracies need active, informed and responsible citizens – citizens who are willing and able to take responsibility for themselves and their communities and contribute to the political process.

These capacities do not develop unaided. They have to be learned. While a certain amount of citizenship may be picked up through ordinary experience in the home or at work, it can never in itself be sufficient to equip citizens for the sort of active role required of them in today's complex and diverse society.

If citizens are to become genuinely involved in public life and affairs, a more explicit approach to citizenship education is required – this approach should be:

- **inclusive** – an entitlement for all young people regardless of their ability or background
- **pervasive** – not limited to schools, but an integral part of all education for young people
- **lifelong** – continuing throughout life.

> We should not, must not, dare not, be complacent about the health and future of British democracy. Unless we become a nation of engaged citizens, our democracy is not secure.
>
> Lord Chancellor, 1998

How does it benefit young people?

Citizenship education benefits young people by helping to address the outcomes for well-being in the *Every Child Matters* programme.

It helps them to develop **self-confidence** and successfully deal with significant life changes and challenges such as bullying and discrimination.

It gives them a **voice** – in the life of their schools, in their communities and in society at large.

It enables them to **make a positive contribution** – by developing the expertise and experience needed to claim their rights and understand their responsibilities, and preparing them for the challenges and opportunities of adult and working life.

> Citizenship is an opportunity for me to explore my social and political views, something young people have been deprived of in the past.
>
> David, Youthcomm,
> **Citizenship News**

Who else does it benefit?

Citizenship also brings benefits for schools, other educational organisations and for society at large.

For schools and other educational organisations, it helps to produce motivated and responsible learners, who relate positively to each other, to staff and to the surrounding community.

For society, it helps to create an active and responsible citizenry, willing to participate in the life of the nation and the wider world and play its part in the democratic process.

> Citizenship is becoming a cornerstone subject in our education system – and rightly so. After its introduction only a few years ago we have seen schools and students embrace the subject unlike perhaps any other. It is a gateway to a more inclusive society.
>
> Stephen Twigg,
> Former Education Minister

IMPROVING PRACTICE

1 To what extent do you think citizenship education is able to make a difference to:

a) voter turnout?
b) crime rates?
c) attitudes towards politics?
d) race relations?
e) charitable giving?
f) our sense of national identity?
g) the health of the economy?

Is it right to expect citizenship education to affect these things? Why or why not?

2 Should citizenship education be expected to solve social problems? If not, what is its purpose?

3 Which aspects of citizenship do you think are the least likely to be picked up in the home or at work and need to be taught explicitly? How do you suggest these can be taught? What sorts of experience can a school offer that is not generally available in the home or the family?

4 Imagine you are recruiting young people for a new citizenship education course or project. What would you say to promote it, for example, on a poster, in a leaflet or in a prospectus?

Where does citizenship occur?

KEY ISSUES

When does citizenship
education begin?

Where can it be taught?

When does citizenship education begin?

Citizenship education is a lifelong process. It begins implicitly in the home and the immediate neighbourhood – with questions about identity and relationships, making choices and ideas of fairness and of right and wrong.

Where can it be taught?

As their horizons expand, children can be introduced to explicit forms of citizenship education in more formal settings:

1 Citizenship in the early years
Citizenship education contributes to several of the areas of learning set out in the *Curriculum Guidance for the Foundation Stage* – in particular, to:
- personal, social and emotional development
- communication, language and literacy
- knowledge and understanding of the world.

2 Citizenship in primary schools
While not a statutory requirement, citizenship teaching has become an important part of the curriculum in primary schools. At primary level, citizenship education is taught alongside and makes an important contribution to the promotion of pupils' personal and social development, including health and well-being.

The *Framework for PSHE and citizenship at Key Stages 1 and 2* sets out the knowledge, understanding and skills recommended for teaching in four 'strands' (see Appendices 1 and 2 on pages 217 and 219):

- Developing confidence and responsibility and making the most of their abilities
- Preparing to play an active role as citizens
- Developing a healthy, safer lifestyle
- Developing good relationships and respecting the differences between people.

> Schemes of work for key stages 1 and 2 are available at: **www.standards.dfes.gov.uk**

3 Citizenship in secondary schools
At secondary level, citizenship education is a statutory subject for 11 to 16 year-olds. The statutory requirements are set out in the National Curriculum programmes of study in three 'strands':
- Knowledge and understanding about becoming informed citizens
- Developing skills of enquiry and communication
- Developing skills of participation and responsible action.

Apart from the absence of an eight-level scale of achievement, citizenship education is treated exactly the same as other National Curriculum subjects at key stages 3 and 4, including:
- annual reports to parents
- assessment at the end of key stage 3
- GCSE qualification
- Ofsted inspection.

> Schemes of work for key stages 3 and 4 are available at: **www.standards.dfes.gov.uk**

4 Citizenship in other settings

Citizenship education – though not always labelled as such – has long been a mainstay of youth and community work, encouraging young people to play an active part in the life of their communities, through initiatives such as:

- youth conferences, forums and councils
- peer education
- intergenerational work
- participation projects
- community regeneration
- designing and developing youth facilities
- campaigns on national and international issues.

Increasingly, citizenship education is also becoming an important aspect of education in the **formal post-16 sector** – in sixth forms, tertiary and further education colleges, and in vocational training – for example, through:

- enrichment activities
- accredited courses
- conferences and whole-day events
- tutorial sessions
- student councils and forums
- representation on governing bodies and committees
- college campaigns and community action
- citizenship content in vocational courses.

WWW

Guidance for providers of post-16 citizenship programmes is available in **Play Your Part: Post-16 citizenship** at **www.qca.org/uk/citizenship/post16** and **Make It Happen: effective practice in post-16 citizenship** at **www.post16citizenship.org/materials**

IMPROVING PRACTICE

1 Are some aspects of citizenship taught more easily in certain educational settings than others? If so, which and why?

2 In your own practice, to what extent do you build on the work of or collaborate with practitioners from other phases or sectors of education? What could you do to build a greater element of continuity into young people's citizenship experiences?

3 Arrange a visit to observe citizenship practice in a different phase or sector of education, or invite a fellow practitioner from a different phase to talk to you about their work or talk to young people about their prior citizenship experiences.

What is citizenship for?

What is the aim of citizenship education?

Wherever it occurs, citizenship education has the same basic aims and purposes. It is education *for* citizenship – that is, education which aims to help people learn how to become active, informed and responsible citizens. More specifically, it aims to prepare them for life as citizens of a democracy.

Different characteristics are required by citizens in different types of political system. The characteristics required of people living as free and equal citizens in a democratic society differ significantly from those of people living under, say, a totalitarian regime.

Democracies depend upon citizens who, among other things, are:
- aware of their rights and responsibilities as citizens
- informed about the social and political world
- concerned about the welfare of others
- articulate in their opinions and arguments
- capable of having an influence on the world
- active in their communities
- responsible in how they act as citizens.

What are its essential elements?

Citizenship education involves a wide range of different elements of learning, including:

- **knowledge and understanding** – e.g. about topics such as laws and rules, the democratic process, the media, human rights, diversity, money and the economy, sustainable development and world as a global community; and about concepts, such as democracy, justice, equality, freedom, authority and the rule of law

- **skills and aptitudes** – e.g. critical thinking, analysing information, expressing opinions, taking part in discussions and debates, negotiating, conflict resolution and participating in community action

- **values and dispositions** – e.g. respect for justice, democracy and the rule of law, openness, tolerance, courage to defend a point of view, and a willingness to listen to, work with and stand up for others.

How are the different elements connected?

This cube helps to explain the interrelationship between the essential elements in citizenship education and the need to include all of them in a developmental way in every stage of a young person's education.

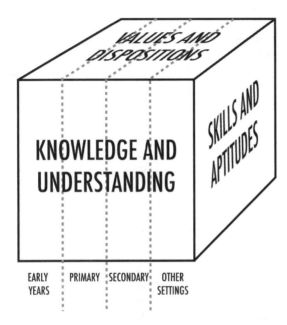

It is artificial to try to separate out the learning of skills from knowledge, knowledge from values and so on. In practice, they are generally learned simultaneously rather than in isolation. For example, in presenting and explaining the findings of a survey to local council officials, young people will be building up their knowledge of local government and its functions at the same time as honing their skills of presentation.

IMPROVING PRACTICE

1 Choose one aspect of citizenship learning – for example, laws and rules – and try to think of different activities through which it might be approached at different stages in a young person's education.

2 What different kinds of citizenship learning do you think might come out of:

a) a debate about immigration?
b) a whole-day event on human rights?
c) a mock election?
d) a visit to a magistrates' court?

How is citizenship learned?

What is the most effective form of learning in citizenship?

The most effective form of learning in citizenship education is:
- active – emphasises learning by doing
- interactive – uses discussion and debate
- relevant – focuses on real-life issues facing young people and society
- critical – encourages young people to think for themselves
- collaborative – employs group work and co-operative learning
- participative – gives young people a say in their own learning.

Learning of this sort requires a certain kind of climate in which to flourish – an environment that is non-threatening, in which young people can express their opinions freely and without embarrassment and use their initiative without undue fear of failure. Such a climate takes time to develop and is built up gradually.

Where does citizenship learning take place?

Citizenship learning takes place in three distinct areas of the life of an educational institution: through its taught curriculum, its culture and ethos, and its links with the wider community. They are increasingly known as the 'three Cs' of citizenship education: curriculum, culture and community.

1   **Taught curriculum**
    First, citizenship learning takes place through the taught, or formal, curriculum of an institution, in the form of:
    - a discrete subject, course, or activity, or
    - an element in other subjects, courses or activities, or
    - a combination of these.

2   **Culture and ethos**
    Second, citizenship is learned through the culture or ethos of the institution – that is, through the values on which the institution operates and the manner in which it goes about its daily business. It is most effective when it takes place in a culture that values young people and encourages them to take an active part in the life of the organisation, through:
    - having a say in their learning – e.g. initiating projects, generating discussion questions, self-assessment
    - playing a part in decision-making – e.g. student forums, school and/or student councils
    - taking on positions of responsibility – e.g. classroom monitor, peer mediator, school councillor.

3   **Wider community**
    Third, citizenship is learned through opportunities for involvement in the local community and the wider world, e.g. through:
    - school linking and exchanges
    - intergenerational projects
    - peer education
    - developing local facilities
    - talking to politicians, police and community leaders
    - campaigns and fundraising.

How do you make it explicit?

If young people are to develop a broad and balanced view of what it means to be a citizen, it is important that these different opportunities for citizenship learning are made explicit and are consistent in the messages they give out.

It is particularly important for the inspection process. Ofsted looks for breadth and balance in citizenship programmes and expects the contributions of different aspects of school life to be identified in written policies.

One way to draw these together is by building them into the assessment process, with young people recording and commenting on their involvement in the life of the organisation and its links with the community as well as on their formal learning.

Another way is by drawing attention to the range of citizenship opportunities available in an institution or project through promotional material, such as course books, prospectuses or citizenship 'manifestos'.

IMPROVING PRACTICE

1   How far do you think the prevailing ethos in your institution reflects the aims and principles of citizenship education in terms of daily practice?

2   What different kinds of citizenship learning do you think are best developed through:

   a) taught curricula?
   b) culture and ethos?
   c) community links?

3   Choose a citizenship project you have been involved in or have observed and evaluate it in terms of the criteria for effective citizenship learning listed here. How well does the project you have chosen stand up to this sort of scrutiny?

What makes citizenship distinctive?

KEY ISSUES

Where does citizenship overlap with other subjects?

Why is it important to distinguish between them?

What is distinctive about citizenship education?

Where does citizenship overlap with other subjects?

Many of the themes explored in citizenship education occur in other areas of education, for example, drug/alcohol education in personal, social and health education (PSHE), communication in key skills, and employment issues in careers education.

There is also considerable overlap between the forms of learning used in citizenship and in other subjects, for example active learning, group work and discussion are common throughout the curriculum in both the formal and informal sector.

> What I can say is that a school providing good citizenship education is also doing well in terms of the **Every Child Matters** agenda of making a contribution.
>
> David Bell, Chief Inspector of Schools, 2005

Why is it important to distinguish between them?

It is important to be aware that just because a certain theme or form of learning occurs elsewhere doesn't necessarily make that activity a *citizenship* activity. Unless you are able to distinguish between citizenship education and other subjects:

- there is a danger that citizenship will be subsumed in other activities and young people won't receive their entitlement to citizenship learning
- you will be unable to make citizenship learning explicit, which is essential if young people are to develop a broad and balanced view of what being a citizen involves and a pre-requisite for inspection
- you will make little progress in your understanding of citizenship issues or how they may be made accessible to young people.

What is distinctive about citizenship education?

Citizenship education is distinguished by its content, focus and approach to learning.

1 **Distinctive content**
   There is a central core of learning – factual and conceptual – not addressed in other school subjects, including:
   - criminal and civil law
   - government and politics
   - electoral systems
   - taxation and the economy
   - role of the EU, the Commonwealth and the UN
   - concepts such as democracy, justice and the rule of law.

2 **Distinctive focus**
   Citizenship education focuses on topical everyday issues that concern young people as citizens – that is, as members of society with legal rights and responsibilities, e.g. education, health care, welfare benefits, public transport, policing, immigration, international relations and the environment.

   These are to be distinguished from issues that concern young people as private individuals – that is, issues which are personal or relate only to family or friends – e.g. applying for a job is a personal issue, the minimum wage is a citizenship one; drinking is a personal issue, the law on alcohol use is a citizenship one; what you look for in a friend is a personal issue, their political opinion is a citizenship one.

3 Distinctive approach to learning

Citizenship learning develops through active involvement. Young people learn what it means to be a citizen through discussions and debates in the classroom, and participation in the life of the school or college and in the wider community. They are given opportunities both to develop their learning and to put it into practice in 'real life' situations.

Citizenship issues are:
- real – actually affect people's lives
- topical – current today
- sometimes sensitive – can affect people at a personal level, especially when family or friends are involved
- often controversial – people disagree and hold strong opinions about them
- ultimately moral – relate to what people think is right or wrong, good or bad, important or unimportant in society.

> **FOCUS**
>
> The ACiS (Active Citizenship in Schools) project talks about making citizenship education **REAL** = **R**elevant, **E**ngaged, **A**ctive **L**earning.

IMPROVING PRACTICE

1 **Consider the following themes:**

   a) **bullying**
   b) **personal safety**
   c) **sex and relationships**
   d) **eating disorders**
   e) **mental health**
   f) **children's rights.**

   For each one, think of issues that might concern young people as citizens (rather than as private individuals).

2 **How would you explain the difference between life as a citizen and life as a private individual to young people?**

3 **Devise a training exercise to help colleagues recognise what is distinctive about citizenship education.**

What citizenship education is and is not

Citizenship education IS NOT:

- optional for students, teachers or schools
- about the indoctrination of young people
- about teachers following a particular political agenda
- to be confused with personal, social and health education (PSHE) or the National Healthy Schools initiative
- to be subsumed into other parts of or a 'bolt-on' to the curriculum
- just about feelings, values, school ethos or circle time
- just about volunteering, charity work and doing 'good deeds'
- solely about what goes on in schools.

Citizenship education IS:

- an entitlement for all young people
- relevant to the everyday concerns and experiences of young people
- about helping young people to think for themselves
- progressive and developmental
- active, enjoyable and stimulating
- rigorous and challenging
- a real curriculum subject with a clear aim and a distinctive core which includes a defined knowledge and understanding component
- co-ordinated and taught by skilled teachers who have specialist knowledge and the necessary skills, approaches and confidence
- about contributing to raising school standards and student achievement
- an essential part of the school curriculum, which links the curriculum, school culture and the wider community
- of benefit to young people, teachers, schools and their wider communities
- about contributing to creating more effective partnerships between schools and their wider communities
- a lifelong learning process.

Chapter 2:
Laying the Foundations

Introduction

> A main focus of citizenship education should be to empower children. Even at this young age, they should feel that they can have an influence on their community and environment

Emma Valerio, **Advice to a Primary School**,
London Metropolitan University, 2004

No one becomes an active citizen by accident. Like everything else, it has to be learned. This chapter is concerned with citizenship learning in the foundation stage (3 to 5 year-olds) and in key stages 1 and 2 (5 to 11 year-olds).

It is relevant to anyone involved in teaching, leading or promoting citizenship education in primary schools, nursery schools and other early education settings.

Contents include:
Citizenship 3–11
The foundation stage
Key stages 1 and 2
Planning for citizenship in primary schools
Citizenship in the primary curriculum
Citizenship in the life of the primary school
Citizenship through community involvement
Circle time, class and school councils
Learning and teaching strategies
Leadership, management and co-ordination
Assessment, recording and reporting
Case studies: 1) Pupil participation
                   2) Pupil involvement in community life
Training exercises: 1) Developing an assessment tool
                   2) Writing a Year 5 report
                   3) Citizenship education through nursery rhymes

The chapter should be read in conjunction with the *Framework for PSHE and Citizenship at Key Stages 1 and 2* (see Appendices 1 and 2 on pages 217 and 219) and *Introducing Citizenship: A handbook for primary schools* (A&C Black, 2001).

Citizenship 3–11

KEY ISSUES

Why teach citizenship to young children?

How does it benefit them?

What other benefits does it have?

Aren't children too young for this?

Where do you begin?

When do you start using the word 'citizen'?

REMEMBER

At the age of ten, children are generally considered by the law to have reached the age of criminal responsibility.

Why teach citizenship to young children?

While young children pick up a certain amount of citizenship learning through their families and communities, it can never be enough to prepare them for their active role as citizens in today's complex, fast-paced and diverse society. Citizenship experiences need to be connected and built upon as young people progress through their education.

> If children are to be empowered as citizens then they need to learn in an environment that recognises them as citizens; treats and respects them as citizens and provides opportunities to practise and then develop skills which make people responsible citizens.
>
> **Time for Rights,** Unicef and Save the Children, 2002

How does it benefit them?

Citizenship education benefits children by helping to address the outcomes for well-being in the Every Child Matters programme.

It promotes a safe environment and helps children to develop a positive sense of self and deal with issues such as bullying and discrimination.

It helps them to learn how to express their opinions and ideas, and understand and make informed choices about their communities and the environment.

What other benefits does it have?

Citizenship education helps to promote positive behaviour and relationships, supports inclusion and equal opportunities, and links schools and other early education settings with parents, neighbours and community partners.

Aren't children too young for this?

While they may lack knowledge and experience to deal with citizenship issues expressed in adult terms, children are quite capable of making sense of them when presented within familiar contexts, for example, learning about the law through agreeing class rules, talking to a community police officer or listening to and discussing a story about a child who steals.

Where do you begin?

Citizenship education begins with children's existing knowledge, skills and understanding, for example with what they think is fair and unfair about the world they live in.

Children are exposed to citizenship issues from a range of sources – family, peers, community and media as well as school. Contrary to opinion, children's awareness is not restricted to their immediate surroundings. They know about a range of regional, national, European and global issues – such as crime, war and natural disasters – and often have a rudimentary knowledge of politics, for example about the Prime Minister or the Queen. For this reason, citizenship education often begins with activities designed to establish prior learning, such as:

- brainstorming
- interpreting an incident, story or picture
- drawing or writing a spontaneous response to a question
- 'rounds' – everyone in turn contributing something they know about a topic.

When do you start using the word 'citizen'?

Initially, language is learned through use, not definitions. It is important, therefore, to familiarise children with the use of key words like 'citizen' and 'active citizen' from the earliest years. One way is through examples, such as pointing to an example of respectful behaviour and explaining 'that's how good citizens behave', or saying 'this is how citizens decide' during a circle-time discussion.

IMPROVING PRACTICE

1   Ask your pupils to list some things they think are unfair:

   a) at home
   b) in school
   c) in their neighbourhood
   d) in the wider world.

   Choose two or three of their suggestions and think of activities you could use to help pupils begin to explore them.

2   Find a picture or a story to illustrate a topical citizenship issue – local, national, European or global. Brainstorm with your pupils what they know about this issue.

3   At what age would you expect children to be able to use terms like:

   a) 'fairness'?
   b) 'rights and responsibilities'?
   c) 'democracy'?
   d) 'government'?

The foundation stage

KEY ISSUES

What does citizenship involve in the foundation stage?

What kinds of learning is it concerned with?

How is it learned?

How does it contribute to the statutory 'areas of learning'?

What about the 'early learning goals'?

What does citizenship involve in the foundation stage?

Citizenship education in the foundation stage is about helping children to begin to understand what it is to be a member of a community.

What kinds of learning is it concerned with?

Citizenship education is concerned with a range of ways of learning at the foundation stage, including:

1 Finding out about:
- home and family life
- people and places in the neighbourhood
- roles people play in community life
- issues affecting children locally and in the wider world.

2 Understanding:
- how one's actions affect others
- how others are different and need to be treated with respect
- why rules are important.

3 Being able to:
- express opinions and explain views
- listen to others
- talk about issues of fairness, right and wrong
- agree and follow rules
- take and share responsibility
- work as part of a group.

> Much of citizenship in the early years is about socialisation, the need for give and take in play situations and learning to take responsibility in ways which contribute to the well-being of their widening community.
>
> Hampshire County Council, in **Citizenship Education: A planning framework for citizenship in schools**, 1998

How is it learned?

Citizenship education at the foundation stage is learned through:

1 **Curriculum activities** – such as:
- stories – e.g. about fair/unfair situations
- puppets – exploring issues of right/wrong through characters
- role play – activities like shopping, or using public transport
- photographs, videos, TV and newspaper stories – on topical issues affecting children
- visits – to events/places in the neighbourhood
- visitors to the school – e.g. community leaders, police officers, nurses
- games – encouraging cooperation, collaboration and making rules
- play – learning to give and take
- circle time – discussing real issues relating to the classroom or the wider community.

2 Initiating activities and **making choices** – such as:
- choosing play partners
- selecting materials
- deciding on games to play
- voting on a group issue
- electing a representative for the class/school council.

3 Taking responsibility – such as:
- agreeing rules
- tidying up after an activity
- fetching items needed
- acting as register monitor
- looking after pets
- welcoming new children and showing them round.

How does it contribute to the statutory 'areas of learning'?

Citizenship education contributes to several of the areas of learning in the foundation stage curriculum, in particular:
- Personal, social and emotional development
- Communication, language and literacy
- Knowledge and understanding of the world.

What about the 'early learning goals'?

Citizenship learning can be used to provide evidence of achievement towards a number of the early learning goals, such as:
- knowing classroom rules and being able to offer explanations about why it is important to keep them – e.g. explaining how running in the classroom could cause an accident
- being aware of consequences of words and actions – e.g. explaining how to make the room safer for a child with a visual impairment
- using language to imagine and recreate roles and experience – e.g. role-playing a 'lollipop person' on duty at a road crossing.

IMPROVING PRACTICE

1 Think of some children's stories that deal with fair/unfair situations. Choose one and consider how you could use it to develop citizenship learning. Which early learning goals could this contribute towards?

2 What kinds of citizenship learning could you build into a role play on children and parents? How would you do this? Which early learning goals could this contribute towards?

3 Which of the curriculum activities listed here do you use in your current teaching? Choose one with which you are less familiar and plan some citizenship learning around it.

KEY ISSUES

What is the legal status of citizenship at key stages 1 and 2?

How is it different from PSHE?

Why is it important to distinguish between them?

Does it have to be assessed?

Will it be inspected?

What is the legal status of citizenship at key stages 1 and 2?

At key stages 1 and 2, citizenship education is part of the **non-statutory Framework for PSHE and citizenship** that came into effect alongside the revised curriculum in August 2000 (Appendices 1 and 2 on pages 217 and 219).

The knowledge, understanding and skills to be taught in PSHE and citizenship are set out in the non-statutory framework as four interrelated 'strands':

1 Developing confidence and responsibility and making the most of their abilities
2 Preparing to play an active role as citizens
3 Developing a healthy, safer lifestyle
4 Developing good relationships and respecting the differences between people.

How these are taught is left to the judgement of the school and the needs of its pupils and local community.

How is it different from PSHE?

Citizenship education and PSHE overlap in a number of ways in primary school, for example, in their emphasis on values and attitudes and their concern to empower pupils to act effectively and with self-confidence. However, citizenship education differs from PSHE in terms of:

- **Focus**
  While PSHE deals with issues of personal decision-making and interpersonal relations, citizenship education focuses on the pupil's **public** or **social self**. It deals with rules and laws, rights and responsibilities in school and the community, looking after the neighbourhood and the environment, and so on. It helps pupils to make sense of topical issues that they hear about, e.g. natural disasters, vandalism or racism.

- **Content**
  Citizenship education also has a distinct **core of learning** – about how democracy works, the law and how it affects people, voting, political institutions, how the country is governed, and international organisations.

- **Approach**
  Citizenship education is learned through **active involvement** – through research and enquiry, discussions and debates, and participation in the life of the school and the community.

Why is it important to distinguish between them?

It is important to distinguish between citizenship education and PSHE in order to ensure proper provision of each component in the framework.

> In most schools, the citizenship element of the non-statutory guidelines for PSHE and citizenship has not been thought through sufficiently. Provision for citizenship education remains very vague and important themes are omitted. These include work on laws, democracy and democratic institutions, different identities of the United Kingdom (schools generally deal with bullying, but far less so with racism), sustainable development and the media.
>
> Ofsted, 2002

Does it have to be assessed?

There are currently no statutory requirements for an end of key stage assessment in PSHE and citizenship at key stages 1 and 2. However, schools are required to keep records of the progress of all pupils and report this to parents, PSHE and citizenship included.

Will it be inspected?

Ofsted inspects the implementation of the Framework for PSHE and citizenship in accordance with the *Framework for the Inspection of Schools in England* since September 2005 (www.ofsted.gov.uk).

IMPROVING PRACTICE

1 Look at the sections on 'breadth of study' in the non-statutory Framework for PSHE and citizenship (Appendices 1 and 2, pages 217 and 219). To what extent do you provide these opportunities for pupils in your school? Do you think more could be done to extend this provision? If so, what?

2 Using the non-statutory framework, draw up some learning objectives specific to citizenship for the following activities:

a) a discussion about behaviour and school rules
b) an event to raise money for charity
c) a project on an historical issue, e.g. poverty or child labour
d) a meeting of the class council
e) an assembly about a significant historical figure, e.g. Martin Luther King or Anne Frank.

Say how you would organise the activity so as to achieve these objectives.

Planning for citizenship in primary schools

Why is it important to develop a whole-school approach?

While the citizenship element in the PSHE and citizenship curriculum has definite content – that is to say, knowledge, skills and understanding to acquire – it is clearly more than a 'subject'. It involves a wide range of learning activities and opportunities throughout the school both within and beyond the formal curriculum. A whole-school approach is essential in order to be able to integrate these different activities into a coherent programme that makes sense to everyone involved.

Case studies of a whole-school approach to planning provision for citizenship in primary schools can be found in **Appendix 2** of **Citizenship: a scheme of work for key stages 1 and 2: www.standards.dfes.gov.uk/schemes2**

What are the basic elements?

There are three basic elements in a whole-school approach to citizenship education:

1. **Citizenship in the curriculum**
2. **Citizenship in the life of the school**
3. **Citizenship through community involvement.**

Each is important in its own right and should be given due attention in the planning process.

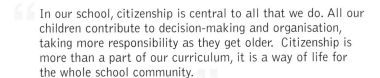

> In our school, citizenship is central to all that we do. All our children contribute to decision-making and organisation, taking more responsibility as they get older. Citizenship is more than a part of our curriculum, it is a way of life for the whole school community.

Dame Mavis Grant, Headteacher, Canning School, Newcastle-upon-Tyne

Where do you start?

The way to start is with an **audit** of what your school is already providing, for example through:

- separate PSHE and citizenship lessons
- project work
- opportunities in other subjects – including literacy and numeracy
- suspended timetable activities
- positions of responsibility
- community-based activities and visits
- class and/or school councils
- circle time
- assemblies
- European and international links.

On the basis of the audit, you can draw up a scheme of work for each year. The scheme of work should contain all your school's planned learning opportunities for citizenship, including in the taught curriculum, in the life of the school and through community involvement. It should be broken down into manageable activities that can be delivered, assessed and evaluated, including, for example, class projects such as 'My Family', or a specific discussion focus for circle time.

WWW
Exemplar schemes of work for citizenship in primary schools are available in
Citizenship: a scheme of work for key stages 1 and 2:
www.standards.dfes.gov.uk/schemes2

Who needs to be involved?

To develop a genuinely whole-school approach to citizenship education you need to involve the whole school. This includes **parents** and **non-teaching staff** as well as governors, teachers, classroom assistants and pupils.

You may also wish to involve representatives from local **community groups**. Not only does this generate wider support for your programme, but it also raises awareness of the subject and sends out a clear message about its importance in school life.

You may find it helpful to compile an up-to-date register of contacts that the school can draw upon in planning and developing citizenship.

WWW
A range of contacts for projects across all subjects is available at:
www.csvcommunitypartners.org.uk

IMPROVING PRACTICE

1   Draw up a grid that could be used to audit provision of the citizenship aspects of the Framework for PSHE and citizenship in a primary school. (The Framework can be found in Appendices 1 and 2 on pages 217 and 219.)

2   Which aspects of citizenship do you think are best delivered:

   a) through the formal curriculum?
   b) in other ways?

3   What provision is currently made for the citizenship element in the Framework for PSHE and citizenship in your school? In what ways, if any, do you think this provision could be improved? What and who might this involve?

Citizenship in the primary curriculum

How can citizenship be integrated into the primary curriculum?

There are a number of ways of integrating citizenship education into the primary curriculum, including through:

- separate lessons
- project work
- other subjects – including literacy and numeracy
- suspended timetable activities
- assemblies.

How important is it to have separate lessons?

It is not necessary to have separate citizenship lessons, but it is essential to have some discrete time for citizenship at key stage 2. This helps pupils to recognise the distinctiveness of citizenship issues and to develop their citizenship knowledge, understanding and skills.

What role can project work play?

Project work can make a significant contribution to citizenship education in two ways:

1 **Cross-curricular projects with citizenship components, e.g. a project on water that includes questions about pollution, or fluoridisation etc.**
2 **Projects that focus on school or community issues, e.g. on rules (school), or road safety (wider community).**

What opportunities are there in other subjects?

There are opportunities for integrating citizenship education into all National Curriculum subjects, for example:

- **English** – gang warfare and conflict resolution in *Romeo and Juliet*
- **history** – child labour and health in Victorian Britain
- **geography** – global interdependence
- **maths** – use of money in society
- **science** – the natural environment and how people look after it
- **design and technology** – effect of products on how we live
- **RE** – religious identity and diversity
- **music** – cultural identity and diversity
- **ICT** – researching topical issues via the internet
- **art and design** – using imagination to understand other people's experiences.

How this is done will vary from school to school, depending on the needs of the pupils and the expertise available.

Citizenship education in turn is able to contribute to aspects of the National Literacy and Numeracy Strategies – such as:

- understanding, using and writing non-fiction texts
- developing technical vocabulary
- planning, drafting, revising and editing writing
- using numeracy to develop financial capability
- employing data-handling skills to present the results of research.

REMEMBER

Contributions from other subjects only become citizenship education when they deal with issues that are topical and relate to real-life concerns. For example, work on a current natural disaster or current issues relating immigration and discrimination could form part of a study on the Irish famine in key stage 2 history.

What about suspended timetable events?

Suspending the timetable and focusing the class or whole school on a single theme for a day or a week is a good way of creating time for citizenship learning and allows for more extended learning activities.

It offers opportunities for pupils to plan and work together, and take more responsibility for their own learning. Examples might include:

- a children's rights day
- a mock election
- a visit to a police station
- a visit to a museum
- a charity week.

WWW | Further examples of themed activity days or weeks can be found in the QCA booklet, **Taking Part: developing opportunities for children to participate: www.standards.dfes.gov.uk/schemes2**

How can assemblies contribute?

Assemblies are particularly useful for dealing with topical issues – either in the school community or the wider world particularly if they involve some follow-up, i.e. – are not 'one-offs'. They provide important opportunities for pupils to learn how to organise and make public presentations and develop their presentation skills.

IMPROVING PRACTICE

1 What are the advantages and disadvantages of each of the different approaches to integrating citizenship into the primary curriculum? Which approaches are currently in use in your school?

2 Choose a National Curriculum subject and think of ways in which it might be used to deliver aspects of citizenship at key stages 1 and 2.

Citizenship in the life of the primary school

Why should pupils be involved in the life of their school?

Involving pupils in the life of their school is important because it encourages them to see themselves as members of a community. It helps them to gain confidence and acquire new skills, knowledge and understanding. It has a positive effect on behaviour and contributes towards a more cohesive and inclusive school environment, strongly supporting the outcomes for well-being in the *Every Child Matters* programme.

There is also a legal duty in the Education Act 2002 on local authorities and governing bodies of maintained schools about consulting pupils when making decisions on matters that affect them. DfES published guidance on this in *Working Together – giving children and young people a say*, 2004.

How can they be involved?

Pupils can be involved in school life in two main ways:

1 **Contributing to school decision-making**
2 **Taking on responsibilities.**

What part can pupils play in school decision-making?

Depending on their age and maturity, primary pupils can contribute towards school decision-making on a wide variety of issues, including:
- class and school rules
- lunch-time arrangements
- playground behaviour
- use of school grounds
- equal opportunities/anti-bullying policies
- rewards/sanction systems
- uniform
- homework.

Opportunities for pupil consultation should not be left to chance, but deliberately embedded into daily practice, including through the provision of more formal mechanisms, such as:
- group discussions
- circle time
- class and school councils
- questionnaires
- suggestion boxes.

What kinds of responsibilities can they take on?

Depending on their age and maturity, primary pupils can take on a wide variety of responsibilities both in class and the school as a whole, including:
- peer reading/education
- peer mediation
- buddies to younger children in the playground
- class/school councillors
- visitor guides
- lunch-time helpers
- recycling monitors
- pupils as researchers

- taking assemblies
- running a school newspaper/website
- class monitors.

It is important to give everyone in a class a special responsibility of some kind.

What about assemblies and special activities?

Assemblies and other off-timetable activities – such as charity weeks or mock elections – provide many opportunities for pupils to take on and share responsibilities.
They can be involved in the planning and organising of events at many levels, including:
- producing manifestos or campaign appeals
- drawing up checklists
- enlisting volunteers
- sharing out tasks
- making telephone calls
- inviting outside visitors
- confirming arrangements or getting rooms ready.

> Wroxham is a school full of lively, engaged pupils and teachers who know their views will be taken seriously, and that they have a real role to play in decision-making. Colourful, well-planned, child-made displays adorn classrooms and halls. Signs of participation are everywhere. On one bulletin board children have posted proposed names for the breakfast club (Brain Food Café is one). There is a postbox where children voted on Y6 garden plans, following a special meeting of Y6s to explain the alternatives to reception pupils, so that they would also be able to understand the choices. And, of course, the newly renovated KS2 toilets.
>
> Lorna Reed, Headteacher, Wroxham School,
> TES (Times Educational Supplement), 14 March 2003

IMPROVING PRACTICE

1 What are the most influential decisions that have been taken in your school recently? In how many of these, if any, were pupils involved? Do you consider this amount of involvement to be satisfactory? Why or why not?

2 Draw up a list of aspects of school life that you think pupils should:

   a) decide for themselves
   b) be consulted on but not make the final decision.

3 Think of ways in which pupil involvement in school life could be linked to citizenship learning in the formal curriculum. How could you bring out these links in your classroom? Think of some examples.

Citizenship through community involvement

KEY ISSUES

Why is community involvement important?

Is it just about 'doing good'?

Does it only apply to the local community?

In what ways can pupils be involved?

Does it mean you have to go out of school?

Why is community involvement important?

Community involvement is important because it helps pupils see themselves as members of wider communities.

Is it just about 'doing good'?

Community involvement is not so much about 'doing good' as a way of providing pupils with opportunities to grow in confidence and acquire the skills, knowledge and understanding that go with active citizenship, for example, organising an old people's party provides an ideal opportunity to consider the needs of another group and how society treats it.

Does it only apply to the local community?

Young children's concerns are not restricted to their immediate surroundings – home, school and neighbourhood. Through the media (TV, radio, newspapers and internet) they are aware of and concerned about a range of **local, regional, national and international issues**, such as poverty, disease and discrimination, and should be encouraged to engage with these whenever possible.

> **WWW**
>
> *Make The Link*
> The Make The Link section on the **Times Educational Supplement** website **(www.tes.co.uk/Make_The_Link/)** provides information on organisations which can match British schools with a suitable partner overseas. It provides you with an opportunity to exchange information and ideas, helping your school to develop its new links.

In what ways can pupils be involved?

Depending on their age and maturity, primary pupils can be involved in community life in a variety of ways, for example through:
- visits – e.g. to council chambers
- raising money for charity
- twinning with a school in another country or area
- a class or school newspaper
- environmental projects – e.g. cleaning up a local park
- community campaigns – e.g. on road safety
- working with local voluntary, groups and organisations
- researching global issues – e.g. children's rights
- running a mini-enterprise
- linking with local secondary schools.

Does it mean you have to go out of school?

Out-of-school visits provide powerful and unique learning opportunities and it is important to build these into the citizenship element of the PSHE and citizenship curriculum where possible. However, at primary level it is likely that community involvement will mainly be mediated through school-based activities, such as:

- visitors to the school
- writing letters/e-mails
- internet research
- pen friends
- school twinning
- links with local NGOs and charities.

Whatever the level of involvement, it is important to make sure pupils:

1 **have opportunities for negotiating and deciding their role**
2 **feel they are 'making a difference'**
3 **are given time to share, reflect on and record what they have learned, e.g., in the form of a piece of writing, a presentation, a display or a citizenship portfolio.**

WWW

A list of questions that help pupils to reflect on their involvement in school life can be found in **Citizenship: a scheme of work for key stages 1 and 2: www.standards.dfes.gov.uk/schemes2**

FOCUS

Marchwood Junior School has developed strong links with the local parish council as part of its Good Citizens Partnership Project. The school opens its doors to village activities, and pupils and parents are encouraged to contribute to council decisions and to the **Village News Magazine**.

IMPROVING PRACTICE

1 **Look at the Framework for PSHE and citizenship (Appendices 1 and 2 on pages 217 and 219) and identify the elements you think are most effectively developed through community involvement.**

2 **What different sorts of citizenship learning could pupils acquire by:**

   a) raising money for charity?
   b) linking with a school in Africa?
   c) tree-planting in the local park?

3 **Think of some ways in which community involvement could be used to enhance learning in National Curriculum subjects or the National Literacy and Numeracy Strategies. What would you need to do to bring out these links in the classroom?**

Circle time, class and school councils

KEY ISSUES

What can circle time contribute to citizenship learning?

How is this achieved?

How do school councils complement circle time?

At what age can children take part in a school council?

What makes a school council effective?

What about class councils?

What can circle time contribute to citizenship learning?

Organised in the right kind of way, circle time helps pupils to:
- take more responsibility for and become more engaged with the life of their school and the wider community
- develop the basic skills of communication and democratic decision-making and confidence to put them into practice.

How is this achieved?

To achieve this, you need to:
- create opportunities for pupils to talk about issues affecting the life of the school or the wider community – e.g. school meals, travel to school, or topics in the news
- structure their discussion around citizenship concepts – e.g. fairness, rights and responsibilities.

Allowing pupils to raise issues for discussion through a suggestion box can be a useful way of addressing 'difficult' issues. It gives pupils anonymity, and helps you to filter out issues that are best dealt with one-to-one.

How do school councils complement circle time?

School councils help pupils to learn about aspects of democratic procedure that are difficult or impossible to build into circle time, such as:
- speaking at hustings
- electing officers – e.g. chair, secretary, treasurer
- drawing up an agenda
- taking minutes
- acting as representatives, consulting and giving feedback
- surveying opinion, speaking persuasively and voting.

At what age can children take part in a school council?

Pupils can benefit from the experience of being part of a school council at any age – even in the nursery/reception class. While they may not always be able to act as representatives in the full sense of the term, there is much for younger pupils to learn just from taking part and seeing what others do.

What makes a school council effective?

Effective school councils tend to:
- be elected – with hustings and a secret ballot
- have clear rules – about what can and can't be discussed/decided
- be representative – not individuals pursuing their own agenda
- have easily identifiable officers – e.g. wear badges
- meet regularly – say, once a fortnight
- have real power – enable pupils to make real decisions e.g over a budget
- be underpinned by work in class – making learning explicit
- be vehicles for 'two-way' communication – between pupils and staff.

> They [the staff] were concerned about children telling
> teachers what should be done and worried about who would
> be elected. But in fact the children were very discerning in
> their choices … Learning they have to work within
> constraints is part of it. And they also learn that I have
> constraints imposed on me as well.
>
> Susan Barker, Headteacher, St Peter's CE Primary School, Wallsend

What about class councils?

Class councils are a natural extension of circle time and can help to inform and support the
work of a full school council. They can also provide an important layer of decision-making in
their own right. Class councils are sometimes more effective than school councils at dealing
with issues that apply at the level of the class, for example, seating arrangements, pupil
behaviour or individual needs.

IMPROVING PRACTICE

1   Think of some citizenship issues appropriate for a circle
    time discussion in your school. What makes them
    citizenship issues?

2   Look at the Framework for PSHE and citizenship
    (Appendices 1 and 2 on pages 217 and 219).
    Highlight the kinds of learning you think pupils can
    acquire through participation in a class or school council.
    What implications does this have for the way that class

    and school councils are organised?

3   What sorts of issues do you think a class or school council
    should be allowed and not allowed to:

    a) discuss?
    b) decide for itself?

    Then ask a group of pupils whether they agree with your
    choices.

Learning and teaching strategies

KEY ISSUES

What kinds of learning and
teaching are important in
citizenship?

What sort of methods can you
use?

How important is written
work?

What is the role of reflection?

What kinds of learning and teaching are important in citizenship?

Citizenship education emphasises learning and teaching that is based on **active
involvement** in **real-life issues** facing pupils at school and in the wider community, for
example, racist name-calling, graffiti, childrens' rights, crime, injustice and the environment.

It requires an approach to learning and teaching that is:
* active – emphasises learning by doing
* interactive – uses discussion and debate
* critical – encourages pupils to think for themselves
* collaborative – employs group work and co-operative learning
* participatory – gives pupils a say.

FOCUS

Questions to promote citizenship thinking

Do you think it is fair?	Does x have a right to do this?
What would make it fairer?	Where does that right come from?
What would happen if everyone did that?	Does that right bring any responsibilities with it?
Who should have a say about this?	
Who should decide it?	What would be best for everyone?
Should there be a law about it?	What is your reason for saying that?
Whose job is it to do that?	What could you say to persuade someone else?
Who should pay for it?	What things does everyone agree on?

What sort of methods can you use?

A wide range of methods can be used, including:
* group and class discussions
* role play/drama
* reading and discussing
* art work
* investigation and problem-solving
* visitors to the school
* games
* shared writing
* case studies and simulations
* circle time and/or class/school councils
* out-of-school visits.

Activities emphasising use of the imagination – like story, drama or games – help pupils to
learn about citizenship issues they are unable to experience first-hand. They also help to
'distance' them from topics that might otherwise be sensitive to discuss, for example, issues
relating to prejudice and discrimination.

How important is written work?

Written work is important in citizenship education because it is a medium for learning and provides evidence of achievement – as well as being a vehicle for the development of literacy skills. It is also essential for participation in society.

> Pupils should be taught to talk and write about their opinions, and explain their views, on issues that affect themselves and society.

Framework for PSHE and citizenship at Key Stage 2

What is the role of reflection?

Active learning is a **cyclical** process. In order for it to be effective, pupils need time to reflect on and share what they have done and experienced. They also need time to draw out and record what they have learned and consider how this might be applied on future occasions. Ways of encouraging pupils to reflect on their learning include:

- question-and-answer sessions
- discussion
- group presentations
- displays
- citizenship portfolios
- citizenship journals, logs or diaries
- personal reflection.

It is important, wherever possible, to involve pupils in their own learning, for example, through voting on questions to discuss, selecting topics to research or assessing their own achievements.

IMPROVING PRACTICE

1 What sort of everyday, real-life citizenship issues do you think most concern primary pupils:

   a) at key stage 1?
   b) at key stage 2?

   Which of these do you think can be addressed directly and which might be better addressed indirectly through techniques such as story or role play?

2 Choose a citizenship issue – local, national or international – and generate some citizenship questions suitable for pupils at key stage 1 or 2. Use the examples listed above as a guide.

3 Create a writing frame to help pupils draft a letter to their local school meals service reporting the results of a class survey on school dinners.

Leadership, management and co-ordination

What part do headteachers and senior managers play?

Citizenship (and PSHE) has implications for the whole school – for the management and organisation of the school as an institution, as well as for what is planned and taught in the classroom.

For this reason, the part played by headteachers and senior managers is a crucial one, and includes responsibility for:
- developing a whole-school approach to planning citizenship within the PSHE and citizenship framework
- integrating PSHE and citizenship planning into other aspects of whole-school planning
- committing money for resources and staff development
- fostering a school ethos that supports PSHE and citizenship learning.

Creating a citizenship ethos involves more than just drawing up a 'wish-list' of the sorts of values and relationships you want to permeate your school. It means embedding these in everyday practice, for example, by listening to pupils, involving them in school decision-making, providing opportunities for them to take responsibility and giving them a say in the management of their own learning.

Who else needs to be involved?

Ideally, all members of the school community should be involved in the development of PSHE and citizenship policy: teaching and non-teaching staff, parents, governors and community partners, as well as the pupils themselves.

What should a PSHE and citizenship policy contain?

While the contents of **PSHE and citizenship policies** will vary from school to school, there are a number of key features that should be common to all, including:
- aims and objectives
- the framework of values within which your programme is set and how it contributes to the *Every Child Matters* outcomes
- an outline of your programme and how you intend to deliver it
- guidance on teaching methods, including dealing with topical issues
- assessment, recording and reporting
- management and coordination
- monitoring, review and evaluation
- links to other school policies.

Why is it important to have a subject leader?

It is important to have a **subject leader** for PSHE and citizenship to co-ordinate provision across the school. In the absence of such person, provision is likely to be haphazard and poorly defined.

The subject leader's responsibilities include:
- leading policy development
- identifying opportunities for learning
- raising staff awareness and establishing a shared view of best practice
- providing support and training
- managing resources
- co-ordinating assessment, recording and reporting
- making links with external agencies and organisations
- monitoring standards of pupils' work and quality of teaching
- evaluating the programme.

What else do you need?

You also need:
- a development plan – linked to your overall school development plan
- a scheme of work – broken down by year and class
- a system for pupil consultation – e.g. circle time/class or school council
- a resource bank – of stories, books, poems, images and useful websites and organisations.

In addition, it can be helpful to have a small **PSHE and citizenship team** meeting regularly to help focus policy development and delivery across the school, and a link governor to provide support and assist with community links. Guidance in setting up and managing your programme is available locally through your **LA adviser** or **AST (Advanced Skills Teacher)** – if you have one.

IMPROVING PRACTICE

1   Using the notes in this section and the headings in the School Self-Evaluation Tool for Citizenship Education (see Appendix 7 on page 226), assess the development of your school's approach to citizenship education. Identify where you think your school is now and where it needs to go next.

2   What kind of qualities and expertise do you think are required in a subject leader for PSHE and citizenship?

Assessment, recording and reporting

KEY ISSUES

Why assess citizenship?

What are the statutory requirements?

What methods should you use?

How do you collect evidence of attainment?

How do you record progress?

How do you grade attainment?

What about reports?

REMEMBER

Remember, assessing citizenship is not about how 'good' a citizen a pupil is, but about what they know, understand or are able to do as citizens.

Why assess citizenship?

Assessing citizenship helps pupils to recognise and value what they learn, know how they are progressing and set targets for the future. It helps staff to evaluate their citizenship provision and build in continuity and progression. (See Section 5, Chapter 11, page 189).

What are the statutory requirements?

While there are no statutory requirements for the assessment of citizenship at the foundation stage, observations of children's citizenship learning can provide evidence of achievement in the early learning goals and contribute to the Foundation Stage Profile.

There are no statutory requirements for end of key stage assessment in PSHE and citizenship at key stages 1 and 2, but schools are required to keep records of the progress of all pupils and report this to parents – PSHE and citizenship included.

What methods should you use?

A balanced approach to assessment is likely to emphasise:
- informal as well as formal techniques – observation and discussion, not just written exercises
- formative as well as summative assessment – providing pupils with on-going feedback on their progress, not just end of term/year results
- pupils as partners in the assessment process – through self and peer assessment, target-setting and discussion about learning objectives.

How do you collect evidence of attainment?

Evidence of pupil attainment can be collected from a range of sources, including:
- contributions to discussion and debate
- role play and drama
- talks and presentations
- diaries, logbooks or portfolios
- pupil planning of events or visits
- displays or web page designs
- letters or emails to the press or public figures
- photographs and video clips.

How do you record progress?

Methods for recording pupil progress include:
- observation notes – kept by the teacher
- teacher assessment sheets – filled in by the teacher after key activities and shared with pupils
- pupil assessment sheets – completed by pupils after key activities and shared with teachers
- citizenship diaries/logbooks – used by pupils to record their achievements and reflections on their learning
- examples of pupil work – kept either by teachers or by pupils, e.g. in the form of a portfolio.

How do you grade attainment?

There is currently no official eight-level assessment scale for PSHE and citizenship. How attainment is graded is left to the judgement of the school. Whatever system is chosen, however, it is important that grades reflect the key stage statements set out in *The National Curriculum: handbook for primary teachers in England* (See Appendix 5 on page 224). It is also important that:

- there is a clear distinction between levels of attainment
- attainment levels are standard across the year
- the full range of PSHE and citizenship learning is covered.

(See training exercise 1 on page 40).

What about reports?

Reports for PSHE and citizenship may take the form either of a brief, but separate commentary on progress, as for other subjects, or be included as part of the school's report on other activities in the school curriculum. While the exact format is left to the school's discretion, it is important that:

- the citizenship element is clearly identifiable
- pupils have some measure of involvement in the process.

(See training exercise 2 on page 41).

IMPROVING PRACTICE

1   **What kinds of citizenship achievement do you think should be mentioned in a report on PSHE and citizenship? Why?**

2   **How would you respond to the view that assessing citizenship is inappropriate because it will brand some pupils as 'failing citizens'?**

1 Pupil participation

Wroxham Primary School

Pupils at Wroxham Primary School play a real role in decision-making in their school. Six 15-minute circle meeting groups are convened every Tuesday morning. Each has a cross-section of pupils from Years 1 to 6 and is run by Year 6 pupils under the supervision of one of the teachers. At the meetings, pupils have the opportunity to raise issues that make a difference to the life and running of the school. Year 6 explain the alternatives to reception pupils, so they are able to understand the choices. Recent issues raised have included:

- establishing a school radio – where to place speakers, programming etc.
- developing the breakfast club
- need for a bicycle rack – so parents don't have to drive to school
- Year 6 garden plans.

Teachers at the school are keen to integrate pupil participation into the formal curriculum and to keep learning activities real, for example, pupils drafting letters to audio companies and other electronics firms (to ask for spare equipment for the school radio) as a short SAT-type writing exercise.

Alison Peacock, headteacher, says, 'Citizenship education comes from the ethos of the school.'

St Peter's CE Primary School

The school council at St.Peter's CE Primary School, Wallsend, meets fortnightly to discuss matters and make decisions that affect the school. Two representatives from each class in the upper four years (plus one reserve) are elected annually. Candidates nominate themselves and have to give a short address to their class on what they could do for their school before voting takes place. Council representatives meet with the headteacher, report back to their classmates and note their concerns – organising a class vote if necessary. They then report their classmates' views to the next council meeting.

Headteacher Susan Barker says, 'If children have a say, they are going to take ownership and will want things to work.'

A ten-year old council representative says, 'If you decide something on the school council, it's not like the teacher has decided it – it's a chance to do something that you decide. It makes you want to do it more.'

2 Pupil involvement in community life

City of Southampton Civic Award

The City of Southampton Civic Award to Young People is an award scheme for pupils in primary schools. It was set up initially as a response to the problem that young people have to wait until they are 14 before they can start the Duke of Edinburgh Award.

Key stage 1 (Year 2) pupils must complete three sections:

1   **Public service to their class and their family – minimum of 15 minutes to each per week over one term (very popular with parents!)**
2   **Hobby – maintained throughout one term**
3   **Plan an 'adventure' – may be a special day in school or a school trip, but pupils must be involved in planning and organisation.**

Key stage 2 (Year 6) pupils must complete four sections:

1   **Public service to both the school and the local community – minimum of 12 hours over two terms**
2   **Hobby – physical/ sporting***
3   **Hobby – non-physical***
4   **Adventure training – a 24 hour camp/expedition.**

(* hobbies must be maintained for two terms and at least one should be something new to the pupil.)

Successful pupils receive their certificate in school from a local city councillor. They document their participation through a range of approaches including photographs, video and diaries. At each key stage, they are encouraged to keep a logbook of their activities.

Roy Honeybone, instigator of the award says, 'It [the Award] has simultaneously made the pupils very aware of their responsibilities to one another and to their various communities.'

Training exercises

1 Developing an assessment tool

Study the example below.

1 **What are its strengths and weakness as a tool for assessing citizenship learning in primary schools?**
2 **How far does it fit with current assessment practices in your school?**
3 **What are its implications for learning and teaching approaches?**

SKILLS AREA	1 VERY GOOD	2 GOOD	3 OK	4 NEEDS WORK	EVIDENCE
Demonstrates an understanding of the issues					
Contributes to the discussion					
Argues points logically					
Considers the values involved					
Listens to others					
Is prepared to change his/her mind					
Works in a team					
Is prepared to compromise					

Hilary Claire and Cathie Holden, **Effective Transition KS2 to KS3** (www.citized.info)

2 Writing a Year 5 report

Study the exemplar report below.

1 **What are the advantages and disadvantages of this format for**

   a) class teachers?
   b) pupils?
   c) parents?
   d) the school?

2 **What aspects, if any, would you wish to alter?**

Year 5 Report
Citizenship Education

PUPIL: **CLASS:**

COURSE DETAILS

Citizenship education in Year 5 is provided through:
- circle time
- an environmental project on improving the school groups
- workshops run by members of the fire and rescue service
- a class newspaper
- opportunities to act as a class monitor and participate in the school council.

PUPIL COMMENT

I enjoyed the project on the school grounds because it gave us a chance to go out in the open air. The school looks much nicer now. It was good to see what a difference we made. I also enjoyed taking the photographs of the town for our newspaper. Next year I would like to be one of the reporters.

TEACHER COMMENT

Jimmy enjoys circle time and has made a number of useful suggestions, for instance about behaviour at lunch-time and how teachers mark work. He worked very hard on the environmental project and in our discussions showed just how much he knew about environmental issues and the role of government and public bodies in environmental protection. He is not quite so confident at talking with visitors from the community. Acting as a reporter for the class newspaper next year should help him with this.

Adapted from the QCA booklet, **Citizenship at Key Stages 1–4: guidance on assessment, recording and reporting**, 2002

Training exercises

3 Citizenship education through nursery ryhmes

Think about the nursery rhyme, Humpty Dumpty, and study the questions below:

1 **What age group could you use these questions with?**
2 **What citizenship issues would they help pupils to learn about?**
3 **Which other nursery rhymes could be used in citizenship education? What kinds of citizenship learning could be drawn out of them? Think of some questions you could ask.**

Now try out the questions about Humpty Dumpty with your pupils.

Why do you think Humpty Dumpty was on the wall?

What do you think he might have been thinking or feeling?

Should his parents have warned him about the wall?

Should his friends have stopped him climbing on to it?

Should the wall have had a fence round it to stop people climbing up?

Why do you think there weren't any warning signs?

Who do you think put the wall up? What other dangerous places do you know about? Why are they dangerous?

Whose fault was it that he fell from the wall? His own? His parents'? His teacher's?

If you saw someone have an accident like that, what could you do? Who could help you?

What is the best way to stop this happening again, do you think?

From an idea by Roy Honeybone, editor, **Teaching Citizenship**

Section 3:
Citizenship in Secondary Schools

Chapter 3:
Citizenship in the Taught Curriculum

> In a sense, all those involved with citizenship education in secondary schools – from trainee teachers to senior managers – are learning to teach the subject.
>
> Peter Brett, St. Martin's College, Lancaster in **Teaching Citizenship**, Summer 2004

This section should be read in conjunction with: the programmes of study for citizenship key stages 3 and 4 (Appendices 3 and 4 on pages 222 and 223); *The School Self-Evaluation Tool for Citizenship Education* (see chapter 8); and *Citizenship: Raising the Standard,* a handbook and training video (Citizenship Foundation/Connect Publications, 2005). Helpful advice will also be found in *The Citizenship Co-ordinator's Handbook* (Nelson Thornes, 2003).

Introduction

There are different ways in which a secondary school might deliver the content of the citizenship curriculum: through its taught curriculum, its culture and ethos, and its links with the wider community. This chapter is concerned with the first of these – with how the citizenship curriculum can be implemented within the school timetable.

It is relevant to anyone responsible for teaching, leading, co-ordinating or promoting citizenship in secondary schools.

Contents include:
    Meeting the statutory requirements
    Citizenship and PSHE
    Citizenship as a stand-alone subject
    Citizenship through other subjects
    Tutorial programmes and assemblies
    Suspended timetable events
    Creating a modular course
    Case studies: 1) Suspended timetable events
                     2) Citizenship through history
                      3) Earth Day
    Training exercises: 1) Citizenship and PSHE
                     2) Core and 'carrier' subjects
                     3) Assessing a suspended timetable event

Meeting the statutory requirements

KEY ISSUES

What are the statutory requirements?

How can the taught curriculum deliver these?

Which is the best way?

How much time does it need?

What are the statutory requirements?

Citizenship education is a statutory subject at key stages 3 and 4.

Apart from the absence of an eight-level scale of achievement, it is treated exactly the same as other foundation subjects in the National Curriculum, including:
- programmes of study setting out what students should be taught
- an attainment target, consisting of two end-of-key-stage descriptions, setting out what students are expected to achieve by the end of each key stage
- annual reports to parents
- assessment at the end of key stage 3.

> Schools need to establish high standards for citizenship that are comparable with standards in other subjects.
>
> DfES, 2003

How can the taught curriculum deliver these?

Broadly, there are four ways of delivering citizenship education through the taught curriculum:

1 **Citizenship as a stand-alone subject**
Individual citizenship lessons (or modules in a modular course) are not in themselves a guarantee of quality, but they ensure that the subject is clearly identifiable, allow you to develop a specialist team, simplify monitoring and assessment and help you to cover the aspects of citizenship education not covered in other subjects – e.g. the justice system, elections and the work of parliament.

2 **Citizenship through other subjects**
Subjects that have a close affinity with citizenship education – e.g. PSHE, history, geography and RE – are in principle able to share responsibility for delivering aspects of the citizenship curriculum. They act as 'carrier' subjects for citizenship education. This can help students to see the wider significance of citizenship education and makes the subject more of a whole-school responsibility – but it is unlikely to allow you to deliver the whole citizenship curriculum and poses problems for monitoring and assessment.

3 **Citizenship through the tutorial programme and assemblies**
Form tutors are well placed to deal with topical issues relating to school life and encourage community involvement, but – even with training – it is unreasonable to expect that they will become sufficiently expert to deliver all aspects of the subject to the required standard.

4 **Citizenship through suspended timetable events**
Devoting whole or half days to citizenship is a way of finding extra timetable time, building in flexibility and creating opportunities for extended citizenship activities – but it is no substitute for regular citizenship teaching and can be difficult to assess.

Which is the best way?

No one way is likely to be capable of satisfying the requirements of the National Curriculum by itself. A **combination of approaches** will almost certainly be needed.

The most flexible and practicable approach in most cases will be one which combines:
- a central core of stand-alone citizenship lessons or modules
- supplementary contributions from a few key subjects
- occasional suspended timetable events.

How much time does it need?

There is no statutory time allocation for subjects in the school timetable.

However, given that citizenship education is expected to establish levels of achievement comparable to other National Curriculum subjects, it is likely to need **a minimum of 3% of curriculum time** (an average of 3–4 hours per week, based on a 25 hour week, when contributions from other subjects are included) – probably more.

This is the figure suggested in the DfES and QCA key stage 3 strategy document, *Designing the Key Stage 3 Curriculum*.

IMPROVING PRACTICE

1　What do you see as the main problems of delivering citizenship education through the taught curriculum? How can these problems be overcome?

2　What percentage of curriculum time is currently allocated to citizenship education in your school? Do you consider this to be about right, too much or too little? Why?

3　How could you respond to the view that the secondary-school curriculum is already 'over-stretched' and there is no space available for citizenship education?

Citizenship and PSHE

KEY ISSUES

What are the similarities between citizenship and PSHE?

How are they different?

How can PSHE help to deliver the citizenship curriculum?

Can the whole citizenship curriculum be delivered in this way?

REMEMBER

Although some of its constituent elements are statutory – e.g. sex and careers education – unlike citizenship education, PSHE is not a National Curriculum subject.

What are the similarities between citizenship and PSHE?

Citizenship and PSHE are similar in their emphasis on values and attitudes, and in their concern to empower young people to act effectively and with self-confidence. They are also similar in some of the themes they explore, such as drug abuse and equal opportunities – and their emphasis on active learning techniques like role play and discussion.

How are they different?

What distinguishes citizenship education from PSHE, however, is its focus and content.

1 **Focus**
   PSHE focuses on personal and inter-personal decision-making, while citizenship education deals with **public policy**. One concerns students' choices as private individuals, the other with their choices as citizens – that is, as members of society with legal rights and responsibilities. For example a typical PSHE lesson on smoking deals with the cost to the individual, whereas a citizenship education one focuses on the cost to society – exploring issues such as legislation on smoking in public places or tobacco advertising.

2 **Content**
   There is a **central core of learning** – factual and conceptual – unique to citizenship education that is not dealt with at all in PSHE, e.g. knowledge about central and local government, criminal and civil law, elections and taxation, and concepts such as democracy, justice and the rule of law. (See training exercise 1 Citizenship and PSHE, page 60.)

How can PSHE help to deliver the citizenship curriculum?

Integrating citizenship education into PSHE can be a natural and effective way of delivering important aspects of the citizenship curriculum, provided:
   • it is taught by a specialist team
   • all involved – staff as well as students – understand which elements are citizenship and which are PSHE.

Drugs education, for example, leads naturally to questions about legal rights and responsibilities, the role of public services and the voluntary sector. However, not all of the content of the citizenship curriculum can easily be covered in this way – especially that relating to legal and political understanding.

The most effective way of integrating citizenship education into PSHE is through a modular approach – with stand-alone citizenship modules sitting alongside PSHE ones. This makes the citizenship element easier to identify and simplifies arrangements for monitoring and assessment.

It is important to ensure that there is parity between citizenship and PSHE modules. Citizenship education is not a sub-theme of PSHE, or vice versa. It is also important to ensure that sufficient time is given to written work – often less prominent in PSHE classes.

Can the whole citizenship curriculum be delivered in this way?

While a well-planned and resourced citizenship/PSHE programme, taught by a specialist team, is able to deliver many of the basic elements in the citizenship curriculum, it will usually need to be supplemented by other forms of provision. These could include contributions from other subjects, the tutorial programme and/or special events, in addition to the citizenship learning that takes place through the culture and ethos of the school and its links with the wider community.

IMPROVING PRACTICE

1 Draw up some citizenship learning objectives appropriate for some of the following topics:
   • food
   • work
   • drugs
   • sexuality.

2 Look at the programmes of study for key stages 3 and 4 (Appendices 3 and 4 on pages 222 and 223) and decide which parts you think would be best taught through:

   a) a joint citizenship/PSHE module
   b) a separate citizenship module.

3 What advantages are there in delivering a citizenship/ PSHE programme through a specialist team as opposed to incorporating it in the tutorial programme?

Citizenship as a stand-alone subject

KEY ISSUES

Why teach citizenship as a separate subject?

What benefits does this have?

Which aspects of citizenship are not addressed in other subjects?

How does discrete teaching fit with other forms of delivery?

Why teach citizenship as a separate subject?

Citizenship education is a foundation subject in the National Curriculum. It has a distinctive focus, content and approach to learning, and presents students with important issues that need to be addressed in their own right, for example:

- What does it mean to be a citizen of a society?
- What are my rights and responsibilities as a citizen?
- Who should govern society?
- What kind of society do I want to live in?
- What can I as a citizen do to change the society I live in, and how?

What benefits does this have?

Teaching citizenship as a distinct subject:

- allows you to cover aspects of the citizenship curriculum not dealt with in other subjects, including those relating to politics and law
- allows you to develop a specialist team of staff able to use their expertise for the benefit of all students
- makes it easier to build in continuity and progression, and simplifies monitoring and assessment
- guarantees a minimum entitlement to all students
- gives citizenship education a visible identity and status alongside other curriculum subjects
- can act as a focus for other elements in the citizenship programme, including those learned through the culture and ethos of a school and its links with the wider community.

Which aspects of citizenship are not addressed in other subjects?

There is a significant core of learning – factual and conceptual – unique to citizenship education that is not properly addressed in other subjects. It includes:

- **legal rights and responsibilities** – e.g. consumer rights, children's rights, human rights
- **the justice system** – e.g. criminal and civil law, role of the police
- **political aspects of diversity** – e.g. national identity, inclusion, equality
- **central and local government** – e.g. democracy and other forms of government, making and changing laws
- **the electoral system and the importance of voting** – e.g. forms of representation
- **the work of voluntary groups** – e.g. Amnesty International
- **the significance of the media in society** – e.g. freedom of the press
- **the world as a global community** – e.g. EU, Commonwealth, UN
- **aspects of the economy** – e.g. taxation, public finance and services.

How does discrete teaching fit with other forms of delivery?

There are many different ways of combining stand-alone citizenship education lessons with other ways of delivering the citizenship curriculum.

However, in terms of flexibility and practicability, the most effective is likely to comprise a central core of stand-alone citizenship lessons or modules supplemented by contributions from a few key 'carrier' subjects and occasional suspended timetable events.

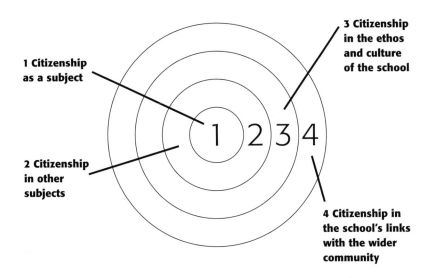

1 Citizenship as a subject

2 Citizenship in other subjects

3 Citizenship in the ethos and culture of the school

4 Citizenship in the school's links with the wider community

This sort of approach makes discrete teaching the lynchpin of the citizenship curriculum, in three ways:

1   It ensures the subject is visible and has a clear identity.
2   It guarantees a minimum entitlement to all students.
3   It acts as a central 'spine' holding together and giving focus to the range of citizenship activities that take place in a school – not only in the timetable, but also through the culture and ethos of the school and its links with the wider community.

IMPROVING PRACTICE

1   What in-school factors are an obstacle to the timetabling of discrete teaching in the citizenship curriculum? What can be done to overcome these?

2   What are the advantages and disadvantages of treating citizenship solely as a stand-alone subject?

3   How can discrete citizenship lessons/modules act as a focus for other aspects of a school's citizenship programme? Think of some practical examples.

Citizenship through other subjects

KEY ISSUES

How can other subjects help to deliver the citizenship curriculum?

Which subjects should be involved?

How can their contribution be co-ordinated?

What is the minimum contribution?

What makes it citizenship?

How can other subjects help to deliver the citizenship curriculum?

Well-planned and organised work within other subjects makes a distinctive and natural contribution to citizenship learning, and helps to strengthen and enrich the citizenship curriculum as a whole. It enables staff to develop citizenship within a broad framework so that students can see its full significance for all parts of life. It is also a way of finding curriculum time for citizenship where there is serious pressure on the timetable.

Which subjects should be involved?

The subjects involved are a matter for the school. There is no statutory regulation about this. In practice, it is probably better to restrict it to a few 'carrier' subjects – though it would be wrong to rule out any subject on principle.

A **carrier subject** is one that has a natural affinity, or overlaps in curriculum content with citizenship education, e.g. history, geography and RE.

Four or five high-quality contributions a year are likely to be more effective than a large number of ill defined or superficially connected ones.

Trying to map citizenship on to the entire school curriculum produces so many links that is very difficult to manage within a coherent framework, and presents serious problems for monitoring and for assessment, recording and report-writing. The situation is exacerbated in key stage 4, where demands of public examinations make this kind of mapping exercise virtually impossible.

In any case, it is highly unlikely that the whole content of the citizenship curriculum could be delivered through the taught curriculum alone – additional forms of provision will almost certainly be needed to satisfy the requirements of the National Curriculum.

> " ... the more fragmented the programme, the more difficulty there is in achieving overall coherence. In some schools the programme is so dispersed that pupils are unaware that they have studied citizenship at all. "
>
> Ofsted, 2004

How can their contribution be co-ordinated?

The need to make links between contributions from different subjects underlines the need for a **citizenship co-ordinator** with sufficient management status to negotiate and plan with other staff.

The process of co-ordination is simplified and the subject gains a clearer identity when citizenship teaching in other subjects is linked to a central core of discrete citizenship lessons. Cross-curricular links are reciprocal. Just as other subjects can enrich discrete citizenship teaching, so discrete citizenship teaching can enrich citizenship teaching in other subjects.

(See Training exercise: Core learning and carrier subjects, page 61.)

What is the minimum contribution?

As far as planned contributions are concerned, the minimum should be **not less than a lesson per subject**. In most cases, it will be more – at least two or three lessons, or a citizenship lesson in two or three different modules.

What makes it citizenship?

It is essential to make sure that connections made with the citizenship curriculum are genuine ones. Learning objectives should be expressed in terms of the National Curriculum programmes of study for citizenship and made explicit in lesson planning.

> In the schools where worthwhile subject contributions are being made, substantial sections of the programme of study have been identified, appropriately modified or augmented and schemes of work added to the existing departmental schemes.
>
> Ofsted, 2003

Work on cross-curricular skills – such as argument and debate, or research and analysis – should not be classed as citizenship unless it is based on a citizenship issue or has a definite citizenship focus.

IMPROVING PRACTICE

1   Study the key stage 3 and 4 programmes of study for citizenship (Appendices 3 and 4 on pages 222 and 223) and map out the areas of potential overlap with other subjects.

2   What can be done to help students recognise that they are 'doing' citizenship when it is being taught through another subject?

Tutorial programmes and assemblies

How can tutorial programmes help to deliver the citizenship curriculum?

Tutorial programmes can help to deliver the citizenship curriculum in three main ways:

1 **Laying the foundations of citizen identity**
   Seeing oneself as a citizen is more than just understanding what a citizen is – citizenship has to be experienced. With their emphasis on personal development and concern for the individual, tutorial programmes are well placed to develop this sense of identity.

2 **Helping students learn about the democratic process**
   Through participation in class or school councils and consultations, students in form groups are able to gain first-hand experience of democratic procedures and the challenges of making them work efficiently and fairly and to the benefit of everyone concerned. They are also able to develop the skills needed for participation in these kinds of procedures.

3 **Providing opportunities for community-based activities**
   Tutorial programmes allow students to discuss topical issues of common concern to their peers – whether relating to the school as a whole or to the wider community. They allow students to use these discussions as a basis for school or community-focused action, such as improving the school environment, school linking or charity support.

What part can assemblies play?

Year or whole-school assemblies can help you to:
- provide opportunities for students to have the experience of making individual/group presentations to a large audience
- make efficient use of outside agencies/speakers
- create a sense of solidarity amongst students and staff.

Assemblies are particularly useful for extending student participation in school and community issues, for example, as forums for feedback from student councillors, for consultation or presentations of student research.

Can the whole citizenship curriculum be delivered in this way?

While tutorial programmes and assemblies can be a useful location for certain types of citizenship learning, it is unwise to rely on them as the main vehicle for the delivery of your citizenship curriculum, for several reasons:
- There is simply not enough time available to satisfy the demands of the National Curriculum programmes of study for citizenship education and attend to all the other demands of tutoring.
- Given the numbers involved, it is unreasonable to expect to be able to provide all form tutors with the level of training they need to deliver essential aspects of the citizenship curriculum such as political and legal understanding.
- It is unlikely that form tutors will approach citizenship education with the same enthusiasm and level of commitment they bring to their own subject when it represents such a small part of their overall responsibility in school – an issue already facing many schools that rely on their tutorial programme to deliver PSHE.

Schools that rely, or are thinking of relying on their tutorial programme as the main vehicle for the delivery of the citizenship curriculum should consider seriously the effectiveness of the teaching that is likely to result, and the extent to which it will satisfy the Ofsted expectation that standards of attainment in citizenship education should be as high as in other subjects.

> Some of the weakest lessons were in tutor time, with pupils' experience limited by the lack of commitment of some teachers and the inadequate time available.
>
> Ofsted, 2003

IMPROVING PRACTICE

1 Choose one of the citizenship programmes of study – key stage 3 or 4 (Appendices 3 and 4 on pages 222 and 223) – and identify the elements you think:

   a) could be taught effectively through a tutorial programme
   b) would be taught more effectively in some other way.

   What implications does this have for current practice in your school?

2 What obstacles do you think face a school seeking to move away from reliance on the tutorial programme as the main vehicle for the delivery of its citizenship curriculum? How could these obstacles be overcome?

Suspended timetable events

How can suspended timetable events help to deliver the citizenship curriculum?

Suspended timetable events allow you to:
- explore citizenship issues in more depth
- relate learning to 'real-life' situations
- make better use of outside agencies and speakers
- arrange visits off campus
- generate press interest and positive publicity
- create a sense of common purpose among students and staff
- plan activities that are memorable and fun.

What form can they take?

Common types include:
- **student consultations** – e.g. on school rules, anti-bullying policies
- **fundraising events** – e.g. Red Nose Day, Children in Need
- **simulations** – e.g. mock elections, mock trials
- **debates** – e.g. formal debates, *Question Time*-style debates
- **conferences** – e.g. on human rights, youth crime
- **community projects** – e.g. Make a Difference Day, inter-generational events
- **visits** – e.g. magistrates' court, council chambers.

How regular should they be?

Successful events need detailed planning and a high level of commitment from a range of individuals. It is unlikely, therefore, that you will be able to organise more than three or four in any one year.

Where do you start?

Start with a planning team, including, where appropriate, representatives of external agencies and community groups. Help is available from citizenship organisations, such as CSV and Changemakers. Local trainee citizenship teachers may also be willing to be involved.

A strong element of student participation is crucial. Students may be involved in a range of ways – appropriate for their age and maturity – from choosing a theme to booking speakers and running workshops.

Opportunities for students to reflect on their learning both at the planning stage and after the event are essential and should be built in from the start.

Factors that increase the likelihood of your event being a success include:
- a clear focus
- contributions from a range of subjects
- a variety of learning approaches
- linking to local/national events or consultations
- inviting in local agencies/speakers
- using municipal venues
- involving the local media.

What makes it citizenship?

Just because a day is memorable and fun does not mean it is citizenship education. Learning objectives should be clearly identified and expressed in terms of the National Curriculum programmes of study for citizenship and made explicit in the planning process. Issues dealt with should be genuine citizenship issues, i.e. ones that deal with students' interests and concerns as members of society with legal rights and responsibilities, not merely as private individuals.

What drawbacks are there?

A whole-day event may appear to be equivalent to one hour of citizenship a week for 5 weeks, but in reality this is unlikely to be the case. Long periods of time often elapse between events, making connected learning difficult to establish. There are problems with continuity and progression, and also with monitoring and assessment.

Suspended timetable days do make a valuable contribution to citizenship learning, but they are never a substitute for regular citizenship teaching (See training exercise 3: Assessing a suspended timetable event on page 62).

> ### REMEMBER
>
> Raising money for charity may be a worthwhile aim in itself, but it is not citizenship education unless it leads to citizenship learning, for example, about the nature of the cause, the process of advocacy or the role of charities in society.

IMPROVING PRACTICE

1   Sketch the outline for a day's event on a citizenship theme of your choice. Map it against the key stage 3 or 4 programme of study for citizenship. How can you ensure that students know they are 'doing' citizenship?

2   What forms of assessment can be used to assess citizenship learning acquired from a special day or event? What sorts of evidence can you collect and how can you collect it?

Creating a modular course

KEY ISSUES

How could you construct a modular citizenship course for key stage 3?

How should the modules be structured?

How might such a course be enriched?

How much time will it need?

How could you construct a modular citizenship course for key stage 3?

One way of constructing a modular course at key stage 3 is to incorporate individual citizenship modules in a joint PSHE and citizenship programme taught by a specialist team.

Example of a modular approach to citizenship education at key stage 3

TERM/YEAR	YEAR 7	YEAR 8	YEAR 9
AUTUMN	**1 Citizenship** **The school community**: anti-bullying; school council; school rules (rights and responsibilities, resolving conflict)	**7 Citizenship** **The local community**: sport and leisure; community action – e.g. public transport as a local issue and as a political issue (local government, public services)	**13 Citizenship** **Social action**: case studies – e.g. animal rights; campaigning organisations – e.g. RSPCA (voluntary agencies)
	2 PSHE	**8 PSHE**	**14 PSHE**
SPRING	**3 Citizenship** **Young people and the law**: crime and the neighbourhood; policing; youth justice system; mock trial (criminal justice)	**9 Citizenship** **Having a say**: who runs the country?; a national political issue; how parliament decides; political parties (parliament, central government, voting)	**15 Citizenship** **Current affairs**: what happens in the news; freedom of speech; censorship (media in society)
	4 PSHE	**10 PSHE**	**16 PSHE**
SUMMER	**5 Citizenship** **Equal opportunities**: fighting injustice; disability rights; race and gender; anti-racism (diversity)	**11 Citizenship** **Families**: parental responsibilities; children's rights; NSPCC; domestic violence; children at risk; foster care and local authority care (civil law, legal and human rights)	**17 Citizenship** **International affairs**: poverty and wealth; fair trade; child labour and slavery; international aid – who pays? (global community)
	6 PSHE	**12 PSHE**	**18 PSHE**

How should the modules be structured?

The content of the citizenship curriculum in this example is addressed indirectly in terms of **themes**, for example 'the law', 'families', 'having a say'. Structuring modules around themes is a way of engaging student interest and ensuring that learning is child-centred ('bottom-up' not 'top-down'). It is also a way of relating it to issues that are topical and in the news.

Taken together, the modules shown here would cover most of the main areas of knowledge and understanding specified in the programme of study at key stage 3, at the same time as developing the skills of enquiry and communication, as well as of participation and responsible action.

How might such a course be enriched?

The basic timetable shown here might be enriched in the first instance by contributions from other relevant subjects – say, a commitment from three or four interested subject departments to deliver two hours of explicit citizenship teaching in each year.

It might also be enriched through the tutorial programme and/or suspended timetable events – say, one per year group.

PSHE modules might also include citizenship issues where appropriate, for example, when tackling topics like drugs, domestic violence, equal opportunities, work-related learning and so on.

How much time will it need?

The example shown here assumes joint provision of one hour per week for citizenship and PSHE. If these core modules were enriched by work in other subjects, the provision would be likely to be somewhere in excess of 3% of curriculum time, based on a 25-hour week.

IMPROVING PRACTICE

1 What are the advantages and disadvantages of delivering the key stage 3 citizenship curriculum in this way?

2 What in-school factors might create an obstacle to the introduction of a citizenship programme like this? What could be done to overcome them?

3 Think of some alternative 'themes' for citizenship modules and map them on to the key stage 3 programme of study (Appendix 3 on page 222). For which year groups are they most appropriate?

---

1 Suspended timetable events

Penketh and Culcheth High Schools

Two citizenship ASTs collaborated to produce a jointly planned and co-ordinated programme of suspended timetable/enrichment days across a range of core citizenship themes, enhancing the discrete and cross-curricular provision for citizenship within the students' regular timetables:

Year 7 Crime (involving local police, Youth Offending Teams and Magistrates' Association)
Year 8 'Make a Difference' Day
Year 9 Parliament and Voting (incorporating a mock election)
Year 10 Racism, Human Rights, Prejudice and Discrimination
Year 11 European or Media and Communication Day

'Make a Difference' Day

Supported nationally by CSV (Community Service Volunteers), this varies from year to year. One year, Penketh High School students researched the use and conservation of water in the UK and the Third World, producing wall displays and making information leaflets for primary schools, using resources and a presentation from WaterAid. Another year, both schools organised Fair Trade Days using a resource pack from Comic Relief. Students in both schools have since lobbied for fair trade chocolate to be sold in their canteens.

2 Citizenship through history

Trinity High School, Redditch

Year 9 pupils undertake an eight to ten-week unit in history on 'Protest', based on Peterloo, Luddites, Chartists and Suffragettes. It starts with a visit to the Peoples' History Museum in Manchester where students take part in a 'living history' performance with actors in role as the black Manchester Chartist William Cuffay and the local suffragette, Hannah Mitchell.
Citizenship activities which build upon students' historical learning include:

- using the six points of the Chartists' 'Peoples' Charter' to explore the role of Parliament today, considering the merits of the case for voting at 16 and to create a contemporary Peoples' Charter with links to Year 8 elections for representatives on Manchester's Youth Council
- considering the role of the law in protecting children's and workers' rights then and today
- discussing the purpose and effectiveness of trades unions today
- evaluating tactics used by pressure groups.

The school is looking to identify one piece of 'in depth' citizenship work undertaken in history to include in students' citizenship portfolios.

3 Earth Day

Swanshurst School, Birmingham

When Doug Smith was asked to produce a citizenship education experience for over 300 Year 8 students he decided to focus on sustainability. He began planning Earth Day (Eco Awareness Rather Than Harm) in September for the following July, with the help of a colleague from the Connexions service with good links to business and industry.

There would be six 45-minute sessions in the day. Four sessions would be delivered by local groups, including Birmingham City Council, Oxfam, Islamic Relief, Friends of the Earth, and Fair Trade — each student experiencing four workshops on a carousel basis. The fifth session would involve student evaluations and generating their own sustainability projects. The sixth session would allow them to present these to the rest of their peers. An 'eco-group' would be established to carry forward the most popular suggestions. A BT award of £2000 was to enhance significantly the day and its outcomes.

Doug wrote a script on the theme of sustainability and commissioned a group of students from a local college to make a documentary-style video, consisting of interviews with the site manager, teachers, students and others.

The day itself was very successful. The final session proved to be the climax, with 360 students, workshop presenters, teachers and others packed into the school hall. Twenty presentations on ideas for sustainability were made by pairs of students and judged by some of the presenters. The winners each received a block of fair trade chocolate, and all participating students went home with a recyclable bag and a fairly-traded banana.

As a direct outcome of the day, the school has established a paper recycling scheme and is working with a local charity to recycle cans and mobile phones as a fund raiser.

Training exercises

1 Citizenship and PSHE

Study the grid below showing how citizenship issues are to be distinguished from PSHE ones.

1 **Divide into groups – each with a copy of the grid below.**
2 **Groups generate their own questions to fill in the blanks in the grid.**
3 **Groups return to the plenary and share their questions.**
4 **Groups select one of the issues and sketch out two lesson plans using some of the questions generated – one for PSHE, one for citizenship education.**

THE ISSUE	PRIVATE	PUBLIC
Smoking	How does smoking damage your health?	Do you think smoking should be banned from all public places, including pubs and restaurants?
Work		
Drugs and alcohol		
Personal safety		
Gambling		
Bullying	What should you do if you are bullied?	
Parenting		
Education		Should students have to pay fees for higher education?
Sexual health/ health issues		

2 Core and 'carrier' subjects

Study the diagram showing how contributions from other subjects can be linked to an essential core of discrete citizenship teaching.

1 **Choose some of the subject disciplines in the 'Others' box and suggest areas in which they might also make a contribution to citizenship learning.**
2 **Which do you think are the most important links? Why?**

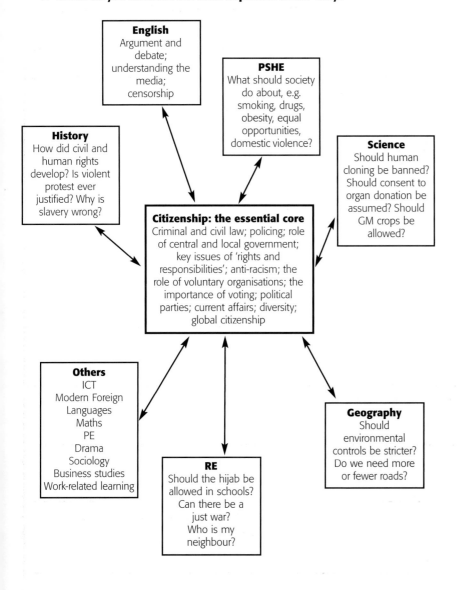

English
Argument and debate; understanding the media; censorship

PSHE
What should society do about, e.g. smoking, drugs, obesity, equal opportunities, domestic violence?

History
How did civil and human rights develop? Is violent protest ever justified? Why is slavery wrong?

Science
Should human cloning be banned? Should consent to organ donation be assumed? Should GM crops be allowed?

Citizenship: the essential core
Criminal and civil law; policing; role of central and local government; key issues of 'rights and responsibilities'; anti-racism; the role of voluntary organisations; the importance of voting; political parties; current affairs; diversity; global citizenship

Others
ICT
Modern Foreign Languages
Maths
PE
Drama
Sociology
Business studies
Work-related learning

RE
Should the hijab be allowed in schools? Can there be a just war? Who is my neighbour?

Geography
Should environmental controls be stricter? Do we need more or fewer roads?

3 Assessing a suspended timetable event

Study the plan below and consider:

1   **What forms of assessment are being used to assess citizenship learning here?**
2   **What type of evidence is being collected, how and by whom?**
3   **How does the evidence collected relate to the learning and teaching activities?**
4   **How useful do you think this sort of tool is for planning other suspended timetable events?**

Students help to plan and participate in a Human Rights Day.

Learning outcomes

Students can explain specific examples of human rights issues and recognise a range of views on such issues.

Students demonstrate skills related to organising and running an off-timetable event, negotiating their own contribution.

Students can meet deadlines and negotiate for more time if needed.

Students can work independently and as members of teams.

Assessment opportunities	*Evidence*	*By whom*
Observation: teachers and other adults, for example mentors, use observation sheets to record students' contributions to planning the day and then provide feedback to students.	Observation sheets and mentor assessment forms.	Teachers
		Mentors
Self-assessment sheets and diaries: students keep their own self-assessment record.	Student self-assessment sheets or diaries.	Students
	Teachers' notes and record grids.	Peers
Reflection: during the de-brief students reflect on their learning and plan ways to improve, discussing this in small groups observed by teachers or other adults.	Display of students' work. Articles written for school newsletter or local newspaper, etc.	
Follow-up: students carry out follow-up activities, for example, writing an account of the day for the school newsletter or local newspaper, designing a human rights web page, producing a display for the rest of the school, arranging an assembly about the work of an organisation such as Amnesty International.		

QCA Key stage 3 scheme of work for citizenship, 2003 (from an original idea by Chris Waller)

Section 3:
Citizenship in Secondary Schools

Chapter 4:
Citizenship through Other Subjects

Introduction

Well-planned and organised work within other subjects makes a distinctive contribution to citizenship learning, and helps to strengthen and enrich the citizenship education curriculum as a whole.

However, for contributions from other subjects to be officially classified as part of the school citizenship curriculum, simply identifying common concerns or points of contact between subjects is not enough. The citizenship element must be the significant part of the lesson.

This chapter examines ways in which different subjects are able to assist in the delivery of the citizenship curriculum and briefly outlines some of their key strengths and weaknesses. It is primarily intended for subject teachers and managers, and citizenship co-ordinators, but has application for anyone else involved in teaching, leading or promoting citizenship in secondary schools.

Contents include:
    Citizenship through history
    Citizenship through geography
    Citizenship through Religious Education
    Citizenship through English
    Citizenship through science
    Citizenship through ICT
    Citizenship through maths
    Citizenship through art and design
    Case study: Designing a sensory garden – a cross-generational design and
                 technology project.

Citizenship through history

How can history help to deliver the citizenship curriculum?

It is difficult to understand contemporary institutions, such as parliament or the monarchy, without knowing something about their historical development. History supplies examples from the past that provide a context for students' understanding of citizenship issues in the present.

What does it have in common with citizenship?

History and citizenship education share:
- **concepts** – e.g. power, authority, law, governance, representation, freedom, protest
- **skills** – e.g. research, analysis, expression, empathy, discussion, debate.

What can citizenship offer to history?

Citizenship education can bring increased relevance to history lessons and help students to understand why it is important to study history.

How should the links be made?

For contributions from history to be officially classified as part of the citizenship curriculum, simply identifying common concerns is not enough.

The Citizenship element should be:
- the significant part of the lesson
- linked to the rest of the citizenship curriculum
- planned in association with the citizenship co-ordinator.

Learning objectives should be expressed in terms of the National Curriculum programmes of study for citizenship and made explicit in lesson planning.

Links can be made in terms of:
- concepts – explaining characteristics of concepts through past contexts, e.g. justice, authority, equality
- patches – two or three lessons with a more specific 'citizenship orientation', e.g. the Holocaust or human rights
- strands – revisiting aspects of citizenship across a key stage, building and developing understanding, e.g. democracy
- a local dimension – history contributing to active involvement in the local community, e.g. intergenerational projects.

As a rule of thumb, history only becomes citizenship education when it is used to inform debates on topical issues and events.

WWW

The QCA history subject notes provide examples of opportunities for delivering citizenship through history. Exemplar units can be downloaded at: **www.standards.dfes.gov.uk/word/secondaryschemes/citsubject_hist.doc**

Examples of citizenship opportunities in history

HISTORY	CITIZENSHIP OPPORTUNITIES
Concept Justice in the Middle Ages	• Develop concept of justice and the law; idea of trial by jury • Link to whether you can get justice more easily today; • Debate future of trial by jury
Patch Nazi Germany and the Holocaust	• Compare authoritarian with democratic government; why some Germans supported the Nazis • Link to authoritarian governments today • Link to racism and anti-semitism today
Strand Year 7 – power of medieval kings Year 8 – Civil War, 1688 – power moving to parliament Year 9 – struggle for vote in nineteenth century, Chartism, women's suffrage	• Notion of who has power in people's lives; who makes laws • Link to how laws are made today • Understand how parliament developed; struggle between king and parliament • Link to role of the monarch today • Notion of democratic representation and active engagement in politics • Link to lowering the voting age
Local World War Two – researching experience of local people Memories of migration to Britain	• Interview elderly people to collect memories; setting up website for local people • Link to community participation, community heritage, intergenerational projects

IMPROVING PRACTICE

1 Choose two or three key citizenship concepts and devise ways of introducing them into a history lesson, e.g. a card sort activity.

2 Choose a unit of work from the history curriculum and give it a 'citizenship orientation'. Work out the citizenship learning objectives and decide how you could make it clear to students that they are 'doing' citizenship.

Citizenship through geography

KEY ISSUES

How can geography help to deliver the citizenship curriculum?

What does it have in common with citizenship?

What can citizenship offer to geography?

How should the links be made?

FOCUS

Key concepts in geography that relate to citizenship

Change
Interdependence
Sustainability
Development
Urbanisation
Community
Human rights
Globalisation

REMEMBER

Work on complementary skills – such as research and analysis – can only be classed as citizenship if it is based on a citizenship issue or has a definite citizenship focus.

How can geography help to deliver the citizenship curriculum?

Geography:
- helps students to understand the impact of economic activity on people and communities
- brings out the relationship between local, national and global development
- shows that citizens can have an effect on their communities and the wider world
- explores issues of sustainable development
- promotes respect for other people/cultures and for the environment.

What does it have in common with citizenship?

Geography and citizenship education share:
- **concepts** – e.g. human rights, community, interdependence
- **skills** – e.g. research, analysis
- **content** – e.g. world as a global community, challenge of global interdependence
- **themes** – e.g. transport, housing
- **learning approaches** – e.g. enquiry-based learning, issue-led investigation.

What can citizenship offer to geography?

Citizenship education can:
- bring increased relevance to geography lessons
- help students understand the importance of geography
- promote understanding of development issues – e.g. fair trade
- encourage students to participate in local environmental projects – e.g. recycling, conservation.

How should the links be made?

For contributions from geography to be officially classified as part of the citizenship curriculum, simply identifying common concerns is not enough.

Lessons should have a specific 'citizenship orientation', for example, they should relate to citizenship concepts such as justice or human rights, or incorporate 'citizenship-driven' activities such as a discussion on debt cancellation in a unit on globalisation.

The citizenship element should be:
- the significant part of the lesson
- linked to the rest of the citizenship curriculum
- planned in association with the citizenship co-ordinator.

Learning objectives should be expressed in terms of the National Curriculum programmes of study for citizenship and made explicit in lesson planning.

QCA subject notes for geography provide examples of opportunities for delivering citizenship through geography. Exemplar units can be downloaded at:
www.standards.dfes.gov.uk/word/secondaryschemes/citsubject_geog.doc

Examples of citizenship opportunities in geography

GEOGRAPHY	CITIZENSHIP OPPORTUNITIES
Global dimension Globalisation	• Investigate global clothing industry • Consider pay and conditions of workers • Cost – benefit analysis for countries • Concept of ethical trade and fair trade • Reflect on ethics of boycotting companies who pay low wages or endanger the health of workers
Sustainability	• Investigate deforestation • Link to wood use in UK • Relate to pollution/global warming • Consider what Britain should do to promote sustainability • Consider action we can take in the local community
Local dimension Local amenities	• Investigate whether local amenities meet needs of local community • Prepare a report for the council suggesting how services could be improved • Consider who should pay • Find out how councils are financed
High street/town centre improvement schemes	• Investigate a local improvement scheme – take photographs, carry out a survey • Identify problems/suggest solutions • Reflect on decision-making when budgets are limited • Consider who makes the decisions and how local people can make their views heard
Local development	• Plan a simulation/role play of a new development, e.g. a supermarket • Consider how different interest groups are involved • Reflect on how decisions should be taken

IMPROVING PRACTICE

1 **Choose two or three of the key concepts listed here and consider how you could develop these in a geography lesson to promote citizenship learning.**

2 **Choose a unit of work from the geography curriculum and give it a 'citizenship orientation'. Work out the citizenship learning objectives and decide how you could make it clear to students that they are 'doing' citizenship.**

Citizenship through Religious Education

KEY ISSUES

How can Religious Education help to deliver the citizenship curriculum?

What does it have in common with citizenship?

What can citizenship offer to Religious Education?

How should the links be made?

How can Religious Education help to deliver the citizenship curriculum?

Religious Education:
- helps students to understand the part played by religion in social and political life
- encourages moral reflection on issues relating to public life
- provides opportunities to meet with individuals from a range of religious and ethnic communities.

What does it have in common with citizenship?

RE and citizenship education both deal with issues that are essentially moral – issues on which people often have strong and conflicting opinions. They adopt the same 'open' approach to moral issues, trying not to influence students' opinions unfairly, but helping them to learn to think for themselves.

RE and citizenship education also share:
- **content** – e.g. diversity of life in the UK, human rights, the world as a global community, the importance of resolving conflict fairly, the work of voluntary groups
- **skills** – e.g. research, analysis, expression, empathy, discussion and debate
- **attitudes** – e.g. openness, tolerance, mutual respect.

What can citizenship offer to Religious Education?

Citizenship education can:
- bring increased relevance to RE lessons
- help students to understand why it is important to study religious traditions
- provide opportunities to discuss topical social and political issues from a range of standpoints – religious and secular.

REMEMBER

Work on complementary skills – such as discussion and debate – can only be classed as citizenship if it is based on a citizenship issue or has a definite citizenship focus, e.g. a discussion of the right of soldiers to refuse to go to war on grounds of conscience.

How should the links be made?

For contributions from RE to be officially classified as part of the citizenship curriculum, simply identifying common concerns is not enough.

Lessons should have a specific 'citizenship orientation', for example, they should relate to topical issues and events such as the expansion of faith schools or the celebration of Holocaust Day, or incorporate 'citizenship-driven' activities such as a discussion on the law on blasphemy.

The citizenship element should be:
- the significant part of the lesson
- linked to the rest of the citizenship curriculum
- planned in association with the citizenship co-ordinator.

Learning objectives should be expressed in terms of the National Curriculum programmes of study for citizenship and made explicit in lesson planning.

A QCA exemplar unit of work on **RE** and citizenship education can be downloaded at:
www.standards.dfes.gov.uk/word/secondaryschemes/citsubject_re.doc

Examples of citizenship opportunities in Religious Education

RELIGIOUS EDUCATION	CITIZENSHIP OPPORTUNITIES
Forgiveness	• Youth justice system – sentencing of offenders.
Martin Luther King Mahatma Gandhi	• Human rights, political protest, civil disobedience – is it ever right to break the law?
Religious aid agencies, e.g. Salvation Army, Islamic Relief	• Work of voluntary groups, public services – how much should the government do for us? • Giving to charity – a citizen's duty?
Religion in the news	• Media portrayals of different religions – how accurate? • Faith schools – good or bad for society?
Jihad, just war, pacifism	• Discuss the legitimacy of a current conflict
Religious symbols	• Should the hijab be allowed in schools?
Christianity	• Religion in politics – bishops in the House of Lords, state occasions, e.g. Remembrance Day

IMPROVING PRACTICE

1 **Choose an RE topic you currently teach and consider how it might be adapted to contribute to the citizenship curriculum. Work out the citizenship learning objectives and explain how you would make it clear to students that they are 'doing' citizenship.**

2 **Draw up a list of the citizenship links that can be made with the following RE topics:**

   a) creation stories
   b) the Holocaust
   c) a world religion, e.g. Sikhism.

   Which of these links could you incorporate into your RE curriculum, with which year group(s) and how?

Citizenship through English

KEY ISSUES

How can English help to deliver the citizenship curriculum?

What does it have in common with citizenship?

What can citizenship offer to English?

How should the links be made?

How can English help to deliver the citizenship curriculum?

Novels, short stories, poetry and drama:
- provide contexts through which students can explore citizenship ideas and values
- throw a powerful light on issues of social and political significance
- make controversial subjects easier to discuss by embedding them in human situations – e.g. racism
- create defining images of complex ideas – e.g. of totalitarianism and individual freedom in George Orwell's *1984*.

Examples of citizenship opportunities in English

NOVELS	CITIZENSHIP OPPORTUNITIES
Noughts and Crosses **Malorie Blackman** Set in a sci-fi alternative world segregated into noughts (second class citizens) and crosses (dominant class)	• Explores racial prejudice and the determination to act justly
Animal Farm **George Orwell** Animals take over their farm with the intention of creating a society where all are equal	• Explores the notion of an equal society, rights and responsibilities, justice and the nature of authoritarianism
To Kill a Mockingbird **Harper Lee** Lawyer in segregated southern states of America defends a black man accused of murder	• Explores racism and the notion of equality before the law, courage to defend a point of view, determination to act justly
Goodnight Mister Tom **Michelle Magorian** Widower takes an evacuee into his home during World War Two	• Explores rights and responsibilities, commitment to active citizenship, tolerance, belief in human dignity

What does it have in common with citizenship?

English and citizenship education share a common interest in the media. Media studies activities that contribute to the citizenship curriculum include:
- **analysing advertisements** – how they impact on young people and society
- **examining news values** – how some stories are given preference over others
- **studying TV soaps** – how they cover topical issues, e.g. HIV, homophobia.

There are also close connections between the skills that both subjects seek to develop. En 1, 2 and 3 (as specified in the citizenship programmes of study) are closely aligned to the citizenship skills of enquiry and communication, and participation and responsible action. English and citizenship education share the same focus on analysing texts and sources of information, detecting bias, arguing a case, structuring talks and speeches, and writing to persuade.

What can citizenship offer to English?

Citizenship education offers:
- a context for developing English skills
- a rationale for analysis of the news media
- topics relevant to students' lives
- important themes for literature and drama.

How should the links be made?

For contributions from English to be officially classified as part of the citizenship curriculum, simply identifying common concerns is not enough.

Lessons should have a specific 'citizenship orientation', for example, they should relate to citizenship concepts such as justice or human rights, or incorporate 'citizenship-driven' activities such as an analysis of the use of rhetoric in a political speech.

The citizenship element should be:
- the significant part of the lesson
- linked to the rest of the citizenship curriculum
- planned in association with the citizenship co-ordinator.

Learning objectives should be expressed in terms of the National Curriculum programmes of study for citizenship and made explicit in lesson planning.

> **REMEMBER**
>
> Work on complementary skills – such as discussion and debate – can only be classed as citizenship if it is based on a citizenship issue or has a definite citizenship focus, e.g. a discussion on racism set in the context of school policy.

IMPROVING PRACTICE

1 **Choose a novel, such as** When Hitler Stole Pink Rabbit **by Judith Kerr, or an autobiography, such as** Coming to England **by Floella Benjamin. Identify some citizenship themes or concepts that could be drawn out and developed through the story.**

2 **Plan a short unit of work for English – say, two or three lessons – based on a topical social issue. Work out the citizenship learning objectives and explain how you would make it clear to students that they are 'doing' citizenship.**

Citizenship through science

KEY ISSUES

How can science help to deliver the citizenship curriculum?

What does it have in common with citizenship?

What can citizenship offer to science?

How should the links be made?

FOCUS

Links in key stages 3 and 4 (single science)

• **Sc1 Ideas and evidence** KS3 1a) and 1c); and KS4 1a)–d): the development of scientific ideas, experimentation and evidence, work of scientists, scientific controversies

• **Sc2 Life processes and living things** KS3 2m) and n), 4a), 5a); and KS4 3g) and 4c): immunisation, variation, genetic engineering, the impact of humans on the environment and sustainable development

• **Sc4 Physical processes** KS3 5a)–c); and KS4 4b): energy resources

• **Breadth of study** KS3 and 4 a)–c) a: application, benefits and drawbacks of scientific and technological developments related to the environment, health and quality of life

How can science help to deliver the Citizenship curriculum?

Modern society continually throws up issues in personal and public life that require an understanding of science that is coupled with the skills of moral discourse and the ability to make critical judgements.

What does it have in common with citizenship?

Points of contact between science and citizenship education include:
- **ethical dilemmas requiring scientific literacy** – e.g. use of animals or human tissue in research
- **issues about science and the environment** – e.g. global warming
- **the impact of technical advances on society** – e.g. internet
- **the control of science** – e.g. allocation of research funding.

What can citizenship offer to science?

Citizenship education can bring a human dimension into science. It helps students to:
- reflect on and discuss the social consequences of science
- appreciate the crucial role that science plays in the world
- see that science is controversial and that scientists have different viewpoints and disagree about evidence and risk.

If you lack confidence in handling discussion about the social dimension of science:
- start with a limited number of topics, giving one or two lessons a definite 'citizenship-orientation'
- ask a humanities teacher about appropriate teaching strategies.

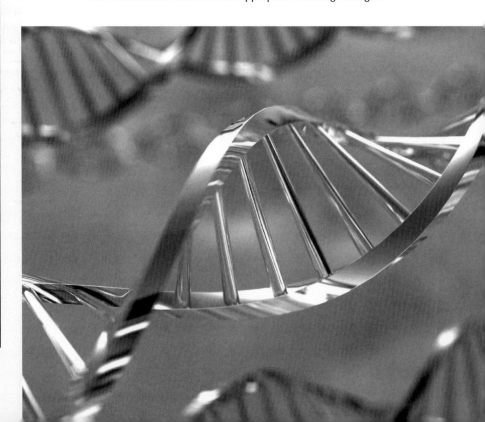

How should the links be made?

For contributions from science to be officially classified as part of the citizenship curriculum, simply adding a few discussion points at the end of the lesson is not enough.

The citizenship element should be:
- the significant part of the lesson
- linked to the rest of the citizenship curriculum
- planned in association with the citizenship co-ordinator.

Learning objectives should be expressed in terms of the National Curriculum programmes of study for citizenship and made explicit in lesson planning.

WWW

The QCA scheme of work 'What's in the public interest?' provides a template for studying current and controversial public issues with a science dimension: **www.standards.dfes.gov.uk/schemes2/citizenship/cit20/** For other relevant materials and activities, see: **www.sycd.co.uk**

Examples of citizenship opportunities in science

SCIENCE	CITIZENSHIP OPPORTUNITIES
Variation	• Understanding reasons for racial differences in terms of inherited characteristics • Variety of ethnic identities in UK
Immunisation	• Debate about vaccination – public good and private interest; recently MMR
Genetics	• Debate about gene therapy to prevent diseases; use of embryos; notion of designer babies • Genetic screening, how it might be used by employers/insurance companies
Genetically-modified food	• Cloning animals and humans • Arguments for and against GM crops, including environmental impact • Debate about selling GM foods in UK supermarkets
Energy resources	• What happens when certain energy resources run out? • Impact of energy generation on environment – how to minimise this • Rights and responsibilities of humans to change lifestyle – local and global implications

---

IMPROVING PRACTICE

1 Plan a citizenship activity to accompany a unit of work from the science curriculum. Work out the citizenship learning objectives and decide how you could make it clear to students that they are 'doing' citizenship.

2 How could you respond to the view that it is 'not the science teacher's job to teach ethics'?

Citizenship through ICT

KEY ISSUES

How can citizenship and ICT (Information and Communications Technologies) complement each other?

How should the links be made?

How can citizenship and ICT (Information and Communications Technologies) complement each other?

ICT is a skills-based subject that seeks raw material from a range of other subjects for its own subject matter.

Citizenship education and ICT can complement each other in four main ways, by:

1 Providing a context for information-based activities
   Citizenship education helps students develop their skills of 'exchanging and sharing information' by introducing topical material they are likely to find interesting. Students can research issues, evaluating different sources, and sharing and debating their findings, e.g. the age of consent or human rights abuse.

2 Developing ICT skills
   Citizenship education gives purpose and direction to activities that develop ICT skills, for example:
   • using search engines to research current issues
   • word-processing a persuasive document
   • making presentations where technical skills are developed alongside the need for a logical line of argument
   • developing a discussion forum for the school council or school website
   • creating websites that have a real audience.

3 Constructing and interpreting databases
   The ability to use, handle and interpret sets of figures – including the use and abuse of statistics – is an important aspect of the citizenship curriculum. ICT teaches the skills involved in setting up databases and constructing and manipulating spreadsheets. Citizenship education can provide the data for ICT activities and give the lesson a real sense of purpose, e.g. data on crime or health statistics.

4 Evaluating the tools and uses of ICT
   Citizenship education provides a vehicle for students to evaluate critically the use of ICT tools, e.g. advantages and disadvantages of e-voting. They can also look at the social implications of new developments in ICT, such as:
   • the impact of ICT in globalisation
   • how personal data is collected and used, e.g. by the police or government agencies
   • use of the world wide web for pornography or terrorism.

How should the links be made?

The key question for you as an ICT teacher is how formal a contribution you wish to make to citizenship education.

Many ICT departments use citizenship issues as a context for information-based activities. However, for contributions from ICT to be officially classified as part of the citizenship curriculum, simply using citizenship issues as a contextual device is not enough.
The citizenship element should be:
* the significant part of the lesson
* linked to the rest of the citizenship curriculum
* planned in association with the citizenship co-ordinator.

Learning objectives should be expressed in terms of the National Curriculum programmes of study for citizenship and made explicit in lesson planning.

FOCUS

Students at South Dartmoor Community College operate a citizenship discussion forum on the college website. The 'OffTopic' section on the website ranges over a variety of topics, e.g. racism, fox hunting, communism, genetic engineering and the Iraq war. Students use aliases and anyone who wishes to use it has to register with the (staff) website manager first. There are a number of ground rules, e.g. about language and respecting other people's opinions – otherwise the forum is entirely controlled and moderated by students. The forum includes a section where teachers can set homework and offer web links for projects and assignments. Nat Parnell, website manager, says, 'It's a good way for students to communicate and there's some serious discussion on there. It's about giving people a voice and that surely is what we mean by citizenship.'

IMPROVING PRACTICE

1   **Choose a topic from the ICT curriculum and consider how it might be adapted to contribute to the citizenship curriculum. Work out the citizenship learning objectives and decide how you could make it clear to students that they are 'doing' citizenship.**

2   **What sorts of citizenship learning can be developed from student involvement in a school website?**

Citizenship through maths

FOCUS

Crime statistics

Ask your students to compare the official police and Home Office figures with those from the British Crime Survey. Discuss the social construction of these figures: the reasons for the differences and how the figures change when the definition of a crime changes. A social scientist should be able to help you with this.

How can maths help to deliver the citizenship curriculum?

Figures and statistics play a prominent part in debates in the public arena. They are used as platforms for persuasive argument and are subject to manipulation and obfuscation. Mathematics has a unique contribution to make to citizenship education in helping students to interpret data and understand big numbers and how they are calculated.

Equally important is an understanding of probability and risk which are crucial in ethical debates on issues such as health, for example, immunisation, disease and genetically modified food.

What can citizenship offer to maths?

Citizenship education can give maths increased relevance by providing it with real-life contexts and showing why an understanding of maths is important to our lives and in making decisions.

One area where maths and citizenship education come together in a practical way in school is in student participation in budgeting for citizenship activities. This includes anything from student-organised fundraising events and school trips to students managing a budget allocated to their school council.

How should the links be made?

The key question for you as a maths teacher is how formal a contribution you wish to make to citizenship education.

Many maths departments teach units on data-handling skills and use a citizenship context for these. However, for contributions from maths to be officially classified as part of the citizenship curriculum, simply using citizenship issues as a contextual device is not enough.

The citizenship element should be:
- **the significant part of the lesson**
- **linked to the rest of the citizenship curriculum**
- **planned in association with the citizenship co-ordinator.**

Learning objectives should be expressed in terms of the National Curriculum programmes of study for citizenship and made explicit in lesson planning.

Examples of citizenship opportunities in maths

MATHS	CITIZENSHIP OPPORTUNITIES
Ma4 – applying and handling data Collecting, interpreting, discussing and making inferences from data Representing data in different graphical forms	• Crime statistics • Global statistics related to poverty, health and the environment • Statistics relating to the economy and how it functions
Ma2 – Using and applying number Looking at big numbers and considering what these mean Concepts of proportion and ratio Adding and subtractions, percentages, fractions and decimals	• Elections – various computations, e.g. turnout figures and percentage swings needed for a majority, proportional versus first-past-the-post systems • Global figures on debt, diseases like AIDS/HIV, world trade, migration • Fair trade – breaking down the cost of products to show proportions taken by different groups and organisations • Personal finance – budgeting, interest rates on credit cards and loans, working out percentages on sale goods, impact of debt on families

WWW

A video case study of a Year 8 lesson on citizenship through maths, analysing data protection issues using spreadsheet functions of sum, average, minimum and maximum, is available at:
www.curriculumonline.gov.uk/CaseStudies/citizenshipcasestudy.htm

IMPROVING PRACTICE

1   Choose a topic from the maths curriculum and consider how it might be adapted to contribute to the citizenship curriculum. Work out the citizenship learning objectives and decide how you could make it clear to students that they are 'doing' citizenship.

2   Think of some topical issues where the application of different concepts of 'average' has important social implications. Choose one and work it up into a lesson. How could you make the social implications explicit?

Citizenship through art and design

KEY ISSUES

How can art and design help to deliver the citizenship curriculum?

What can citizenship offer to art and design?

How should the links be made?

FOCUS

Citizenship education through photography

Photography is an excellent medium for exploring citizenship issues – from collecting evidence of the state of the school environment or local amenities to documenting public events such as marches or demonstrations. The process of choosing what to photograph and how to photograph it enables students not only to engage with the social and political world around them, but also to understand the impact of visual media upon society. Editing, selecting and captioning images for display provide important opportunities for students to reflect upon the issues they are studying and how they might respond to them.

How can art and design help to deliver the citizenship curriculum?

Art and design is a vital and vibrant part of every society, reflecting the ideas, beliefs and values of citizens in the past and present.

It can contribute to the citizenship curriculum by:
- providing a visual medium through which students can reflect on and articulate citizenship issues
- supplying visual stimuli that provide a context for students' understanding of citizenship issues
- developing students' visual literacy skills and ability to communicate views about the built environment and its role in society
- helping students to understand the role of art and design in political protest and campaigning
- promoting appreciation and respect for cultural diversity – through studying the art and craft of different societies and ethnic groups.

What can citizenship offer to art and design?

Citizenship education provides a context for art and design work and involves students in a critical discourse about the world they see around them.

It also helps students to recognise how artists and craftspeople have an important role to play in the well-being of society.

What sort of links should you make?

The key question for you as an art and design teacher is how formal a contribution you wish to make to citizenship.

All art and design makes references to citizenship issues from time to time. However, for contributions from art and design to be officially classified as part of the citizenship curriculum, simply making reference to citizenship issues is not enough.

The citizenship element should be:
- the significant part of the lesson
- linked to the rest of the citizenship curriculum
- planned in association with the citizenship co-ordinator.

Learning objectives should be expressed in terms of the National Curriculum programmes of study for citizenship and made explicit in lesson planning.

Examples of citizenship opportunities in art and design

ART AND DESIGN	CITIZENSHIP OPPORTUNITIES
Art of different cultures	• Learning about the lifestyle and values of other cultures • Understanding how art and craft is linked to religious beliefs and rituals • Issues of diversity in society
Art and the built environment	• Understanding the impact of the built environment on the quality of life in society • Developing visual literacy skills to be able to articulate views about the urban environment
Art and the media	• Understanding how photographs and visual images are used in the media – newspapers, magazines, advertisements – to convey messages to different audiences
Art and politics	• Understanding how the visual arts can be used in political protest and campaigning – posters, graffiti art, TV campaigns

WWW

Schemes of work for citizenship through art and design at key stage 3 are available at: **www.standards.dfes.gov.uk/schemes2/citizenship/sec_art**

IMPROVING PRACTICE

Choose a topic from the art and design curriculum and consider how it might be adapted to contribute to the citizenship curriculum. Work out the citizenship learning objectives and decide how you could make it clear to students that they are 'doing' citizenship.

Designing a sensory garden: a cross-generational design and technology project

Hazel Grove High School

Year 9 pupils were involved in a competition to design a sensory garden/quiet area within the school grounds over three lessons during Technology Week. Working in small teams, they were briefed by the grounds staff on issues such as accessibility, site restrictions, possible construction materials and plants. Age Concern provided expertise about planting and design constraints.

The relatively short timescale of the project and the bringing in of external expertise encouraged the students to ask questions and think around the problem creatively. Some students prepared 3D graphic designs using ICT. Many of their ideas were incorporated into the final design, for example the concept of concentric circles, opportunities for the playing of music, the layout and spacing of benches and raised gardens to allow wheelchair access. Additional elements were contributed by the science and food technology departments, for example a solar system design built into the stonework flooring and a herb garden.

Citizenship dimensions of the project included working on a 'real' issue and consulting with future users of the area and finding out about their needs and rights, for example space requirements for wheelchair users. They also learned about the work of voluntary groups such as Age Concern.

In feedback sessions, students said how much they liked being involved with something that was actually going to be built and mentioned their increased respect for the role of the school grounds staff. They felt they had learned from having to think about the problem of wheelchair access and the way that they had to integrate a number of different skills.

The positive collaboration between the school and Age Concern has led to planning for an ambitious Lottery-funded Heritage project – 'Young Roots' – incorporating curriculum links to local history, dance, music and ICT as well as citizenship education. Both the school and Age Concern see many citizenship benefits in breaking down generational barriers through practical projects such as these.

Chapter 5:
Citizenship in the Life of the School

Introduction

Student involvement in the life of the school is an integral part of the citizenship curriculum in secondary schools. It not only reinforces what is taught in the classroom, but also acts as a source of 'real', everyday citizenship learning in its own right.

This chapter considers ways in which students can contribute to decision-making in, and the running of, schools and how these can be integrated into the wider citizenship curriculum.

It is relevant to anyone responsible for teaching, leading or promoting citizenship in secondary schools.

Contents include:
- Creating a citizenship ethos
- Student consultation and decision-making
- Students in positions of responsibility
- Involving students in learning
- School/student councils
- Case studies: 1) Special needs fair trade shop
                 2) Peer counselling
- Training exercise: Students as researchers

Creating a citizenship ethos

KEY ISSUES

What is meant by the ethos of a school?

What sort of ethos is a citizenship ethos?

How does it contribute to citizenship learning?

How do you create a citizenship ethos?

Where do you start?

What is meant by the ethos of a school?

The ethos of a school is its social, moral, spiritual and cultural environment. It is the way the school goes about its daily business: the messages sent out by its rules, procedures and fundamental values; how its different members relate to one another and the part they play in school life – staff, students, governors and parents. It is sometimes known as the school culture or climate.

What sort of ethos is a citizenship ethos?

A citizenship ethos is one that embodies the values of **democratic citizenship**.

It is an ethos which upholds high standards of fairness and respect for human rights, and in which everyone involved is valued equally and encouraged to take an active part in the life of the school.

It gives students a strong voice in the life of school and encourages them to support their communities and the environment – supporting and, crucially, 'adding value' to the *Every Child Matters* agenda by providing opportunities for students to reflect on their participation."

> I would like to make the link between 'participation' in citizenship and the 'making a contribution' element of **Every Child Matters**. Making a contribution involves 'asking children and young people what works, what doesn't and what could work better, and involving them on an on-going basis in the design, delivery and evaluation of services.
>
> David Bell, Chief Inspector of Schools, 2005

How does it contribute to citizenship learning?

Students learn implicitly from what they see and experience in the daily life of the school, as well as from what they are taught explicitly in the classroom.

It is through seeing and experiencing citizenship in 'real' action in the everyday environment of the school – its structures and relationships – that students begin to learn what it is to be a citizen. They need to become aware that they are members of a community with rights and responsibilities, and have the opportunity to acquire the knowledge and skills needed to exercise these.

> Schools that model democratic values by ... inviting students to take part in shaping school life are most effective in promoting civic knowledge and engagement ... and [their students] are more likely to expect to vote as adults than other students.
>
> Torney-Purta et al.,
> **Citizenship and Education in Twenty-Eight Countries:**
> **civic knowledge and engagement at age fourteen**, 2002

How do you create a citizenship ethos?

Creating a citizenship ethos involves more than just drawing up a 'wish-list' of the sorts of values and relationships you would like to permeate your school. It means embedding these values and relationships in concrete practices and procedures – in particular, through providing opportunities for students to:

- **play a part in decision-making** – e.g. about uniform, codes of conduct, school food, the school environment
- **take on positions of responsibility** – e.g. as peer educators, associate governors, student councillors
- **manage their own learning** – e.g. through self/peer assessment, setting learning targets.

Research suggests there is an association between schools that encourage student participation and overall academic achievement, attendance and general discipline.

Where do you start?

A good place to start is with a review of your school's current ethos. There are a number of mechanisms you can use to collect evidence about this, including:

- focus groups
- questionnaires and surveys
- governors' visits
- inspection reports
- 'student pursuits' – shadowing students and observing at first hand how they experience school.

What is important is that students are involved in the process from the outset.

School ethos or culture can be assessed, planned for, implemented, monitored and evaluated like any other aspect of a school's work. It should be referenced in the citizenship education policy and development plan, and strongly linked to the school improvement plan, as well as featuring explicitly in the school prospectus.

IMPROVING PRACTICE

1 Draw up a list of values that you think characterise a citizenship ethos. For each one, think of some concrete steps that can be taken to embed it in the life of a school.

2 What aspects of the citizenship programme of study do you think a citizenship ethos contributes most towards? Why?

3 What do you see as the biggest obstacles to developing a citizenship ethos in a school? How can these obstacles be overcome?

Student consultation and decision-making

KEY ISSUES

Why should students be
consulted about school issues?

What sort of issues can they
be consulted on?

What methods can you use?

How far can students be
involved in actual decision-
making?

How does this fit into the
wider citizenship curriculum?

Why should students be consulted about school issues?

Students should be consulted about school issues because:
- they have a right to be involved in decisions that affect them
- it is an important opportunity for citizenship learning
- it improves relationships and promotes dialogue in school.

It is also a legal requirement. The Education Act (2002) requires governing bodies of
maintained schools and LAs to take account of guidance from the Secretary of State for
Education and Skills about consulting with pupils in matters that affect them.

The DfES guidance document, **Working Together: giving children and young
people a say**, is available at **www.teachernet.gov.uk**

What sort of issues can they be consulted on?

There is a wide range of school issues that students can and should be encouraged to
express their opinions about, including:
- school rules, sanctions and rewards
- anti-racist, anti-bullying and equal opportunities policies
- drugs, sex and relationships education
- learning and teaching methods
- dress codes
- curriculum content and structure
- social facilities/out-of-school hours activities
- induction of new students and student welfare
- parents' evenings
- staff appointments
- travel to school
- school mission statements, development and improvement plans
- applications for specialist school status.

> " Children have a right to express their views on all matters of
> concern to them, and to have those views taken seriously in
> accordance with their age and maturity. "
>
> Article 12, UN Convention of the Rights of the Child

What methods can you use?

Methods you can use include:
- class and school councils
- group discussions
- student working parties
- planning groups
- questionnaires/surveys
- suggestion boxes.

You can also build consultation into the formal curriculum, for example an art/photography
project drawing attention to problem areas in the school.

How far can students be involved in actual decision-making?

Students need to know exactly what their role is in school decision-making. This includes what they are entitled to comment about but have no power over as well as what they are allowed to decide for themselves. This is also a useful lesson for their involvement in life beyond school.

While they should not have the final say in appointing staff, for example, student committees can nevertheless provide valuable feedback to governors through their involvement in the appointment process.

How does this fit into the wider citizenship curriculum?

Giving students a say in the running of their school presents important opportunities for acquiring the skills, knowledge and understanding of citizenship through action. To make the most of these opportunities, students need to be able to see the 'bigger picture'. This means building time into lessons and/or tutorial periods for students to:
- discuss what they should be consulted about and how
- consider the current state of consultation and decision-making in school
- suggest how it might be improved in the future
- reflect on their personal involvement
- record their views or what they have learned.

Students doing GCSE Citizenship Studies can use the consultation process as the basis for a coursework assignment, for example a survey on personal safety in school.

IMPROVING PRACTICE

1 What are the most influential decisions that have been taken in your school recently? How many of these, if any, were students involved in? Do you consider this amount of involvement to be satisfactory? Why or why not?

2 Which methods of student consultation do you see as most appropriate to your school? Why? Who is best placed to implement them – governors, SMT, teachers, the students themselves or someone else?

3 Draw up a plan of action to ensure that student consultation is included in your school improvement/ development plan.

Students in positions of responsibility

KEY ISSUES

Why should students be
encouraged to take on
positions of responsibility?

What sort of responsibilities
are students capable of?

Can students be involved in
staff appointments?

Can students be school
governors?

How does this fit into the
wider citizenship curriculum?

Why should students be encouraged to take on positions of responsibility?

Taking on positions of responsibility helps students to:
- see themselves as active members of a community
- grow in confidence and maturity
- acquire new skills, knowledge and understanding
- prepare for the world of work and/or continuing education and/or training beyond school.

It has a positive effect on general discipline and helps to create a more cohesive and inclusive school.

What sort of responsibilities are students capable of?

Depending on their maturity and experience, students are capable of taking on a whole range of different responsibilities in school, for example:
- organising events
- welcoming/supporting new pupils
- leading assemblies
- reception duties
- acting as visitor guides
- peer counselling/mediation
- managing school websites/newsletters
- running after-school clubs
- working on recycling/environmental projects
- running a school shop
- helping to develop school prospectuses/promotional material
- peer education
- acting as class representatives/student councillors
- sitting on school working parties
- contributing to everyday school management.

What is important is that students are fully briefed about their responsibilities, are given support and training, have the opportunity to discuss and receive feedback on their experiences and can include them in their personal portfolio and/or progress file.

Can students be involved in staff appointments?

Students can be involved in staff appointments by:
- helping to draw up job descriptions
- conducting their own interviews
- giving feedback on demonstration lessons
- observing candidates as they show them round the school.

Can students be school governors?

Under-18s cannot be school governors, but they are allowed to be '**associate members**' of the governing body. As such, they are entitled to attend full governing body meetings (apart from the discussion of confidential issues) and become members of governing body committees – though they do not have voting rights. (Statutory guidance is available to download at **www.standards.dfes.gov.uk/federations/pdf/Collaboration_20 Guidance.pdf?version=1)**

How does this fit into the wider citizenship curriculum?

Encouraging students to take on positions of responsibility presents important opportunities for acquiring the skills, knowledge and understanding of citizenship through action. To make the most of these opportunities, students need to be able to see the 'bigger picture'.

This means building time into lessons and/or tutorial periods for them to:
- discuss the responsibilities students should have
- consider their current responsibilities
- suggest how these might be developed in the future
- reflect on their personal involvement
- record their views and what they have learned
- celebrate their involvement and achievement.

FOCUS

At Lawrence Sheriff School, elected members of the school council interview candidates for teaching posts and then pass on their comments to the senior management team before they interview the candidates.

REMEMBER

It is important to distinguish between positions of responsibility that all students in a year are able to experience, and ones that are only available to a few. The former may be included in your 'core' or 'entitlement' citizenship provision, but the latter are better designated as 'enrichment'.

IMPROVING PRACTICE

1   What types of responsibility do students already have in your school? To what extent are they aware that these are part of your citizenship provision and their citizenship entitlement?

2   What types of student responsibility require training? Who should be responsible for this training and how should it be delivered?

3   What types of responsibility do you think all secondary school students should be entitled to experience? Why?

4   What opportunities are there in your school for students to see the 'bigger picture' in lessons – to discuss, reflect on, record and celebrate the responsibilities they have taken on?

Involving students in learning

KEY ISSUES

What does it mean to involve students in learning?

How do they benefit from this?

What forms can this take?

What about the curriculum?

How does this fit into the wider citizenship curriculum?

What does it mean to involve students in learning?

Involving students in learning means:
- consulting them about what and how they are taught
- helping them to understand what they need to do to succeed
- encouraging them to play a part in the learning and teaching process.

Giving students a real say in their learning is essential to 'personalised learning', i.e. tailoring education to individual needs, interests and aptitudes. For details, see **www.standards.dfes.gov.uk/personalised learning/**

How do they benefit from this?

Involving students in learning helps to improve their achievement and increase their motivation to learn – not only in citizenship education, but across the curriculum.

> The aim is to enable pupils to understand themselves better as learners and so take greater control of and responsibility for their learning, transferring and applying a widening repertoire of learning approaches in different subjects and contexts.
>
> DfES, 2004

What forms can this take?

Students can be involved in learning in three main ways:

1 **Playing a part in policy development** – e.g. being consulted about course content, teaching methods, problem behaviour, class groupings, homework

2 **Taking responsibility for delivery** – e.g. peer education, peer assessment, delivering aspects of citizenship education, such as reporting back on projects and coursework, carrying out school/student surveys and investigating local and community issues

3 **Managing their own learning** – e.g. voting on questions for class discussion, self-assessment, commenting on the pace of teaching, negotiating learning targets and how to achieve them, choosing topics to research, designing research methods.

Teaching staff may sometimes feel uneasy about the prospect of young people having a more significant role in the management and delivery of learning and teaching. This is perfectly understandable: it represents a shift in the traditional teacher–student relationship. Change of this kind takes time and depends on the creation of a climate of mutual trust in which everyone involved – staff and students alike – feels valued and able to contribute to the life of the school community.

What about the curriculum?

While the National Curriculum is a legal requirement, how it is timetabled and delivered is left largely to the school. There is plenty of scope, therefore, for involving students in curriculum planning and evaluation – not just in citizenship education but in the curriculum as a whole.

Students are able to contribute to school development and improvement plans, review policies and schemes of work.

How does this fit into the wider citizenship curriculum?

Involving students in learning presents important opportunities for acquiring the skills, knowledge and understanding of citizenship through action.

To make the most of these opportunities, students need to be able to see the 'bigger picture'.

This means building time into lessons and/or tutorial periods for students to:
- discuss how students should be involved in learning
- consider their current level of involvement
- suggest how these might be developed in future
- reflect on their personal involvement
- record their views and what they have learned
- celebrate their involvement and achievement.

IMPROVING PRACTICE

1   What do you see as the main obstacles to involving students in learning in a secondary school? How can they be overcome?

2   To what extent are students currently involved in learning in your school? Do you think this level of involvement is about right or is there room for improvement? If so, how?

3   Think of ways in which students might be involved in drawing up a key stage 3 or 4 scheme of work for citizenship education.

4   How do you respond to the view that involving students in learning is an 'unnecessary distraction' or that students 'are not in a position to criticise what they do not yet fully understand'?

School/student councils

KEY ISSUES

Why is it important to have a school/student council?

How much power should it have?

What makes a school/student council an effective one?

How does this fit into the wider citizenship curriculum?

Why is it important to have a school/student council?

A school/student council:
- gives students a voice
- helps students to see themselves as active members of a community
- teaches students democratic skills and about the democratic process
- improves decision-making generally in the school.

> The students picked the décor for the new toilets. It hasn't been graffitied or vandalised once.
>
> Sarah Purtil, Kingsbury High School in **TES** (**Times Educational Supplement**), 14 February 2003

How much power should it have?

Students need to be clear about what their council can and cannot discuss or decide. There are certain issues affecting students that students themselves have no formal right to decide, for example dress codes. However, there is nothing to prevent a school council from discussing such issues and passing their comments to the SMT or governing body.

> At Deptford Green School we aim to build a culture in which students have a say in the life of the school. The key to this is our school council.
>
> Pete Pattison, Citizenship Co-ordinator, Deptford Green School

What makes a school/student council an effective one?

Effective school/student councils:
- have clear terms of reference – avoiding unrealistic expectations
- are elected – preferably in a secret ballot with hustings
- have written constitutions – regulating number of representatives, powers, elections and meeting schedules
- are genuinely representative – e.g. involve special needs students
- are accountable – ensuring the whole student body is involved
- are backed by the SMT – endorsing council decisions as much as possible
- have an adult facilitator – giving technical help/guidance and monitoring progress
- have elected officers – e.g. a chair
- meet regularly – a minimum of twice every half-term
- use formal procedures – e.g. minutes
- don't have too many members – around 20 gives everyone a chance to contribute
- involve all students – through regular consultation/feedback
- are properly resourced – preferably with a budget and/or fundraising capacity and access to IT and photocopier
- are given training – e.g. in meeting protocol
- have a good communications system – through tutor periods and/or assemblies, a council notice board, school website or newsletter
- are actively promoted – by the SMT in school and externally through prospectuses, promotional material and press releases
- are integrated into the school's overall decision-making process – e.g. representatives involved in staff or curriculum planning and review meetings.

How does it fit into the wider citizenship curriculum?

Having a school/student council presents important opportunities for acquiring the skills, knowledge and understanding of citizenship through action.

To make the most of these opportunities, students need to be able to see the 'bigger picture'.

This means building time into lessons and/or tutorial periods for students to:
- discuss what a school council is for and how it should operate
- consider the effectiveness of their present school council
- suggest how it might be improved in the future
- reflect on their personal involvement
- record their views and what they have learned
- celebrate their involvement and achievement.

IMPROVING PRACTICE

1 **List some of the skills, knowledge and understanding you think students can acquire through participation in council activities. Which aspects of the citizenship curriculum does a school/student council contribute most towards?**

2 **What sorts of things should a school/student council be allowed and not allowed to:**
a) discuss
b) decide?

Why? Who should have the final say about this?

3 **How can you make sure it isn't the same few students being involved year after year?**

1 Special needs fair trade shop

St Christopher's Special School

Students at St Christopher's Special School, Wrexham, have opened a fair trade shop in their school and trained students from other schools in how to do the same – with the help of representatives from Traidcraft and the Co-op.

At the opening of their fair trade shop, Traderite, by the local MP, Ian Lucas. students performed a play called *Spread The News* and displayed their dedicated website. The Deputy Mayor presented Fair Trade Coalition certificates to students and representatives from two other schools. Fair trade scones biscuits, tea and coffee were served to those attending.

Subsequently, students presented four fair trade assemblies in local primary schools – encouraging pupils to visit St Christopher's with a view to opening their own shops.

Special events were organised for Fair Trade Fortnight including:

- tea and coffee tasting
- a dance for adults to promote fair trade - serving fair trade wine
- locally produced beer, cheese and fair trade grapes
- a penalty shoot-out at half time advertising fair trade during a local football match.

What have the students learned from their fair trade shop?

In addition to learning about issues of fair trade, students have been able to develop their maths skills. The shop forms a basis for entry level maths coursework, including analysis of questionnaire data, developing a business plan, ordering items, and completing the daily and weekly accounts and stock checks. The students learn about bank accounts and it is planned to use any profits to purchase shares in Traidcraft, allowing students to track these ethical shares against non-ethical shares over time.

The whole project qualified for a BT Citizenship Award. The £2 000 grant was spent on equipment for the shop, stock and the launch reception. The most successful BT award projects qualify for one of three national £10 000 awards. You can find out more information at **www.bt.com/education/schoolsawards.**

2 Peer counselling

Frederick Gough School, Bottesford

Peer counselling can be an effective way of dealing with bullying and associated problems in school. It is especially designed to meet the needs of students who would rather speak about issues of a personal nature to a peer than to an adult.

At Frederick Gough School, potential peer counsellors are recruited through a Year 9 assembly on the aims of peer counselling and the type of person who might make a good counsellor. Information is sent out to Year 9 and a meeting is held for those interested.

Volunteers are asked to write a short letter (with guidance from a form teacher and possibly their parents/guardians) saying why they think they would make a good counsellor. Subsequently, four or five students are selected – following a letter of consent from parents/guardians.

Training with an outside agency takes place in the spring term. It consists of ten one-and-a-half hour sessions after school dealing, among other things, with issues of confidentiality and what can and can't be discussed with fellow students. Those completing the course receive a certificate.

New peer counsellors start work in September. They begin by briefing new students and their parents and going round all Year 7, 8 and 9 forms to show their faces and tell people how to make an appointment should they need one.

Students who would like to make an appointment go to the counselling office at break where they can speak to one of the peer counsellors and arrange a lunch-time session. During the sessions, the peer counsellors make notes on who they have seen, when and what they have discussed – each has their own personal book which is kept locked away for privacy when not in use.

The role of the staff member in charge is a key one – not least to provide support mechanisms for the peer counsellors themselves and to deal with child protection issues should they arise.

Further details of this scheme can be found in *Teaching Citizenship*, issue 1, Summer 2001.

Training exercise

Students as researchers

Study the text on Hastingsbury Upper School below.

1 **What are the potential benefits of setting up a Students-as-Researchers group in a secondary school? Could there be any disadvantages? If so, do you think the benefits outweigh the disadvantages or vice versa?**
2 **Do you agree with Brian Roberts that there are 'no real areas where students can't be involved in the decision-making in school'? Why or why not?**
3 **What different aspects of the citizenship curriculum can a Students-as-Researchers group contribute towards? What does this imply for the remit and methods employed by such a group?**
4 **What issues, if any, do you think would be worth students investigating in your own school?**

Students as Researchers at Hastingsbury Upper School

The 'Students-as-Researchers' movement is arguably amongst the most significant student participation developments in recent years because of its potential to re-draw organisational lines of responsibility and accountability in school.

Hastingsbury Upper School in Bedford was one of the first schools in England to set up a 'Students-as-Researchers' group. The group developed out of a sub-committee of the student council. The students involved collect and analyse information and evidence on specific school issues and report their findings to students and staff.

One of the issues they have investigated is the structure of the school day. Students felt there was a problem getting from one lesson to the next and suggested that a five-minute gap between lessons would help.

More controversially, student researchers sit in lessons as non-participant observers to investigate issues of learning and teaching. After a certain amount of resistance initially, this has now been generally accepted by teaching staff as helping to create a better learning environment in the school as a whole. Students now have a better understanding of how the school works and staff have access to a wider range of student perspectives.

Brian Roberts, Vocational and Careers Officer, says, 'There are no real areas where students can't be involved in the decision-making in school.'

Further details of this scheme will be found in the handbook and training video, *Citizenship: Raising the Standard* (Citizenship Foundation/Connect Publications, 2005).

Section 3:
Citizenship in Secondary Schools

Chapter 6:
Citizenship through the Wider Community

Introduction

Providing opportunities for student involvement in the community beyond the school is an essential part of the citizenship curriculum in secondary schools, alongside classroom teaching and participation in school life.

This chapter considers different ways in which student involvement in the wider community can contribute to citizenship learning, and how this may be integrated into the wider citizenship curriculum.

It is relevant to anyone responsible for teaching, leading or promoting citizenship in secondary schools.

Contents include:
> Why community involvement?
> Forming local partnerships
> European and international links
> Case study: A whole-school approach to global citizenship

Why community involvement?

Why is community involvement important?

Student involvement in the community beyond the school is an essential requirement of citizenship as a National Curriculum subject.

> Pupils should be taught to:
> * negotiate, decide and take part responsibly in both school and community-based activities
> * reflect on the process of participating.

Key stage 3 and 4 citizenship programmes of study

It helps students to:
* see themselves as members of society
* gain new skills, knowledge and understanding
* grow in confidence as individuals
* prepare for life after school.

In doing so, it strongly supports the outcomes for well-being in the *Every Child Matters* programme.

Is it just about 'doing good'?

Community involvement is not so much about 'doing good' as about helping students to develop the capacity to be active citizens, with the confidence to feel that they can make a difference.

While it is perfectly proper to encourage students to engage in activities directly aimed at making a difference to society, it is important to remember that there are many different forms of community involvement and each can contribute to citizenship learning in a different way – for example, what students get out of interviewing a police officer will be quite different from what they learn from organising a local campaign – but each may be valuable in its own right.

Does it only apply to the local community?

Community involvement applies to the national, European and global community as much as to the local one. There is a close connection between the different types of community to which we belong and students should be alerted to this, for example by reflecting on local and national responses to global disasters or injustices.

How can students get involved?

Students can be directly involved in community
life through, for example:

- environmental projects
- campaigns
- peer education
- youth/community forums
- intergenerational activities
- community arts events
- school linking
- charity weeks.

Does it mean you have to go out of school?

Out-of-school visits and activities provide powerful and unique learning opportunities
and should be built into the citizenship curriculum wherever possible, for example
trips to magistrates' courts.

Clearly, there are practical limits, but it is not unreasonable to expect a minimum of one or
two citizenship-related visits per student per year – or to plan citizenship outcomes for a
similar number of out-of-school activities in other subjects.

However, the vast majority of student contact with the wider community is likely to take
place through **the community being brought into the school**, for example through:

- discussions with visitors about community issues
- writing letters to the papers or to politicians
- publishing or contributing to community newsletters
- internet research about issues in the public domain
- e-mail communication with community-based organisations
- video conferencing – e.g. with students in other countries/regions.

How does this fit into the wider citizenship curriculum?

To make the most of their community learning, students need opportunities for negotiating
and deciding their involvement, and for reflecting on the process of being involved. This
means setting aside time for preparation beforehand and for sharing and recording learning
after the event, for example in a citizenship portfolio.

> ### REMEMBER
>
> In order for an activity to
> count as part of your official
> citizenship curriculum, it – or
> an equivalent activity – should
> be experienced by all students
> in the year.

IMPROVING PRACTICE

1 **Identify the elements in the programmes of study for
   citizenship (Appendices 3 and 4 on pages 222 and 223)
   that you think community involvement can make most of
   a contribution towards.**

2 **What kinds of citizenship learning can students acquire
   from:**

   a) **fundraising for charity?**
   b) **linking with a school in another country/region?**
   c) **voluntary work in a care home?**
   d) **tree-planting in a local park?**

Forming local partnerships

KEY ISSUES

What are the benefits of linking up with local groups and organisations?

What kinds of groups and organisations can help?

What about parents?

How can you find out what is available in your area?

What are the benefits of linking up with local groups and organisations?

Links with local groups and organisations are vital in planning opportunities for student involvement in community life. They provide:
- places of interest and relevance to visit
- information about issues and events
- placements for volunteering
- funding and/or sponsorship
- help with classroom and whole-school activities
- expert visitors.

They are also invaluable sources of training and support.

What kinds of groups and organisations can help?

Groups and organisations that can help include:
- Local Authorities (LAs)
- university law and politics departments
- PGCE citizenship students
- local councillors, mayors, MPs, MEPs
- social services, drug and alcohol teams, primary care trusts
- community safety teams, police, fire service
- youth service and Connexions
- professional groups – e.g. magistrates, solicitors, journalists
- shops and businesses
- community and residents groups
- Citizens Advice Bureau (CAB)
- charity and campaign groups – e.g. Amnesty, Groundwork
- church- and faith-based organisations
- local voluntary groups and agencies.

"Developing and sustaining community partnerships must be a priority that is fuelled with adequate resources of time, telephone access and support."

Community Service Volunteers

What about parents?

Parents are members of the community in their own right and can be an important source of help and support with community involvement, for example by:
- organising visits and whole-school events
- making links with local organisations and businesses
- helping with classroom activities
- contributing to policy development and review.

They also have links to other members of the community who may not have children at school, but possess professional interests and skills they are willing to share.

> " Ensure the relationship with parents and the community is an active one. It is very easy to allow the relationship to slip to one of parents as passive receivers or helpers rather than one of contributors and partners. "
>
> School Self-Evaluation Tool for Citizenship Education available at www.dfes.gov.uk/citizenship

How can you find out what is available in your area?

To find out quickly what is available in your area, look in local directories or visit your local library or local council website.

You could also contact your LA cltizenship adviser, local National Healthy Schools Standard leader or Advanced Skills Teacher for Citizenship (if your LA has one) – or see if there any local support groups or networks for citizenship education.

FOCUS

The Stoke Cross-Community Citizenship Education Forum links over 50 local and community organisations that have an interest in supporting citizenship education in schools.

WWW

National organisations that can help include:
- **National Association of Volunteers Bureaux (www.navb.org.uk)**
- **National Council for Voluntary Organisations (www.ncvo-vol.org.uk)**
- **National Council for Voluntary Youth Services (www.ncvys.org.uk)**

A range of contacts for projects across all subjects is available at:
www.csvcommunitypartners.org.uk

One way of encouraging local groups and organisations to become more involved in your citizenship programme is through the development of a **citizenship 'manifesto'**. Developed through consultation with students, teachers, parents and community partners, a citizenship manifesto is a concise public document that sets out student entitlement to citizenship education. It offers a guarantee of action which the school is willing to make to its stakeholders and which stakeholders in turn are willing to offer to the school.

IMPROVING PRACTICE

1 Think of ways in which you might involve a local residents group in your citizenship programme. What different aspects of the citizenship curriculum could it help you with?

2 Which aspects of the key stage 3 and 4 programmes of study for citizenship (Appendices 3 and 4 on pages 222 and 223) do you think local groups and organisations can help you with most?

3 How can you encourage parents to become more actively involved in your citizenship programme?

European and international links

KEY ISSUES

Why is it important to make European and international links?

How can you involve students in European and international issues?

What role can other school subjects play?

Why is it important to make European and international links?

Making European and international links is an essential requirement of citizenship as a National Curriculum subject.

> At key stage 3, pupils should be taught about:
> - the world as a global community and the political, economic, environmental and social implications of this
> - the role of the EU, the Commonwealth and the UN.
>
> At key stage 4, pupils should be taught about:
> - the UK's role in Europe, including the EU, and relations with the Commonwealth and the UN
> - the wider issues and challenges of global interdependency and responsibility, including sustainability and Local Agenda 21.
>
> Citizenship programmes of study

It is also important because:
- UK citizens are EU citizens
- the actions of UK and EU citizens impact on citizens of other countries and the global environment
- the UK is a member state both of the UN and the Commonwealth, and of other international organisations, such as the Council of Europe, North Atlantic Trade Organisation (NATO) and the World Trade Organisation (WTO).

How can you involve students in European and international issues?

There are four main ways of involving students in European and international issues:

1 Personal connections
Students should be encouraged to reflect on direct links with their personal lives, for example:
- where their clothes and other possessions come from
- family and friends living or working in other countries
- foreign holidays
- overseas recipients of their fund-raising.

2 Connections with the life of the school
Students can consider European and international implications of school policy and practice, for example relating to:
- transport
- energy use
- waste management
- purchasing
- grounds maintenance.

3 Simulations
Students can stimulate European or international situations or events whether actual – such as meetings of the UN, or of Commonwealth heads of state, or the G8 Summit – or imaginary – such as taking on the roles of the management of an imaginary UK factory (students investigate where their raw materials come from and the relation between overseas producers and the consumers who buy their products in the UK).

4 School-linking

Linking with schools in other countries, through pen pals, e-mailing, interactive websites and video-conferencing is rewarding. In countries where lack of resources makes web-based linking difficult, contact is often more effectively maintained through student-produced CD-ROMs backed up by e-mail.

To find out more about school-linking, contact:
- The Global Gateway (www.globalgateway.org.uk)
- The British Council (www.britishcouncil.org/education)
- Comenius School Linking (www.socrates-uk.net/comenius)

What role can other school subjects play?

School subjects able to introduce an element of globally-related citizenship education include:
- business studies – e.g. international trade
- geography – e.g. sustainable development
- science – e.g. environmental issues
- history – e.g. international conflict.

FOCUS

A teacher at Solway Community School in Silloth, exchanged with a teacher from Mexico City and brought the link back into her school via the school council. Student councillors reported back to their class, chose topics for discussion with their Mexican peers, printed e-mails for display, and collected information about Silloth for dispatch to Mexico.

WWW

For advice on global links, visit:
www.globaldimension.org.uk
www.globalgateway.org.uk

Or see:
DfEE, **Developing a Global Dimension in the School Curriculum** – download at: **www.teachernet.gov.uk/doc/1837/dfeeguid.pdf**
Development Education Association, **Citizenship Education: the global dimension, guidance for key stages 3 and 4** – download at: **www.citizenship-global.org.uk**

IMPROVING PRACTICE

1 How can you make the citizenship learning opportunities created by school-linking available to all your students, not just to the few?

2 Draw up a list of the potential links between the community around your school and other countries. How could you incorporate these links into your citizenship curriculum?

3 Which other subjects can provide elements of globally-related citizenship education? Identify two or three and consider how you would ensure that 'real' citizenship learning took place through such curriculum provision?

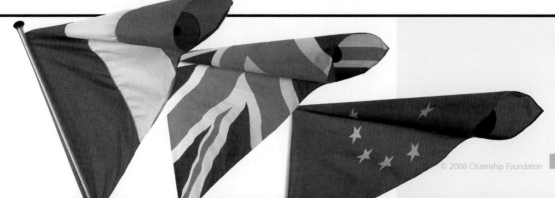

Case Study

A whole-school approach to global citizenship

Altrincham Girls Grammar School

Altrincham Girls Grammar School, a specialist language college, provides a model of what can be achieved by a school committed to developing a deep-rooted sense of global citizenship in young people.

The school has been involved in a wide range of international initiatives, including twinning with schools in South Africa and Beijing, work experience placements in the EU, a World Challenge Expedition to Ecuador and links to a number of European schools through a Comenius project. Funding was secured through involvement in a development education programme supported by the Department for International Development (see www.dep.org.uk/projects/developingcitizenship.htm) and part of the Global Footprint initiative (see www.dep.org.uk).

A Human Rights Week enabled students to experience the 'Escape to Safety' mobile exhibition organised by Global Link (see www.globallink.org.uk), on what it is like to flee persecution and seek asylum. Year 11 students studied human rights in RE, the school Amnesty group led assemblies and a representative from the Law Society spoke about human rights legislation.

Year 9 took part in an international Europe Day, supported by the EU's schoolnet (see www.futurum2004.eun.org). Form groups researched different countries, prepared presentations and set up a display as part of a European bazaar. There was a graffiti wall for comments, a European collage and a vote on the euro (rejected by a ratio of 5:1!).

Global citizenship issues are incorporated within the formal curriculum through geography and, at key stage 3, discrete citizenship lessons. The geography department has identified explicit citizenship accreditation lessons contributing to the students' Progress File, for example in Year 7 a role play on 'should Antarctica be protected?' Year 9 have focused on fair trade – establishing a fair trade stall at school and making a presentation on fair trade campaigns relating to chocolate bars and coffee.

Staff commitment to the international dimension begins with the head and SMT and is apparent at all levels of the school. Knowledge and experience of other countries, cultures and languages are central to the ethos of the school and have helped to make it genuinely outward-looking.

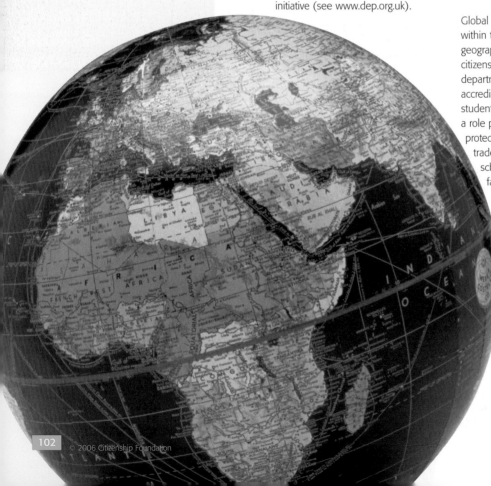

Section 3:
Citizenship in Secondary Schools

Chapter 7:
Learning and Teaching Strategies

Introduction

Citizenship education emphasises approaches to learning and teaching based on real-life, everyday experience and active involvement.

This chapter considers the sorts of approaches to learning and teaching that are most appropriate for citizenship education and reflects on their implications for practice, both for individual teachers and for the school as a whole.

It is relevant for anyone involved in teaching, leading, co-ordinating or promoting citizenship education in secondary schools.

Contents include:
- Learning climate
- Topical and controversial issues
- Active learning
- Group discussions and debates
- Developing discussion skills
- Project work
- Written activities
- Training exercises: 1) Assessing group work through peer assessment
  2) Assessing discussion and debating skills
  3) An essay-writing frame

Learning climate

What sort of school climate encourages citizenship learning?

Citizenship learning is most effective when it takes place in a climate that is non-threatening, in which students can express their opinions freely and without embarrassment and use their initiative without undue fear of failure.

How do you develop this?

Such an atmosphere takes time to develop and is built up gradually. Strategies that help include:

- ground rules – best when students are allowed to develop and test their own
- paired/small group work – less threatening than having to face a large group
- conducive seating arrangements – creating a more open and inclusive atmosphere, e.g. a circle for discussion
- warm-ups and de-briefs – helping students to get to know and trust each other and feel included
- giving everyone something to do – preventing individuals feeling left out and building up a sense of group solidarity, e.g. voting or 'round robins'
- achievable goals – creating a feeling of success/avoiding a sense of failure
- catering for different learning styles – a range of activities employing different kinds of learning, e.g. visual, physical, written or oral.

How do you deal with racist or insensitive comments?

Almost any issue can prove sensitive to specific individuals, especially those that relate to personal identity and behaviour, or family lifestyle and values.

To minimise the risk, make yourself aware of the religious and ethnic differences and different experiences of the groups with whom you work. Establish clear ground rules on how insensitive comments are to be dealt with, for example 'no put-downs', or 'don't get personal'.
Remarks that are racist, sexist, homophobic or demeaning in other ways should be challenged and dealt with firmly.

Dealing with racist remarks raises difficult issues for the teacher. What constitutes a racist remark can be matter of perception. What is offensive to one person may be a lawful – albeit extreme – political opinion for another. Direct confrontation can make students feel 'got at' and risks alienating them and their families. It can also make students on the receiving end of racist remarks feel they are always treated as victims.

While it is always important to challenge remarks of this nature, you are more likely to encourage young people to re-evaluate their views if you are able to keep open the possibility of dialogue by, for example:
- challenging racist remarks indirectly – e.g. 'Where did you get that view from?' or "Why do you think it is all right to say that?'
- making it clear that everyone has racist thoughts and feelings of some kind – e.g. 'Is there anyone here who has never had a racist thought?'
- giving students a role in dealing with it themselves – e.g. through circle time, student councils or committees
- exploring the issue in the wider citizenship curriculum as a justice or equality issue – e.g. through role play or case studies
- evaluating the kind of beliefs and values encountered in these sorts of situations – e.g. through literature, film or drama

---

REMEMBER

A written race equality policy is required by law in all schools and also by local authority services. You should make yourself familiar with this and other equal opportunities policies, and any formal procedures that are in place in your organisation for recording and dealing with incidents relating to them.

IMPROVING PRACTICE

1   Devise a group activity to help students establish their own ground rules for classroom work. What mechanisms could you use to help them review and amend their rules on subsequent occasions?

2   What issues of class management are raised by gender differences? How can they be overcome?

3   How would you respond to a student who says, 'I'm a racist and I'm as entitled to express my views as anyone else – it's a free country'?

Topical and controversial issues

KEY ISSUES

What makes issues topical and controversial?

Why teach about them?

How do you avoid bias?

Can you express your own views?

FOCUS

Section 407 of the Education Act 1996 requires that, where political or controversial issues are brought to students' attention, students must be offered a balanced presentation of opposing views.

FOCUS

Section 406 of the Education Act 1996 forbids the promotion of partisan political views in the teaching of any subject in schools.

What makes issues topical and controversial?

Topical and controversial issues are issues which are current and about which different groups disagree and hold strong opinions. They divide society and arouse strong feelings and/or deal with fundamental questions of value and belief, for example immigration, abortion, gay rights.

Why teach about them?

Topical and controversial issues are part of life. Students are aware of and want to talk about and understand such issues. To shelter students from them is to leave them ignorant about some of the major issues of the day and unprepared to deal with them.

How do you avoid bias?

While there is no 100 per cent foolproof system for avoiding bias, there are strategies that help to minimise it, including:

- making sure all sides of an argument are heard
- presenting opposing views in a balanced way
- not presenting evidence as if it is incontrovertible
- challenging popular/conventional views
- not setting yourself up as the sole authority on a subject
- not presenting opinions as if they are facts
- establishing a climate in which all feel able to contribute.

By far the most important, however, is to **equip students with the ability to recognise bias themselves**, for example, by:

- comparing news stories from different media/websites
- studying images in magazines
- exploring the use/abuse of statistics
- setting exercises to distinguish fact from opinion.

Can you express your own views?

It would be quite wrong, as an educator, to express your own personal views on an issue in such a way as to undermine the ability of students to think critically about it. In secondary schools, it could also be against the law.

However, expressing an opinion is not necessarily the same as advocating it. Teachers can also express personal opinions for educational reasons, for example to provoke discussion or introduce new or unfamiliar ideas.

This is perfectly valid, providing you make sure that you are not thereby unintentionally introducing bias in some other way – for example through tone of voice or emphasis – or encouraging students to break the law.

Ultimately, whether you choose to reveal your own opinions depends on:

- how likely you are to influence the student(s) as a result
- how comfortable you feel personally about revealing them.

Opportunities for expressing personal opinion are likely to become more frequent as students grow older and less susceptible to adult influence. Broadly, there are three approaches to teaching controversial issues:

1 Neutral – expressing no personal views at all
2 Balanced – presenting a range of views, including ones you may disagree with personally
3 Committed – making your own views known as a participant in the group.

Used in isolation or rigidly each approach has its shortcomings – but used judiciously and/or in combination all can help to minimise the risk of biased teaching.

IMPROVING PRACTICE

1 What are the respective advantages and disadvantages of:

a) a neutral approach?
b) a balanced approach?
c) a committed approach?

Do these vary with the age and maturity of the student? If so, how?

2 Should students be free to express whatever opinions they like in citizenship lessons? Why or why not?

3 Do students have a right to know the personal views of their teachers? Why or why not?

4 Are there any topical and/or controversial issues on which it is inappropriate for educators to be neutral? If so, which and why?

Active learning

KEY ISSUES

What is active learning?

Why is it important in citizenship education?

What does it involve?

How does it work?

What is active learning?

Active learning is learning by doing. It is learning through experiencing situations and solving problems for yourself, instead of being told the answers by someone else. Active learning is sometimes referred to as experiential learning.

Active learning may lead to but is not the same as 'active citizenship'. 'Active citizenship' refers to any way in which a citizen can be actively involved in the life of the community – locally, nationally or internationally. Active learning is a means by which citizens acquire the expertise and experience needed to do this.

Why is it important in citizenship education?

Active learning is important in citizenship education because being a citizen is essentially a practical activity – it is something we 'do'.

We learn about democracy by engaging in the democratic process, how to debate by taking part in debates, and what it is to be responsible through the exercise of responsibility.

What does it involve?

In citizenship education active learning refers both to learning which is achieved directly through engagement with real issues and events and that which is achieved indirectly through the use of activities based on imagined or hypothetical situations.

1 **Real issues and events**
   Involving students in real issues and events in the life of their school or the wider community gives them first-hand experience of citizenship in action. Opportunities include involvement in:
   • school democracy – e.g. class and student councils
   • local democracy – e.g. youth councils, area forums
   • peer mentoring – e.g. playground buddies
   • community events – e.g. Make a Difference Day
   • campaigns – e.g. about public transport, or personal safety
   • regeneration projects – e.g. recycling, conservation
   • public consultations – e.g. lowering the voting age
   • charity support – e.g. Comic Relief.

2 **Imagined or hypothetical situations**
   Involving young people in imagined or hypothetical situations enables them to experience vicariously aspects of citizenship they are unable to experience first-hand, including through:
   • picture books – e.g. *Where the Wild Things Are*
   • role play and simulations – e.g. mock trials and elections
   • drama and story – e.g. *Animal Farm*
   • games – e.g. trading games.

At key stages 3 and 4 pupils should be taught to:
- negotiate, decide and take part responsibly in both school and community-based activities
- reflect on the process of participating.

Citizenship programmes of study

How does it work?

Active learning is a **cyclical** process. In order for it to be effective, students need time to reflect upon what they have done and experienced. They also need time to draw from what they have learned and to plan how they can apply this in future situations.

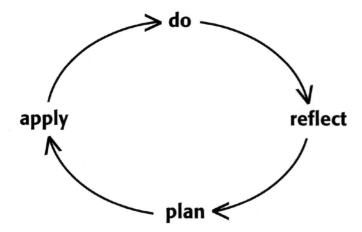

The crucial part of the active learning cycle is the element of **reflection**, sometimes referred to as de-briefing. It is in the de-briefing process that students become conscious of what they have learned and their experience becomes a genuinely educational one. Activities to stimulate reflection on learning include:
- one-to-one or group interviews
- discussion
- presentations
- journals, logbooks or diaries
- displays or exhibitions
- videos.

IMPROVING PRACTICE

1 What activities could you use to help students reflect on the citizenship learning they have acquired through designing and carrying out an investigation into safe routes to school?

2 For what sorts of citizenship learning is simulated experience more appropriate than actual experience? Think of some specific examples and the kind of activities that might be used to provide this experience.

3 What is the role of the teacher in facilitating active learning in citizenship education? Does it depend on the age of the students? If so, how? How would you build active learning into citizenship education for:

a) Year 7 (11–12 year-olds)?
b) Year 10 (14–15 year-olds)?

Group discussions and debates

KEY ISSUES

Why is group discussion important in citizenship?

What form should it take?

What is the optimum size for a group discussion?

Why is group discussion important in citizenship?

Group discussion is important in citizenship education because it:
- gives students a voice
- is an important vehicle for learning
- is a citizenship skill in its own right.

It is also a requirement of the National Curriculum programmes of study for citizenship.

What form should it take?

Group discussions fall into two main categories:

1 Adversarial – when speakers try to win an argument or vote by asserting a case as forcefully as they can
2 Exploratory – when speakers try to reach a consensus or joint solution to a shared problem by engaging with each other's ideas.

Each is commonly encountered in contemporary social and political life and students need to become familiar with and try out both to be properly equipped for life as citizens in today's society.

What is the optimum size for a group discussion?

There is no optimum size for a group discussion – it depends upon the nature and purpose of the discussion. Different types of group have different functions in the classroom. It is important to be aware of these and be able to deploy a range of types appropriately. The three main ones are:

1 **Pairs**
Students tend to find paired discussion less threatening than speaking to the whole class. It is often used at the beginning of a session to test initial reactions or feelings towards an issue, and to help students develop ideas or arguments they can use in small-group or whole-class discussion later. It also ensures that everyone is engaged.

2 **Small groups**
Working in small groups gives students the opportunity to listen to and interact with a wider range of views and perspectives than is available in paired work. It therefore allows them to give more detailed feedback to the group as a whole. It also helps them to learn some of the skills associated with different roles in a team, e.g. group leader, rapporteur.

3 **Whole class**
Whole-class discussion gives students the experience of speaking in a larger public forum. It gives them an opportunity to hear new ideas and arguments and helps them gauge the range and strength of opinion amongst their peers. Whole-class discussion is often used in citizenship education as a prelude to action, such as letter-writing, instigating a campaign or planning a school or community project.

FOCUS

Formal debates

Formal debates are necessarily adversarial in nature. The aim is to win the argument, not to explore issues for their own sake. Two teams debate a motion, e.g. 'This house believes that GM crops should be banned.' One team speaks in favour and the other against, speakers from each team alternating. Each has an allotted amount of time to speak. Questions are invited from the 'floor', a vote is taken and the motion is either carried or rejected.

REMEMBER

Not all all discussions are citizenship discussions. A discussion is only a citizenship discussion if it has a citizenship focus – i.e. it relates to a topical political, moral, social or cultural issue, problem or event – and engages students as citizens (rather than as private individuals).

IMPROVING PRACTICE

1 What different problems of management arise in paired, small-group and whole-class discussions? What can be done to overcome these?

2 In your own classroom or your school as a whole, what proportion of discussion work is adversarial and what proportion is exploratory? Do you consider this ratio to be satisfactory? Why or why not?

3 Choose a citizenship topic and plan two discussion activities – one adversarial, one exploratory in nature – appropriate for:

a) paired
b) small group
c) whole-class discussion.

4 How would you respond to the criticism that discussion is 'all talk and no action'?

Developing discussion skills

KEY ISSUES

What sorts of skills are needed in citizenship discussions?

How can you help students to develop these?

How do you get a discussion going?

What sorts of skills are needed in citizenship discussions?

Effective citizenship discussion depends upon a number of skills and aptitudes – general and specific to citizenship – including:

- social and communication skills – e.g. speaking clearly, taking turns and making appropriate eye contact
- use of appropriate vocabulary – e.g. terms such as 'citizen', 'public interest', 'common good'
- recognition of different forms of argument – e.g. 'slippery slope', 'lesser of evils'
- debating techniques – e.g. ability to argue a case, negotiate consensus, recognise and use rhetoric.

How can you help students to develop these?

Launching students into debates on challenging and controversial topics totally unprepared is a recipe for chaos. It is wrong to assume that the ability to participate in a discussion somehow develops naturally in students, for example it just 'rubs off'. Students need to be taught how to discuss. Strategies to help include:

- setting limited, achievable goals – e.g. a successful ten minute discussion is better than a half-hour one that is a failure
- making the purpose clear – don't just say 'discuss x (a topic)', specify the questions to be discussed
- using discussion cards – makes the activity less abstract (and gives students something to do with their hands!)
- assigning roles – e.g. chair, note-taker, rapporteur
- repeating/maintaining ground rules – better still, involve students in enforcing their own
- making it relevant – relate discussion topics to students' experience and interests
- giving everyone something to say – e.g by voting or 'round robins'
- making it fun – e.g. using TV formats, such as *Question Time*, *Room 101*
- re-arranging seating – a circle or horse-shoe is usually best
- devising appropriate questions – ones that are simple, easy to understand and go to the heart of a topic, e.g. 'Why should people pay tax?'
- encouraging students to generate the questions – allow them to devise their own questions on a topic and vote on which to discuss.

How do you get a discussion going?

REMEMBER

You should encourage students to talk to each other in a discussion rather than to the teacher, for instance, by insisting they always respond to previous contributors, e.g. 'I agree /disagree with x ...', or 'picking up on what Y said ...'

To get a discussion going:

- find a stimulus that raises the issues to be discussed in an interesting way – e.g. a story, article, video-clip, photograph, unusual fact or an activity like a role play
- draw out the issues – e.g. identifying pros and cons, developing arguments for and against, listing/prioritising points
- allow time to think – a few minutes for silent reflection or jotting down ideas guarantees everyone has something to say
- make it topical and controversial – choose a topic on which students are likely to have different opinions (if they all agree there will be nothing to discuss!)
- don't speak too much yourself – allow space for the students to talk
- wait before intervening – gives more thinking time and encourages the reluctant to speak
- de-brief – encourages reflection on the process of discussion work.

IMPROVING PRACTICE

1   Choose a citizenship topic and draw up a vocabulary list appropriate for a particular age group. How could you encourage students to use these in discussion?

2   Choose a citizenship topic and devise some questions that are 'simple', 'easy to understand' and 'go to the heart' of the topic.

3   Observe a discussion led by a colleague, or ask a colleague to observe one of yours. Compare the amount of time students spend focusing on the teacher when speaking to the amount of time they focus on their peers.

4   Develop some general questions you could use to stimulate a citizenship discussion. For example, 'Can you say why you think that?', 'Who has rights in this situation?' or 'What would make the situation fairer'?

Project work

Why is project work important in citizenship?

Project work is important in citizenship education because it is:
- a form of active learning
- an opportunity for students to take responsibility for their learning.

Student investigation of a citizenship issue is also an essential 'coursework' component in GCSE Citizenship Studies.

What can students learn from it?

Project work helps students to develop a range of citizenship skills, including:
- research – e.g. drawing up questionnaires, carrying out interviews and surveys, using libraries, doing internet searches
- analysis – e.g. interpreting evidence, using statistics, recognising bias, summarising findings, making recommendations
- presentation – e.g. writing reports, public speaking, making handouts, preparing OHTs and Powerpoint displays.

Project work also helps students learn how information is collected and presented for public use in society, in particular by businesses, government and the media.

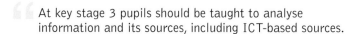

> At key stage 3 pupils should be taught to analyse information and its sources, including ICT-based sources.
>
> At key stage 4 pupils should be taught to research a topical political, spiritual, moral, social or cultural issue, problem or event by analysing information from different sources, including ICT-based sources, showing awareness of the use and abuse of statistics.

Citizenship programmes of study

What other benefits does it have?

Project work can be a powerful motivator for citizenship learning. Allowing students to use their initiative on an issue that concerns them can stimulate them to find out more about how their community is run, what barriers there are to change and how these might be overcome.

It also has a valuable role to play in the consultation process. Students are able to research information useful for decision-making in schools and other organisations and in the community at large.

FOCUS

At Deptford Green School all students take GCSE Citizenship Studies. Coursework revolves around choosing a local issue, researching the facts and presenting a case to a local 'decision-maker'. Students visited the Convoys Wharf development site, researched and discussed its development, and formulated and presented their views. They are now working on a project to consult with young people across four schools on a proposed local Sixth Form Centre.

What are the most effective forms of project work?

The most effective forms of project work are:

- youth-led – giving students a say in the choice of topics, research methods and ways of presenting their findings, appropriate to their age and maturity
- group-based – working with others helps students cope in unfamiliar and challenging situations and develop new social and communication skills
- action-orientated – integrated into some form of school or community-based action, e.g. a consultation on teaching methods, transfer between schools
- tightly-structured – project aims should be manageable and clear at the outset, research methods appropriate and practicable, deadlines set and individuals allocated to identifiable roles, and, where necessary, given training.

While a certain amount of adult support is almost always necessary at the beginning of a project, students should be encouraged to take increasing responsibility as time goes on.

IMPROVING PRACTICE

1 Draw up a checklist of questions to help students develop a proposal for a citizenship project.

2 Choose a citizenship project – say, a review of a school's behaviour policy, or an investigation into a health and safety issue – and list the different kinds of citizenship learning that might be drawn from it. What would you need to do to ensure that this learning took place? How would you make students aware that it was citizenship learning?

3 Consider ways in which student project work might be used to inform a school and its local community's consultation processes, for example on the timing of the school day, student voice, facilities for young people in the local community.

Written activities

KEY ISSUES

Why is writing important in citizenship?

What can it help students to learn?

What other benefits does it have?

Why is writing important in citizenship?

Writing is important in citizenship education because it:
- gives students a voice
- is a medium for learning
- is a way of recording achievement
- is a vehicle for the development of literacy skills.

It is also a requirement of the National Curriculum programmes of study for citizenship.

> At key stage 3, pupils should be taught to justify in writing personal opinions on topical issues, problems and events.
>
> At key stage 4, pupils should be taught to express, justify and defend in writing personal opinions on topical issues, problems and events.
>
> Citizenship programmes of study

What can it help students to learn?

Written work can help students to develop a wide range of citizenship skills, including how to:

- explain an opinion/argue a case/defend a view
- analyse information and its sources
- draw up an agenda/keep the minutes of a meeting
- make an application for funding/sponsorship
- write a news release
- produce publicity/campaign materials
- write content for a website
- draw up a questionnaire
- write a report
- produce handouts/presentations
- draft petitions/manifestos.

It is important that students learn how the written word is used to provide information and affect public opinion in society, in particular through the media, including the internet. It can also act as a vehicle for self-reflection and critical thought on citizenship issues, for example, through:

- personal writing – e.g. diaries, journals, logs
- creative writing – e.g. stories, raps, poetry
- extended writing – e.g. essays, critiques.

What other benefits does it have?

Written work has an important part to play in the assessment of citizenship learning. It is a source of evidence about students' achievements, and it can be used to test levels of knowledge and understanding, as well as skills of enquiry and communication, either individually or collaboratively in the form of paired or group assessment exercises.

It can also be used as the medium for an on-going dialogue between students and citizenship teachers, in which students are able to express their learning needs, receive feedback on progress and set themselves new targets to achieve.

FOCUS

Children's Express

Children's Express is a programme of learning through journalism for young people aged 8–18. It is all about getting the message across that young people have things to say on issues that affect them. That is why 'members' (as the young people are called) do most of the work – coming up with the story ideas, as well as running and taking part in Members' Boards where they choose which stories to cover each month.

When doing a story, members don't just sit behind computers or interview people they know. They have to do their own research, write the questions and then do the interviews and roundtables. They also look through the transcripts of the interviews and roundtables with staff and edit down quotes into a final article, which is then sold to newspapers or magazines.

IMPROVING PRACTICE

1 **Do an audit of the kinds of written work currently employed in citizenship education in your school. What does this say about your current practice? How could you ensure you include a range of different written activities over the year?**

2 **Devise a creative writing activity to help students explore a citizenship issue. How could you make sure that this is genuinely an exercise in citizenship learning and not simply an exercise in creative writing?**

3 **Create a writing frame to help young people write a letter to a newspaper or magazine arguing for a change in the law on an issue about which they feel strongly.**

4 **How could you respond to the view that writing is 'boring and kills citizenship education stone dead'?**

1 Assessing group work through peer assessment

Study the information below:

1   **Choose one of the peer assessment methods suggested and use it to try to assess the citizenship learning taking place in a small-group activity.**

2   **After the exercise, consider:**
    - **How well did it work?**
    - **What kind of learning outcomes did it measure?**
    - **What do you see as its main advantages and disadvantages?**

3   **Now ask your students what they thought about it.**

Peer assessment can be particularly useful for assessing citizenship learning through group work, especially skills of participation and responsible action.

By providing them with a checklist and discussing what to look for in group work (including aspects of group dynamics and roles of responsibility), students are able to assess each other's contribution. Group members feed back their assessment to the rest of the group through a **reflection sheet**. Alternatively a student observer can be appointed to each group and feed back his/her assessment through a **group assessment chart** as shown below.

Someone who organised the group	Someone who helped others	Someone who made links to other groups
Someone who helped others stay focused	Someone who asked useful questions	Someone who found useful resources

It is also possible to allocate an overall mark for group work to reflect on individual contributions.

You can do this by basing 80% of the group mark on teacher observation, and asking the group to allocate each member a suitable mark for their contribution using the 20% left over.

Another way is to multiply the mark arrived at through teacher assessment by the number of students in the group and ask group members to allocate the total between them in a way that reflects their individual contribution – setting a limit on the maximum and minimum mark they may give.

2 Assessing discussion and debating skills

Study the assessment tool below.

1 **What do you see as the advantages and disadvantages of using a tool like this for:**

   a) student self-assessment?
   b) peer assessment?
   c) teacher observation?

2 **Try it out in practice and see what your students think.**

What was the discussion or debate about?

In which lesson did you take part in the discussion or debate?

SKILLS FOCUS

Tick the box next to the face which describes your achievement in each of the skills

☹ = not very good   😐 = good   ☺ = brilliant

Planning what to say	☹		😐		☺
Speaking in front of others	☹		😐		☺
Speaking without reading notes	☹		😐		☺
Asking other people questions	☹		😐		☺
Following what others say	☹		😐		☺
Answering others' questions	☹		😐		☺
Encouraging others to contribute to discussion	☹		😐		☺
Summing up at the end	☹		😐		☺
What did you do well in preparation for and during the debate?	☹		😐		☺

SKILLS FOCUS

Which areas do you think you need to work on to develop your debating skills?

What can you do to improve in these areas?

QCA, 2003

3 An essay-writing frame

Study the model writing frame below.

1 **Choose another citizenship essay question, fill in the writing frame appropriately and try it out with a group of key stage 3 or 4 students.**
2 **Does the writing framework work well as it stands or does it need amending in some way? If so, how?**
3 **Are there any kinds of citizenship essay question for which this writing frame would not be appropriate? If so, which?**

'Britain should join the euro today.' Discuss.

The Euro is... EU countries that have joined it include... EU countries that haven't joined it are... In this essay, I aim to...	*Introduction* You use this bit to define any key words from the essay title and explain what you hope to achieve in this essay. This shows you understand the question.
An argument for Britain joining the Euro is... However, an argument against Britain joining the Euro is...	*First paragraph* Go into detail here. Say if you agree with these arguments – and why/why not.
A second argument for Britain joining the Euro is... On the other hand, Britain shouldn't join because...	*Second paragraph* (Repeat as many times as you can.)
My opinion about Britain joining the Euro today is... I believe this because... I do/don't think Britain should [the alternative] because... I believe this because... Overall...	*Conclusion* *Justification* Argue against the theory you don't agree with – say why. 'Because I say so' isn't an argument.

Kevin Newman, St Andrews Boys School, West Sussex

Section 3:
Citizenship in Secondary Schools

Chapter 8:
Management, Planning and Review

Introduction

Effective management, planning and review are essential for a coherent citizenship programme that has a clear identity and makes sense to everyone involved – teachers, students, parents and others.

This chapter considers some of the ways in which the challenge of creating, developing and maintaining a successful citizenship programme can be met.

It is relevant to anyone involved in leading, managing, co-ordinating or planning citizenship in secondary schools.

Contents include:
- A whole-school approach
- The role of the headteacher and SMT
- The citizenship co-ordinator
- Developing a citizenship policy
- Writing a scheme of work
- Planning a lesson
- Monitoring and evaluation
- The self-evaluation matrix
- Ofsted inspections
- Case study: A whole-school approach to citizenship, diversity and race equality

A whole-school approach

KEY ISSUES

Why is it important to develop a whole-school approach to citizenship?

What are the basic issues to consider?

What key elements do you need to have in place?

What are the factors underlying a successful citizenship programme?

Who needs to be involved?

Why is it important to develop a whole-school approach to citizenship?

While citizenship education is a foundation subject in the National Curriculum, it is clearly more than a subject in the conventional sense. It involves a range of activities and opportunities that extend well beyond the normal confines of the classroom. A whole-school approach is essential if these different activities and opportunities are to be integrated into a coherent citizenship programme with a clear identity that makes sense to everyone involved – teachers, students, parents and others.

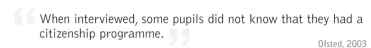

> " When interviewed, some pupils did not know that they had a citizenship programme. "
>
> Ofsted, 2003

What are the basic issues to consider?

Issues to consider include:
- How will citizenship be distinguished from PSHE?
- How will it be delivered across the school?
- Who will teach it?
- How much timetable time will it have?
- Will it have discrete timetable time?
- What kind of resources will it need?
- How much money will it be allocated?
- How will student learning be assessed?
- What sort of professional development will be needed?
- Who will be responsible for the overall programme?

What key elements do you need to have in place?

Key elements that support the development of effective citizenship education include:

1 People/Personnel
- a subject-leader/co-ordinator – the citizenship 'champion'
- a citizenship development group
- a citizenship teaching team
- form tutors providing elements of citizenship through the pastoral programme
- a link SMT member
- a link governor.

2 Documentation
- a citizenship policy
- a scheme of work
- a citizenship development plan
- references to citizenship in school and departmental development plans

3 Systems
- a meeting cycle
- student participation/consultation – e.g. school council
- assessment, recording and reporting
- monitoring and evaluation
- a staff training/development programme.

4 Networks/partnerships
- LA citizenship adviser/AST
- feeder primary schools
- post-16 education and training providers
- teacher trainers – e.g. Citized, higher education, NGOs
- external agencies/initiatives – e.g. National Healthy Schools Standard, Association for Citizenship Teaching (ACT), community partners.

What are the factors underlying a successful citizenship programme?

Factors underlying a successful citizenship programme include:
- a coherent and broad understanding of citizenship education in the school and its wider community
- a participatory ethos reflecting the aims and goals of citizenship education
- strong SMT support
- a confident, well-respected co-ordinator, working in partnership with the SMT
- a dedicated citizenship teaching team
- on-going reflection, planning, and review
- staff training
- time and resources.

Who needs to be involved?

A genuinely whole-school approach to citizenship education involves the whole school, particularly students and staff, but also, as far as possible, governors, parents and community partners.

> Governors, by definition, are active citizens themselves and are likely to take a very active interest in the way their school promotes citizenship education. The governing body could ask one of two governors to take an on-going interest in citizenship education...Governors could also be very effective in helping to link the school with business and community partners.
>
> DfES, **Citizenship Education in Your School: an update for school governors,** 2005

IMPROVING PRACTICE

1 **Using the notes and advice here, evaluate the development of your school's approach to citizenship education. How would you rate your school currently? What priorities do you think it should have for immediate and future development?**

2 **How can you ensure students identify citizenship as a distinct programme in its own right – not just a series of random activities or a sub-set of PSHE?**

3 **How can you raise awareness of citizenship education among governors, parents and community partners?**

The role of the headteacher and SMT

How important is leadership in the delivery of the citizenship curriculum?

The support of headteachers and senior managers is crucial to the effectiveness of a school's citizenship programme.

> Implementation has generally been most effective when a strong lead from senior management has given the subject the necessary status and profile.
>
> Ofsted, 2003

Why is it so significant?

Leadership is especially significant in the case of citizenship education because it is both a new subject and a new type of subject in the school curriculum.

As a new subject, it is not always well understood by teachers, students or parents – yet it is expected to compete for timetable time with existing subjects.

As a new type of subject, it presupposes the involvement of the entire school community – staff, students and parents, as well as individuals and organisations beyond the school.

What is the role of the headteacher and SMT?

The role of the headteacher and senior management team is to:
- promote a vision of citizenship education that is central to the life and work of the school
- make available the time and resources needed to turn this vision into a reality.

It involves:
- showing a level of personal commitment to the subject
- giving citizenship parity of esteem with comparable subjects
- a leadership style that exemplifies citizenship values
- taking a lead in the development and promotion of policy
- familiarising staff with the statutory requirements
- ensuring all staff have opportunities to contribute
- identifying a citizenship co-ordinator and teaching team
- allocating adequate timetable time to achieve curriculum coverage
- encouraging on-going professional development and support
- committing money for staffing and resources
- establishing and supporting a school council
- championing citizenship with parents and the wider community.

> Schools appear to be most successful in developing citizenship education where there is strong senior management support with senior managers promoting citizenship education through active involvement in planning and delivery approaches in partnership with a strong, well respected co-ordinator.
>
> **Citizenship Education Longitudinal Study Report**, NFER, 2004

How else can school leaders support citizenship?

Other ways in which school leaders can support citizenship education include:
- promotional material – including references to citizenship in school prospectuses, brochures and marketing material
- public occasions – incorporating events, such as parents' evenings and open days, into the citizenship programme, e.g. exhibitions, contributions from the school council, celebrations of citizenship projects/achievements
- governors – involving governors in the citizenship programme, e.g. establishing a link governor to help develop community partnerships, liaise with the school council and feed back progress to the governing body
- citizenship manifestos – making a public commitment to citizenship education by drawing up and distributing a school 'manifesto' guaranteeing the core and optional activities students can expect in each year/key stage and the different ways in which community partners can be involved
- specialist status – applying for status as a specialist Humanities college (which can include citizenship education) – information available at http://www.standards.dfes.gov.uk/specialistschools/guidance

IMPROVING PRACTICE

1   How can headteachers 'exemplify citizenship values' in their leadership style?

2   How well is citizenship education supported by senior managers in your school? How far do the headteacher and SMT match up to the list of roles and responsibilities listed here?

3   Draft a short vision statement for citizenship education for inclusion in your school prospectus. How is citizenship education referred to in current promotional material? How far does this reflect actual policy and daily practice?

4   How can a citizenship co-ordinator respond to a headteacher who is ambivalent or antipathetic towards citizenship education? What do you think is the best course of action to take?

The citizenship co-ordinator

Why is it important to appoint a citizenship co-ordinator?

Appointing a member of staff with specific responsibility for co-ordinating and leading citizenship across the school is important if your citizenship programme is to be coherent and have a clear identity.

In the absence of someone to take a lead – whether or not called 'co-ordinator' or 'subject leader' – provision is likely to remain ad hoc, low profile and lacking in effectiveness.

What is the co-ordinator's role?

The co-ordinator's role is to:
- take an overview of citizenship provision across the school
- manage the relationship between its different elements on a daily basis
- 'champion' citizenship at all levels.

Who should this be?

It is preferable that a citizenship co-ordinator or subject leader is someone with management experience. What is more important, however, is that it is someone who:
- has sufficient authority to manage a whole-school approach
- has the active support of the SMT, particularly the headteacher
- has the backing of a citizenship development (policy-making) group
- understands the difference between citizenship and PSHE.

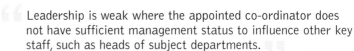

> Leadership is weak where the appointed co-ordinator does not have sufficient management status to influence other key staff, such as heads of subject departments.
>
> Ofsted, 2003

What qualities does the role require?

The citizenship co-ordinator needs to have:
- a clear understanding of the aims and purposes of citizenship education
- a sound grasp of subject knowledge
- a good understanding of appropriate learning and teaching approaches
- skills of curriculum planning and development
- knowledge of assessment strategies.

He or she should be able to:
- support and motivate colleagues
- develop partnerships both within and beyond the school
- champion citizenship at all levels
- lead by example
- command respect from staff and students
- lead training, development and review.

What sort of responsibilities does it involve?

The main areas of responsibility for a citizenship co-ordinator or subject leader include:

1 Policy development – working with the SMT to develop:
   • a citizenship education policy
   • a citizenship education development plan
   • a system for assessing, recording and reporting
   • a system for monitoring and evaluation.

2 Curriculum planning – including:
   • drawing up a scheme of core provision for key stages 3 and 4
   • identifying opportunities for citizenship learning in other subjects
   • identifying opportunities for citizenship learning beyond the classroom.

3 Managing learning and teaching – including:
   • selecting, deploying, and updating resources
   • managing the citizenship budget
   • building/supporting a citizenship teaching team
   • co-ordinating assessment, recording and reporting
   • liaising with the school council.

4 Liaising/communicating – with:
   • SMT
   • subject departments/faculties
   • heads of year/key stage
   • school governors
   • LA adviser/AST
   • feeder primary schools
   • post-16 education and training providers
   • external agencies/initiatives – e.g. local council, police.

5 Training and support – for:
   • citizenship trainees – e.g. PGCE students, NQTs
   • the citizenship teaching team
   • other colleagues within school.

6 Monitoring and evaluation – including:
   • reviewing delivery of the citizenship programme
   • contributing to the school improvement plan
   • preparing for inspection and school self-evaluation.

REMEMBER

Whatever responsibilities are finally decided upon, it is vital that the role of the co-ordinator or subject leader is agreed by the headteacher and made clear to staff at the outset.

IMPROVING PRACTICE

1 What are the advantages and disadvantages of having a citizenship co-ordinator or subject leader who is:

   a) the PSHE co-ordinator?
   b) a head of a humanities subject/humanities faculty?
   c) a member of the SMT?

2 How ought a citizenship co-ordinator to respond to a subject head who refuses to have anything to do with citizenship on the grounds that it is not the responsibility of his/her department?

Developing a citizenship policy

Why is it important to have a citizenship policy?

Having a citizenship education policy helps you to:
- promote a shared vision of citizenship across the school
- show how the various elements in the subject fit together to form a whole
- establish common standards and practices
- create a framework for curriculum development and review
- have a foundation for monitoring and evaluation
- prepare for inspection and school self-evaluation.

How should it be drawn up?

The process of drawing up a citizenship policy is as important as having one. It should be as participative as possible, involving contributions from a range of different individuals and groups, including staff (teaching and non-teaching), students, governors and members of the wider community.

Where do you begin?

The process of drawing up a citizenship policy begins with the identification of a **citizenship development group**. The group should include representatives from the senior management team, the governing body, the pastoral programme, students and staff – and, where possible, parents and community partners – and be serviced by a citizenship co-ordinator or subject leader. The next stage is to conduct a thorough review of your school's existing citizenship provision, including all of the whole-school, extra-curricular and community-based activities with which the school is involved, as well as the opportunities that are offered for students to participate in the organisation of the school.

What should the policy contain?

While the precise contents of citizenship policies are likely to vary, there are a number of key features that all policies should contain. They include:

1 **Cover page – title, e.g. 'Citizenship at _____ School'.**

2 **Context**
- short description of the school and its community
- the aims of citizenship at _____ School
- how it supports the school's core mission and contributes to the *Every Child Matters* outcomes
- background to citizenship in the National Curriculum
- how the Curriculum is delivered within and beyond the classroom.

3 **About the policy**
- rationale – what the policy is for
- how it was drawn up
- who was consulted
- when it was completed
- where it can be obtained
- how and when it will be reviewed
- contact person for comments/feedback.

4 **The policy statement**
  - the aims of citizenship at _____ School
  - how it supports the school's core mission
  - how the curriculum is delivered – within and beyond the classroom
  - approaches to learning and teaching – including topical and controversial issues
  - staffing
  - resources
  - networks/partnerships – e.g. LA, ASTs, community partners
  - staff development
  - management and coordination
  - assessment, reporting and recording
  - monitoring and evaluation
  - links to other policies – e.g. equal opportunities, behaviour policy, key stage 3 strategy, inclusion, health and safety, National Healthy Schools Standard.

5 **Timetable – action to be taken, when and by whom.**

6 **Appendices**
  - National Curriculum citizenship programmes of study
  - overview of scheme of work for key stages 3 and 4.

IMPROVING PRACTICE

1 **Suggest some different ways in which the following might contribute to the development of a school policy for citizenship education:**

  a) students
  b) governors
  c) non-teaching staff
  d) parents
  e) community partners.

2 **How does consulting parents and community partners about citizenship policy differ from involving other stakeholders?**

3 **Devise a set of questions that will enable subject heads and year teams to evaluate the extent to which they are currently contributing to students' citizenship learning in your school.**

Writing a scheme of work

KEY ISSUES

What should a citizenship scheme of work contain?

How should it be structured?

What should it cover?

How do you draw up a unit of work?

What about concepts?

What should a citizenship scheme of work contain?

A citizenship scheme of work should contain all your school's planned learning opportunities for citizenship education across key stages 3 and 4, including:

- separately timetabled provision
- explicit opportunities in other subjects
- suspended timetable events
- activities in the pastoral programme
- active student involvement in the life of the school and wider community.

How should it be structured?

The scheme of work should be broken down into:

- key stages
- years
- terms/half-terms
- units of work/modules.

It should distinguish between core provision (to which all students in a year are entitled) and enrichment activities. It should also have a separate section for on-going activities, such as a school council, with links to specific units of work where appropriate, for example incorporating issues arising out of the work of the school council into a unit on democracy.

 QCA has provided guidance for writing citizenship schemes of work in the form of exemplar units of work and individual subject leaflets. See: **www.qca.org.uk**

What should it cover?

The scheme of work should ensure students have access to all the major topics in the 'knowledge and understanding' strand of the citizenship programmes of study at least once in each key stage. This does not mean that you have to plan a separate unit of work for every topic. Some topics, such as legal and human rights, may occur throughout the key stage. Some, such as the Commonwealth, may only merit a single lesson or part of a lesson. Some may be brought together in the same unit of work, module, or even lesson, for example central and local government in a study of Anti-Social Behaviour Orders (ASBOs).

How do you draw up a unit of work?

Units of work are best drawn up in terms of themes based around the sorts of real-life issues that are relevant to young people, for example youth crime, discrimination, animal rights, environmental change. Five or six lessons is a good length, but there are no hard and fast rules. Planning units of work within larger, over-arching 'year' themes can help to link students' learning in discrete citizenship lessons with learning in related topics in other 'carrier' subjects, Year 7 – Community Issues and Law, Year 8 – Social Justice and Human Rights, Year 9 – Prejudice, Discrimination and Global Citizenship.

What about concepts?

Citizenship concepts may serve as themes on occasions, for example 'equality', 'power', 'government'. However, basing a scheme of work entirely around concepts is unlikely to allow you to cover the range of skills, knowledge and understanding required by the programmes of study.

FOCUS

Checklist

Do all of your units of work:
- draw upon the three strands in the programmes of study?
- contain –
  a) a topical dimension/link?
  b) a range of learning activities?
  c) an opportunity for active participation and/or community involvement?
  d) an opportunity for assessment, review and evaluation?

IMPROVING PRACTICE

1 **Plan a unit of work – say, five or six lessons – on the theme of 'Crime and Punishment'. Try to build in:**

   a) **separately timetabled provision**
   b) **explicit teaching in at least one other curriculum subject**
   c) **an element of active participation and/or community involvement.**

2 **Devise a set of themes – say, one per half-term – for a citizenship scheme of work at key stage 3. Explain how your themes will enable you to cover all the major topics in the key stage 3 programme of study.**

3 **Examine the different learning opportunities for citizenship across each year group in your school. Would having over-arching 'year' themes give greater focus to these opportunities? If so, how could you take this forward in practice?**

Planning a lesson

What are the main elements in a citizenship lesson plan?

The main elements in a citizenship lesson plan are exactly the same as in any other national curriculum subject, namely:
- a set of learning objectives
- an indication of how the objectives relate to the programme of study
- an activity/several activities through which the objectives are to be achieved
- a list of resources needed.

How are the learning objectives expressed?

The learning objectives of a citizenship lesson are expressed in terms of knowledge, understanding and skills.

FOCUS

Example

Lesson focus: How are elections conducted in the UK and what are the arguments for and against electoral change?

Learning objectives
Students should:
- know how elections are carried out in the UK
- understand the concept of representation
- be able to express reasoned views on electoral reform.

Learning outcomes:
By the end of the lesson students will have:
- represented in diagrammatic form how elections are carried out in the UK
- constructed three questions to ask a local councillor about how she represents the views of her constituents
- researched and articulated reasoned views for and against electoral reform.

What does a typical citizenship lesson look like?

A typical citizenship lesson has:
- a starter – engaging student interest, explaining what the lesson is about, reviewing prior learning
- a main activity/activities – the body of the lesson
- a plenary/de-brief – opportunity for students to reflect on and share their learning.

It is important, however, not to be too formulaic: students need variety. Lesson structure will also depend on the amount of time available.

What factors need to be considered in the planning process?

In planning a citizenship lesson you need to consider:
- content – does it relate to the programme of study?
- learning – is it about skills and understanding, or just facts?
- methods – are the methods appropriate to what is to be learned?
- topicality – is there a link to real-life issues?
- relevance – does it relate to students' experience?
- accessibility – do students understand what they are doing and why?
- variation – is there variety in pace, methods, use of media?
- differentiation – will it engage the less able and stretch the gifted?
- participation – are there opportunities for active involvement?
- assessment – are there opportunities to assess learning?

What can you do to engage students?

Ways of engaging students include:
- **encouraging personal involvement** – e.g. drawing on students' own experience
- **setting problems to solve** – e.g. how can we make trials fairer, streets safer, or society more equal?
- **using case studies as well as topical and controversial media stories to provide concrete examples** – e.g. of legal cases, infringements of rights, unfair trading, etc.

IMPROVING PRACTICE

1 Plan a 50-minute citizenship lesson for an age group of your choice on one of the following topics:

   a) identity cards
   b) human cloning
   c) GM crops.

   Assess your lesson plan in terms of the factors listed here.

2 Think of examples of case studies that could be used to engage students on issues related to:

   a) electoral reform
   b) international aid
   c) the United Nations
   d) the jury system.

3 Choose one of the following and consider how you could give it an explicit citizenship focus when planning a lesson on:

   a) sustainable development in geography
   b) human rights in RE
   c) anti-slavery campaigns in history
   d) appreciation/understanding of cultural diversity in English.

Monitoring and evaluation

Why is monitoring and evaluation important?

Monitoring and evaluation is integral to the success of any educational programme. It helps you to:
- identify your strengths and weaknesses
- set realistic targets
- identify training needs
- prepare for inspection and school self-evaluation.

Why is it particularly important in citizenship?

It is particularly important in citizenship education because it:
- is a relatively new subject and still developing
- is delivered in a range of ways – within and beyond the classroom
- focuses on topical and sensitive issues that can quickly date.

What areas do you need to cover?

There are three main areas to cover in monitoring and evaluating your school's citizenship programme:

1 **Citizenship in the taught curriculum**
2 **Citizenship in the ethos and culture of the school**
3 **Citizenship in the wider community.**

In the context of these areas, you will need to consider:
- standards of student achievement
- levels of student satisfaction
- coverage of the programmes of study
- relative emphasis on each of the three strands
- range of learning activities offered
- coherence of the overall programme
- effectiveness and manageability of assessment, recording and reporting
- adequacy of resources
- levels of staff confidence and expertise
- effectiveness of management and co-ordination
- effectiveness of team-building and partnerships
- extent of differentiation and inclusion.

How do you go about it?

Effective monitoring and evaluation is best achieved through a blend of formal and informal methods.

While keeping a watchful eye on developments is a management skill in its own right, some aspects of citizenship require you to have in place a formal system for collecting evidence about progress, for example feedback from students.

End-of-unit evaluations from teaching staff help you to monitor their levels of confidence, identify training and support needs and set targets for further development. Where possible, you should also try to get feedback from parents and others – including your link governor, if you have one. Methods you can use include:

- review meetings
- lesson observations
- samples of student work
- test and/or exam results
- student evaluations/consultations
- liaison with class and/or school council
- questionnaires/surveys
- feedback from parents and community groups.

Whose responsibility is it?

Monitoring and evaluation is primarily the responsibility of the citizenship subject leader/co-ordinator in association with the senior management team.

The process is much enhanced if you have a dedicated citizenship development group and citizenship teaching team in place to share experiences, collect feedback and comment on progress.

What do you do with the information?

Evaluation is not an end in itself, but a means to improving provision and raising standards. It is important, therefore, that the information gained is fed directly back into the planning process – not least in the form of targets for the following year's citizenship development plan.

IMPROVING PRACTICE

1 **What methods can a school use to evaluate the quality of its citizenship provision with regard to:**

   a) student achievement?
   b) assessment procedures?
   c) the work of its school council?
   d) the level and impact of student participation?
   e) community partnerships?

2 **How can you involve students in the evaluation process?**

3 **How effective are monitoring and evaluation in identifying strengths and weaknesses in the citizenship provision in your school? Could the process be improved? If so, how?**

4 **Realistically, what targets do you think your school could set for citizenship development in the next academic year? What factors will determine whether these are achieved?**

The self-evaluation matrix

What is the self-evaluation matrix?

The self-evaluation matrix is a tool that enables schools to chart their progress systematically in developing citizenship education. It is designed to pinpoint strengths and weaknesses across different areas, identify next steps and contribute to school improvement and raising standards.

Who is it aimed at?

In the first instance, the matrix is aimed at headteachers, senior management teams and citizenship subject leaders or co-ordinators. It can also be used by Advanced Skills Teachers, consultants, advisers and inspectors in evaluating schools' progress in implementing the citizenship curriculum.

Why use it?

The matrix provides a ready-made format for monitoring and evaluating citizenship provision that:

- is easy to use
- covers the wider citizenship curriculum, in and beyond the classroom
- allows you to benchmark progress against different levels
- is available both in hard copy and as an interactive version on-line
- is part of a school's approach to self-evaluation across the curriculum
- helps you to address the *Every Child Matters* outcomes.

WWW

The interactive online version of the matrix is available at:
matrix.ncsl.org.uk/curriculum
The facility is available to anyone, but to be able to use it you need to register online first. Copies of the matrix are also available in PDF and Word formats at **www.dfes.gov.uk/citizenship** and at **www.teachingcitizenship.org.uk**

How does it work?

The matrix is divided into six categories:

1 **Vision and policy into practice**
2 **Resources and their management**
3 **Teaching and learning**
4 **Staff development**
5 **Monitoring and evaluation**
6 **Parental and community involvement**

Each category is divided into a number of key areas, which in turn are broken down into a series of levelled statements. To complete each key area, you must decide which statement best reflects the current status of your school. The statements represent four graded levels of provision:

1 **Focusing**
2 **Developing**
3 **Established**
4 **Advanced.**

Completing each category helps you to create a picture of citizenship development in your school, on the basis of which you can take the next steps in prioritising and carrying forward your citizenship agenda.

What can the online facility do?

The online facility allows you to create a citizenship action plan based on where your school is at any one time. Any data you generate is automatically saved, so you are able to revise and edit the plan in the light of on-going self-review and monitoring.

You can input the necessary actions, success criteria, resources needed, level of priority, completion date, and person responsible for the action. Reminder e-mails can be sent to the person responsible for an action if it is not completed by the inserted date. You can view or print out your action plan for the entire matrix, or just for one of the categories. All information saved is confidential and there is an online tutorial for first-time users.

REMEMBER

Note
Student participation does not explicitly appear as a component of the citizenship curriculum in the original version of the matrix – either online or in hard copy. This omission has been addressed in the revised version of the matrix reproduced in Appendix 8 on page 227.

IMPROVING PRACTICE

1 **Study the layout of the matrix carefully. How comprehensive do you think it is? Are all the important aspects of the citizenship curriculum present? If not, what do you think it is missing?**

2 **Choose one of the categories and use the matrix – either the paper or online version – to identify the current position in your school. What priorities does this suggest you should set for the future?**

3 **Student participation does not explicitly appear in the original matrix. If this were added as a separate category what would you include in it at each level?**

4 **How might the matrix be incorporated into the inspection process?**

Ofsted inspections

KEY ISSUES

How will Ofsted report on citizenship?

What kind of evidence will inspectors look for?

What about citizenship taught through other subjects or activities?

What are the main weaknesses commented on in past inspectors' reports?

REMEMBER

In any inspection, citizenship education is treated exactly the same as any other foundation subject in the National Curriculum and the same high standards of achievement are expected.

How will Ofsted report on citizenship?

Under the new arrangements that came into place in 2005, whole-school inspections will be shorter than previously – no more than two days. There will not be time to evaluate individual subjects in detail, but inspectors will want to ensure that statutory requirements are met. Alongside the arrangements for shorter inspections, Ofsted will carry out additional visits to schools to inspect particular subjects and curriculum areas, including citizenship education. Subject inspections will comprise a mixture of lesson observation, discussions with staff and students, and the scrutiny of student's work and subject documentation, such as schemes of work. Typically, a secondary school will have one subject inspected every three years, but any school may be inspected in any subject.

What kind of evidence will inspectors look for?

Under the new arrangements, **school self-evaluation** is the starting point for any inspection. Self-evaluation reflects the importance of the *Every Child Matters* outcomes. In summarising your evaluation of the five outcomes, you should remember to comment not just on what your school has done to promote these, but also the impact this has had on learners. In the case of a subject inspection, inspectors will wish to see your school's self-evaluation form (SEF) and discuss your self-evaluation of citizenship achievement, provision and leadership in the school. This does not mean that everything has to be written down, but you will need to provide some evidence on which to base your discussion, for example:
- a departmental/team review
- a policy statement or 'manifesto'
- a scheme of work
- a system for assessment, recording and reporting
- targets in the school development plan
- student participation in school and/or community-based activities.

Inspectors will look for actions you have taken towards improvement – including evidence of the impact of those actions, especially on student learning – and the way in which the views of students, parents and other stakeholders have been incorporated into your self-evaluation.

Further information about the inspection process can be found at: **www.ofsted.gov.uk**

What about citizenship taught through other subjects or activities?

Where a lesson in another subject is included in your school's citizenship provision, the citizenship content is examined and reported on as though it were a discrete citizenship lesson. Citizenship content should be made explicit to students and citizenship learning objectives included in the lesson plan and assessed separately. The same applies where citizenship is taught through other activities, for example, special events, tutorial/pastoral programmes.

What are the main weaknesses commented on in past inspectors' reports?

The main weaknesses commented on in past inspectors' reports are:
- lack of understanding of the implications of citizenship as a National Curriculum subject
- inappropriate curriculum provision – e.g. citizenship taught solely through a cross-curricular approach, or as subsidiary element in a PSHE programme
- insufficient time allocated to discrete citizenship teaching
- gaps in provision – especially relating to political, legal and financial understanding
- lack of opportunity to enquire into topical and controversial issues
- insufficient emphasis on written work
- failure to address the relationship between the three strands in the programmes of study
- citizenship co-ordinators lacking experience and/or status
- failure to address assessment, reporting and recording procedures
- low expectations compared to other subjects.

IMPROVING PRACTICE

1   **How might citizenship education feature in a school's self-evaluation form (SEF)? What kinds of evidence could be used to support this?**

2   **If the citizenship education in your school were to be inspected tomorrow, what strengths and weaknesses do you think would be highlighted in the inspection report? How would the school take these forward post-inspection?**

3   **Draw up a list of questions that you would ask students about their experience of citizenship education if you were an Ofsted inspector. How would your own students answer these questions?**

A whole-school approach to citizenship, diversity and race equality

Royton and Crompton School

Royton and Crompton is a mixed comprehensive school in Oldham with a strong commitment to a whole-school approach to citizenship education incorporating school culture, community involvement and the taught curriculum.

Citizenship education is deeply embedded in the life of the school. Strategically placed display boards, partly 'owned' and organised by year forums, communicate a range of positive messages round the school, including displays of students' work, equal opportunities posters, photographs from an African Dance Week and a visit from the Kick Racism out of Football campaign. Citizenship education is central to the school's behaviour policy: students gain 'citizenship' points and merits qualifying them for entry in a monthly draw, and there are 'Citizen of the Month' awards.

There is a strong sense of community involvement throughout the school. A 'green group' has used photography to highlight graffiti and rubbish around the school neighbourhood and instigated a clean-up campaign. There are charity fundraising events, for example a shoebox appeal for children in Eastern Europe. Year 10 students run mini-enterprise projects raising money for causes of their choice, which link into their GCSE Citizenship Studies coursework.

In the taught curriculum, citizenship education is part of an integrated PSHE/ citizenship programme at key stage 3, and linked with RE at key stage 4. The school has recently appointed a citizenship co-ordinator, and there are plans to create smaller specialist teams for 'PSHCE' to develop contributions from other curriculum subjects.

The school has incorporated into its key stage 3 PSHCE and RE schemes of work a teaching pack for citizenship developed by Oldham LA's Ethnic Minorities Support Service – *Culture and Diversity: an Oldham focus*. The Year 7 theme is 'Diverse Oldham: Diverse Britain' and students focus primarily upon issues of identity. Year 8 students explore issues of 'Migration and Settlement' – globally and locally. Year 9 includes a Northland/Southland simulation, the creation of a 'Respect for All' school charter and an in-depth study of the future of Oldham after the riots of 2001.

Introduction

Assessment, recording and reporting are essential aspects of learning and teaching in citizenship education.

They help students to recognise and value what they are learning; provide teachers, parents, employers and others with information about student progress and achievement; and finally, raise the profile of citizenship education both in schools and the wider community.

This chapter considers practical ways of assessing, recording and reporting student progress and achievement in citizenship education that will contribute to standards and enhance provision across the school.

It is relevant to anyone responsible for teaching, leading or promoting citizenship in secondary schools.

Contents include:
Why assess citizenship?
Statutory requirements
Assessment for learning
Assessment of learning
Self and peer assessment
Recording progress
Writing reports
Qualifications and awards
GCSE Citizenship Studies
Training exercises: 1) End of unit assessment grid
2) Self and peer assessment questionnaire
3) Assessing persuasive writing
4) Year 7 report
5) Citizenship logbook

Why assess citizenship?

KEY ISSUES

Why is assessment important in citizenship?

What are students assessed on?

How do you build assessment into your programme?

What about learning outside the classroom?

REMEMBER

Assessing citizenship is not about how 'good' a citizen a person is, it is about what they know, understand or are able to do as citizens – as set out in the attainment targets for key stages 3 and 4.

Why is assessment important in citizenship?

Assessment is important in citizenship education because it:
- gives a baseline from which the student can progress
- improves learning and teaching
- enhances the recording and reporting process
- enables the school to evaluate its citizenship programme
- raises the status of the subject in the school and the wider community.

Assessment also has important implications for how you implement your citizenship curriculum. It is impossible to have a coherent assessment system for citizenship education if you do not have a coherent citizenship education programme to assess.

 Assessment is currently a weak aspect of citizenship.

Ofsted, 2003

What are students assessed on?

In citizenship education, students are assessed on what they learn – that is, their growing capacity to think and act as informed and responsible citizens. It is about skills, knowledge and understanding, not about a student's worth or character.

How do you build assessment into your programme?

It is important that assessment is seen not as a 'bolt-on' but as integral to learning and teaching, and planned as part of your citizenship programme from the outset. It should combine two elements:

1 **On-going qualitative feedback** – to enable students to identify their strengths and weaknesses and set themselves targets for further improvement ('assessment for learning')

2 **Occasional checks on performance** – to provide evidence for student records, reports to parents and, in Year 9, the end of key stage 3 assessment ('assessment of learning').

What about learning outside the classroom?

Students should be assessed on what they learn through participation in the life of the school and wider community as well as what they learn in the classroom. They should be able to receive credit for citizenship learning wherever it occurs.

Clearly, some aspects of citizenship education are more difficult to assess than others. The important thing is to select forms of assessment that are fit for purpose – that is, that give you the kind of information you want and achieve what you want to achieve. For example, you are much more likely to be able to chart progress in the skills of 'participation and responsible action' through group discussion or some form of self or peer assessment than you would by setting a multiple-choice test.

In the case of school or community involvement, it is not the extent or the success of the participation that should be assessed, nor, indeed, the willingness to take part – but the skills, knowledge and understanding that students are able to demonstrate as a result.

IMPROVING PRACTICE

1   Draw up an outline for a unit of work – say five or six lessons – on a citizenship topic of your choice for key stage 3 or 4, indicating how you might:

a) give students feedback on their progress/achievement as they go along
b) check how much they have learned at the end
c) evaluate the overall success of your unit of work.

What issues does this raise for assessment in citizenship education?

2   Values, such as tolerance and respect for others, are a vital aspect of citizenship in a democratic society. Do you think schools have a role to play in the development of such values, and, if so, should this kind of learning be assessed? Why or why not?

3   How could you respond to the view that assessing citizenship education is wrong because it brands some young people as 'failing citizens'?

Statutory requirements

What are the statutory requirements for assessing, recording and reporting citizenship?

All secondary schools are required to:
- keep a record of each student's progress and achievement in citizenship education in Years 7 to 11 (students aged 11 to 16)
- include citizenship education in annual reports to parents in Years 7 to 11
- assess each Year 9 student's attainment in citizenship education at the end of key stage 3 (students aged 13 to 14).

There is no statutory requirement for an assessment at the end of key stage 4 (students aged 15 to 16).

On what basis is attainment assessed?

Attainment is assessed on the basis of the attainment target for citizenship education. The attainment target consists of end of key stage descriptions for key stage 3 and 4 (see Appendix 5 on page 224).

The end of key stage descriptions describe the type and range of performance that the majority of students should characteristically demonstrate by the end of the key stage, having been taught the relevant programme of study.

Citizenship is a foundation subject in the National Curriculum and schools are expected to establish standards of assessment comparable with other subjects in key stage 3 and 4.

How should it be graded?

There is no official eight-level assessment scale in citizenship as in other foundation subjects. However, the expectation is that by the end of Year 9 — having been taught the key stage 3 programme of study — student attainment should match the level demanded in other subjects and be broadly equivalent to levels 5 and 6.

The Qualifications and Curriculum Authority (QCA) recommends that attainment in citizenship be graded in terms of whether students are 'working towards', 'working at' or 'working beyond' the level prescribed in the end of key stage descriptions.

 QCA assessment and reporting arrangements are updated annually. For current arrangements, see: **www.qca.org.uk**

An example of how key stage 3 students' knowledge and understanding of voting and the electoral system might be graded after taking part in a mock election.

STUDENTS WORKING TOWARDS	STUDENTS WORKING AT	STUDENTS WORKING BEYOND
• Understand basic terms, e.g. 'vote', 'election', party', 'candidate' • Can name some of the parties involved and recognise one or two differences between their policies • Can explain the basic steps in voting	• Understand more complex terms, e.g. ' policy', 'constituency', 'manifesto' • Can name all the parties involved and distinguish at least one difference between each of their policies • Can explain the basic steps in voting and the arrangements made for voting at a polling station	• Understand a range of abstract terms, e.g. 'party line', 'rhetoric', 'right-wing/left wing' • Can name all the parties involved and distinguish similarities and differences between each of their policies • Can explain the basic steps in voting, the arrangements made for voting at a polling station and when and how elections are called

Work on cross-curricular skills in other subjects, such as argument and debate, or research and analysis, cannot be assessed as citizenship learning unless it based on a citizenship issue or given a definite citizenship focus.

IMPROVING PRACTICE

1 **Look at the end of key stage description for key stage 3. Draw up a list of the kinds of learning opportunities you think students would need to have to gain a successful assessment at the end of Year 9. Are all these opportunities currently available in your school? If not, why not?**

2 **What do you see as the advantages and disadvantages of introducing an eight-level assessment scale in citizenship education?**

Assessment for learning

What is 'assessment for learning'?

'Assessment for learning' is designed to raise students' achievement. It is based on the idea that students will improve most if they understand the aim of their learning, where they are in relation to this aim and how they can achieve it.

It is different from 'assessment of learning', which involves judging students' performance against national standards to provide evidence for student records, reports to parents and, in Year 9, the end of key stage 3 assessment.

What does it involve?

Assessment for learning is an on-going process. It involves:
- sharing learning goals and assessment criteria with students
- providing students with qualitative feedback on their progress and achievement
- encouraging students to discuss their progress
- helping students to their own targets
- enabling students to correct their mistakes when and where they occur
- teaching students self-assessment techniques so they are able to discover the areas they need to improve.

Research shows that involving students in their own learning raises standards and empowers them to take action to improve their performance, and also that learning can be improved, particularly among the less able, by 'no grade' marking.

How can you build it into your citizenship programme?

There are a number of ways to build assessment for learning into citizenship education. They include:

- **explaining learning objectives** – e.g. 'The aim of the lesson is to learn about the advantages and disadvantages of different forms of political action, and whether you think it is ever right to break the law to make the government listen'
- **negotiating learning goals** – e.g. at the outset of a citizenship project on old people in the community, ask students what they want to learn through the project and how they might achieve this
- **sharing specific assessment criteria** – e.g. 'You will be assessed on how well you can explain the differences between the different voting systems, the advantages and disadvantages between them and how clearly you put across your own view'
- **high-level questioning** – to encourage critical thinking, e.g. 'Why do you think there should be a law about x?', 'What do you think would be best for society as a whole in this case?', 'Who in society do you think should be responsible for this? Why?'
- **encouraging student questioning** – to assess their understanding, e.g. 'What questions would you put to the Prime Minister about a topical issue (like terrorism) if you had the chance? Why?'
- **oral feedback inviting student response** – e.g. 'Some people would say that your group's answer to the problem of youth crime would be impractical. How would you respond to this?'
- **relating marking to the learning intention of the task** – e.g. 'Next time try to give more reasons for your opinions'
- **group and plenary sessions** – to review and reflect on learning, e.g. a dedicated session following a 'mock trial' in which students consider what they have learned about the legal system
- **self and peer assessment** – e.g. students commenting on their own or others' participation in a school council with a view to a better understanding of the idea of representation
- **record-keeping facilitating student-teacher dialogue** – e.g. citizenship diaries or logbooks.

> ### REMEMBER
>
> Assessment of learning can often be used to support assessment for learning, e.g. moving an end-of-term test back a few weeks so students have time to go over aspects not fully understood.

IMPROVING PRACTICE

1 **Think of ways in which you might build assessment for learning into:**

   a) **a peer-mentoring scheme**
   b) **a group project to improve the school grounds**
   c) **a visit by a local MP**
   d) **a Human Rights Day.**

2 **How would you respond to the view that assessment for learning is fine in principle, but 'too time-consuming' to implement in practice?**

Assessment of learning

KEY ISSUES

What is 'assessment of learning'?

What does it involve in citizenship?

What sorts of evidence can you use for assessment?

Do you need to set special assessment tasks?

How many pieces of work do you need to assess?

REMEMBER

You will need a written mark scheme or checklist for each sample piece of work or activity you intend to assess formally.

What is 'assessment of learning'?

'Assessment of learning' is judging students' performance against national standards to provide evidence for student records, reports to parents and, in Year 9, the end of key stage 3 assessment.

It is different from 'assessment for learning', which involves providing students with qualitative feedback on their progress in order to improve their achievement.

What does it involve in citizenship?

Assessment of learning in citizenship education involves selecting samples of each student's work and assessing them against the respective end of key stage descriptions.

What sorts of evidence can you use for assessment?

There is a wide range of evidence you can use for assessment, including:
- essays/articles
- letters
- logbooks/diaries
- discussions/debates
- presentations
- role plays
- web pages
- videos
- photography exhibitions
- self/peer assessments
- peer mentoring
- research projects.

The important thing is that the information obtained is objective and reflects student achievement across a range of citizenship activities – within and beyond the classroom.

Do you need to set special assessment tasks?

While it is possible to base assessment of learning on existing work or activities, setting special assessment tasks allows you to focus your assessment on specific citizenship skills or areas of knowledge and understanding.

Examples relating to the three strands in the programmes of study might include:

1 Knowledge and understanding:
   - a true/false or multiple-choice test on children's rights or on definitions of key words such as 'democracy', 'dictatorship', 'monarchy', etc.
   - explaining the background to a topical newspaper headline
   - devising arguments for and against the introduction of a new law such as putting a tax on 'fatty foods'.

2 Skills of enquiry and communication:
   - a draft letter to the Foods Standard Agency about GM foods
   - a presentation on the current law on euthanasia
   - a research report on young people's attitudes towards politics.

3 Skills of participation and responsible action
   • an evaluation of the work of the school council
   • a proposal on how to reduce violence in school
   • a diary recording a community project.

Focusing assessment on specific skills or areas of knowledge and understanding does not mean that the three strands have to be taught separately. As a general rule, knowledge and understanding about becoming an informed citizen is best acquired through developing the skills of active and responsible citizenship.

How many pieces of work do you need to assess?

Assessment of learning should not be based on a single piece of evidence, but on student achievement over time.

A reasonable figure would be **3–5 pieces of evidence** of different types over a year – some of which may be the result of a special assessment task, but not necessarily all.

It is important that students know which pieces of their work are being assessed or when a special assessment task is to take place. One way to do this is for students to have a calendar of citizenship events at the beginning of each term or year, including details of the formal assessments that are coming up. This could take the form of an insert or section in a citizenship diary or logbook.

IMPROVING PRACTICE

1 **Think of some assessment tasks you could use to assess key stage 3 students' knowledge and understanding of:**

   a) **human rights**
   b) **forms of government**
   c) **rights and responsibilities at work.**

2 **What are the problems of assessing citizenship learning that takes place beyond the classroom? How can these problems be overcome?**

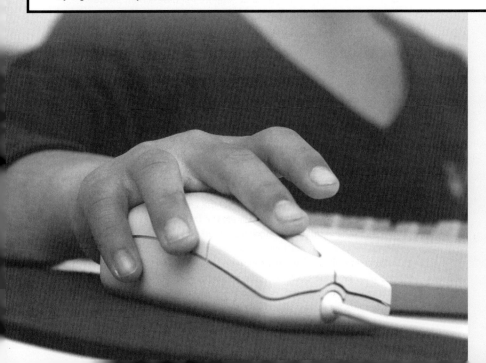

Self and peer assessment

What are self and peer assessment?

Self and peer assessment are when students assess their own and each other's work. They are both types of 'assessment for learning'.

Why are they important in citizenship?

Self and peer assessment are important in citizenship education because they:
- give students more responsibility for their own learning
- help increase motivation
- make a positive impact on achievement
- provide insights into aspects of citizenship education that are otherwise difficult to assess – e.g. group work, skills of 'participation and responsible action'.

What kind of information do they provide?

Self-assessment provides information that is personal to the student. It is a first-hand account of a student's experience of citizenship education or reaction to pieces of their own work.

Peer assessment, on the other hand, should be more objective. It should provide information that can help other students to reflect on their learning.

How do they work?

1 Self-assessment

Self-assessment requires students to understand the success criteria both for specific tasks and for citizenship education as a whole. This does not happen by chance – it has to be built into the learning and teaching process, e.g. by explaining learning objectives and assessment criteria to students at the outset of a task or activity. Strategies that support self-assessment include:
- students negotiating learning objectives and assessment criteria
- regular plenary sessions both during and at the end of tasks
- students marking and grading their own work prior to teacher assessment
- a 'traffic lights' system for students to indicate whether they feel very confident (green), fairly confident (amber) or not confident (red) about the content of a lesson or unit
- self-assessment proformas
- citizenship diaries or logbooks
- citizenship portfolios.

2 Peer assessment

In the case of peer assessment, not only do students need to understand the success criteria both for specific tasks and for citizenship education as a whole, but they also need to be able to apply the criteria appropriately and effectively in the feedback they give fellow students. Peer assessment is a complex process. It is about much more than marking another students' work right or wrong according to a set answer sheet. It should be introduced gradually, and students are likely to need training and practice. One way to do this is through role play, with the class as whole reviewing techniques before doing it 'for real'. Strategies that support peer assessment include:
- students marking each other's work prior to teacher assessment

- 'critical partners' – pairs of students who share and discuss work, and respond to teacher questions and comments together
- peer assessment proformas.

" After a student marking my investigation, I can now acknowledge my mistakes easier. I hope it is not just me who learnt from the investigation but the student who marked it did also. "

Secondary school student as quoted in
Working Inside the Blackbox: Assessment for learning in the classroom, 2002, London: DEPS

IMPROVING PRACTICE

1 Think of ways in which you could build self-assessment into the following activities:

a) a debate on the legalisation of drugs
b) a small-group photography project on local transport
c) a letter to a local paper about a proposed wind farm.

2 Devise a standard proforma that students might use in citizenship education for:

a) self-assessment
b) peer assessment.

3 How could you respond to the view that students' assessments of themselves or of each other are not to be trusted because they are bound to be biased or based on limited knowledge?

Recording progress

What are the statutory requirements for recording progress in citizenship?

All secondary schools are required to keep a record of each student's progress and achievement in citizenship education in key stages 3 and 4.

However, there is no requirement to submit summary data in citizenship education to the national data collection agency.

What are the records for?

Keeping records helps you to:
- collect evidence for reporting to parents, the end of key stage 3 assessment, inspection and school self-evaluation
- involve students in their own learning
- ease transfer between schools and different phases of education
- evaluate your citizenship programme.

What sort of information should you record?

Information recorded should reflect the full range of citizenship provision in your school, including citizenship learning in other subjects, and through special events and other school- and community-based activities.

While the precise amount of detail is a matter for professional judgement, ideally it should include:
- results of assessment tasks
- samples of assessed work
- student reflections on their achievements.

In Year 9 it should also include the end of key stage 3 assessment.

How should it be recorded?

There are different ways of recording student progress in citizenship education, including existing methods, such as the Progress File and Records of Achievement, as well as citizenship-specific methods like citizenship diaries, logbooks and portfolios.

Whichever is chosen, it is important that students are involved in the recording process if they are to benefit from it. There is a strong argument, therefore, for developing a system that uses a combination of methods. This could include:

- **teacher assessment sheets** – filled in after key activities or assessment tasks, but shared with students
- **observation notes** – kept by the teacher
- **student assessment sheets** – filled in by students after specific activities and shared with teachers, either directly or through entries in a citizenship diary/ logbook
- **citizenship diaries/logbooks** – used by students to record citizenship activities and reflections on their learning and the learning of others
- **samples of student work** – kept either by teachers or by students, e.g. in a student portfolio.

What are the benefits of citizenship portfolios?

Citizenship portfolios are samples of documentary and other evidence relating to students' work in citizenship education and collected by them throughout the year, for example pieces of writing, test results, assessments, and material relating to community-based learning such as letters, articles, photographs, etc.

Portfolios are personalised and flexible, and encourage students to become more involved in recording and assessing their own and each other's work. They provide a picture of student achievement across the school and in a range of contexts – particularly, in relation to skills of participation and responsible action, which are otherwise difficult for the teacher to access.

Portfolios can be more than just repositories of completed work. Selecting the items their portfolios should contain and the work they would wish to be judged by can be a learning experience for students in its own right.

> **REMEMBER**
>
> Portfolios need to be regularly reviewed and updated if they are to be effective. It is easy for them to sit in cupboards and be forgotten for months on end.

IMPROVING PRACTICE

1 **What do you think are the main logistical problems in recording student progress and achievement in citizenship education? How can these be overcome?**

2 **Devise a standard proforma for recording student progress and achievement in key stage 3. Who would you envisage filling this in and when?**

3 **How helpful is it for students to bring records of progress in citizenship education with them when transferring from another school (for example, from primary to secondary school)? What does this imply for record-keeping? What messages does it send out to students?**

Writing reports

KEY ISSUES

What are the statutory requirements?

What should reports contain?

What sources of information should they draw on?

Who should write them?

How can students be involved?

What about citizenship taught through other subjects?

REMEMBER

Teacher comments on student participation in school- and community-based activities should make it clear that it is not the degree of participation that is being assessed but the citizenship knowledge, understanding and skills that students have acquired as a result.

What are the statutory requirements?

Schools are required to include citizenship education in annual reports covering students' progress during the academic year, which are sent to parents. The inclusion of citizenship education is a requirement in annual reports for all students in Years 7 to 11 (students aged 11 to 16).

What should reports contain?

What reports to parents should contain about citizenship education is a matter for professional judgement. However, in most cases they are likely to include:
- course details – including how citizenship education is provided in the school, specific topics covered and activities undertaken
- teacher comment – about the progress and achievements students have made, identifying strengths and suggesting areas for further improvement
- an attainment grade – based on the attainment target for citizenship education and expressed in terms of working 'towards', 'at' or 'beyond' what is expected of the majority of young people at that age.

Year 9 reports are also likely to include details of the statutory end of key stage 3 assessment for citizenship.

What sources of information should they draw on?

Reports should draw on the record of student progress and achievements in citizenship education compiled throughout the year. The form this takes will depend upon the recording system in place in your school, but should include evidence from a range of sources, for example:
- teacher assessment
- teacher observations
- self/peer assessment
- citizenship diaries/logbooks
- student personal statements
- samples of assessed work – e.g. in a student portfolio.

Who should write them?

Citizenship reports should be written by the teacher who has been most closely involved in the citizenship education of the student(s) concerned. Who this is will depend upon the way citizenship education is provided in your school. Where there is a specialist team, it should be a citizenship teacher. In the absence of this, the most suitable person is likely to be the form tutor.

How can students be involved?

It is good practice to involve students in report-writing. One way is to include a special section in the report for student comment. This could take the form of a personal statement made by the student on the basis of their citizenship experiences throughout the year. However, this should not be regarded as a substitute for teacher comment. A report consisting solely of a student's personal statement signed by a teacher, for example, would fall far short of the statutory duty owed to parents.

What about citizenship taught through other subjects?

Where aspects of citizenship are taught through other subjects, comments may be included in the reports on those subjects – so long as they are clearly identified as citizenship education and written in terms of the citizenship subject criteria, for example by having a separate section on 'citizenship through history' in a history report.

Generally, however, it is preferable for assessments carried out in citizenship 'carrier' subjects to be collated and reported on by one person, whether a citizenship teacher or the form tutor. It makes for a more coherent citizenship programme overall, for teachers, students and parents.

IMPROVING PRACTICE

1 **What are the advantages and disadvantages of expecting form tutors to write citizenship education reports?**

2 **What do you regard as the main kinds of citizenship education achievements to be included in a citizenship report? Why?**

Qualifications and awards

Why are qualifications and awards important in citizenship?

Qualifications and awards are important in citizenship education because they:
- recognise personal and group achievement
- increase motivation
- improve learning and teaching
- aid assessment, recording and reporting
- raise the profile of the subject.

What sort of qualifications and awards are available?

A wide range of citizenship-related qualifications and awards are available, from local awards offered by community organisations and local authorities to nationally-organised QCA-accredited examinations. Formal qualifications include:
- GCSE Citizenship Studies – a short course assessed by a combination of coursework and final examination
- Entry Level Citizenship Studies – for students likely to find the GCSE short course too challenging, or as accreditation for short projects (Level 1 and 2 qualifications to be available in due course)
- GCSE Integrated Humanities – modules in citizenship combined with other modules in related subjects and curriculum initiatives, e.g. education for sustainable development and enterprise education
- AS Social Science: Citizenship – a more academic course of study addressing citizenship issues through sociology
- International Baccalaureate – includes a requirement for students to record a specified number of hours in CAS activities (Creativity, Action and Service).

Full A-levels and GCSEs in citizenship studies are due to be introduced in 2008.

Other recognised award schemes include:
- ASDAN (Award Scheme Development and Accreditation Network) – focuses on key skills, enabling students from a wide ability range to collect evidence of personal achievement through a variety of activities in PSHE and Citizenship – approved by QCA
- Duke of Edinburgh Award – provides structured opportunities for students to get involved in a range of community projects, and work towards Bronze, Silver or Gold Awards
- Trident Trust: Skills for Life – provides complementary programmes in work experience, personal challenge and community involvement – the Gold Certificate is recognised by many employers
- ACiS (Active Citizenship in Schools Award) – a framework for accrediting 11–15 year-olds for involvement in the life of the school or the wider community, awards given for 25 and 50 hours of volunteering.

REMEMBER

Where citizenship is an element in a joint achievement it can sometimes be possible to accredit citizenship learning through a 'non-citizenship' award, e.g. Duke of Edinburgh Award.

What other ways are there to recognise student achievement?

There are many other ways of recognising student achievement in citizenship education. They fall into two categories:

1 General approaches – such as:
   - assemblies
   - Progress File
   - Records of Achievement.

2 Citizenship-specific approaches – such as
   - in-house awards and certificates (can also be used with Records of Achievement or the Progress File)
   - community awards – generated in partnership with other local schools and the LA, local charities, businesses, trusts or agencies, e.g. Camden Council's Young Citizen of the Year
   - exhibitions and displays
   - congratulatory notes to students and/or their parents.

Wherever possible, you should try to involve students in developing ways through which their achievements are recognised.

For celebratory events, it is often possible to use a local community facility or public building, for example local town hall or council chambers. Students can draw up a list of public figures they would like to invite, for example community leaders, councillors, mayor, MP or MEP, representatives of voluntary agencies.

IMPROVING PRACTICE

1 Consider ways in which you might recognise student achievements in:

   a) a school/student council
   b) a peer mentoring programme
   c) an inter-school 'mock trial' competition.

2 How important is it to celebrate every student's achievement in citizenship education? How is it possible to do this in a large school?

3 How could you respond to the view that formal qualifications encourage 'teaching to the test' and are therefore contrary to the 'spirit' of citizenship education?

GCSE Citizenship Studies

What does Citizenship Studies involve?

Citizenship Studies is a GCSE short course qualification available from the OCR, AQA and Edexcel examination boards.

It may be taught over one or two years at key stage 4 (students aged 14 to 16) and is assessed by a combination of final examination (60%) and coursework (40%) – details at www.qca.org.uk

How much time does it need?

Teachers new to Citizenship Studies are likely to need around two hours per week for a one-year course. Those more familiar with what is required will need less – roughly one or two hours.

Should it be made compulsory for all students?

Making GCSE Citizenship Studies compulsory can help to:
* create more time for citizenship education
* give focus to the statutory requirements
* avoid the need for cross-curricular provision
* provide a structure for learning and teaching and for assessment, recording and reporting
* prevent overlap with general provision (where the exam course is optional)
* raise the profile of the subject
* improve your school's overall exam score.

Some schools may find that linking together the GCSE short courses in Citizenship and RE eases timetabling in key stage 4.

What is the right option for my school?

While Citizenship Studies is intended to satisfy the demands of National Curriculum citizenship insofar as the *taught curriculum* is concerned, it is unlikely by itself to meet the requirements for citizenship learning beyond the classroom.

Making Citizenship Studies compulsory means dealing with large numbers of students, many of whom might not have chosen the course had they had the option. This can pose problems of management, particularly in relation to coursework, as well as raising questions about the sorts of skills and training needed to teach the course.

How can you improve results?

Examiners' reports suggest that the best results are obtained where teachers:
* teach students how to interpret exam questions
* give practice in writing essay-type answers – using writing frames
* show how examples can be used to demonstrate understanding
* emphasise the language and vocabulary of citizenship – pointing out how questions of 'rights', 'responsibility', 'justice', etc arise in different topics
* focus on skills as well as knowledge and understanding
* create their own course by putting together related elements from different sections, rather than slavishly following the syllabus
* study examiners' past reports.

What about coursework?

Candidates are more likely to score highly when coursework is:

- highly structured – e.g. basing coursework on something your school is already doing, such as a charity week, or on a local problem, such as public transport or parking
- clearly based on citizenship issues – simply drawing on something like a work experience diary is not enough – there has to be a specific citizenship focus, e.g. health and safety, employment or consumer law, or equal opportunities provision.

Support for the GCSE short course is available from the awarding bodies in the form of approved textbooks, teachers' guides and training. Contact the subject office for advice or to check that what you are doing is all right.

IMPROVING PRACTICE

1 What logistical problems arise when **GCSE Citizenship Studies** is taught to a whole year group? How can they be overcome?

2 Select some essay-style questions from a past examination paper and create a writing frame to help students to answer them.

3 Write an entry for an examinations booklet explaining what students can expect to gain from **GCSE Citizenship Studies.**

1 End of unit assessment grid

Study the assessment grid below.

1 **What are the advantages and disadvantages of using a grid like this as a tool for end of unit assessment in citizenship education?**

2 **How far does the grid aid the process of:**

   a) giving students feedback on their progress and achievements as they go along?
   b) checking what students have learned at the end of the unit?
   c) evaluating the overall success of the unit of work?

3 **How easily could this grid be applied to end of unit assessment for other citizenship topics?**

Key stage 3

Unit: Crime
Students explore crime and how it affects young people.

Learning outcomes

- Students identify things that young people do that are against the law.

- Students know that there is a difference between crimes and civil offences and between the treatment of each in law.

- Students describe the special measures taken when dealing with young people who have committed crimes.

- Students have accurate information about the measures taken to ensure that people accused of a crime receive a fair trial.

Assessment opportunities	Evidence	By whom
Presentation: students produce and deliver a presentation for other students in which they identify reasons why the peak age for offending is 18.	Presentation. Quiz answer grid. Records kept of small group discussions.	Students Teachers Peers
Quiz: students demonstrate their understanding of the main elements of the youth justice system through a quiz.		
Reflecting: students take part in a group discussion about the justice system from the point of view of fairness to both victim and offender.		

QCA, 2003

2 Self and peer assessment questionnaire

1 **Fill in the questionnaire below.**

2 **What do the answers tell you about:**

a) your attitude towards self and peer assessment?
b) the way citizenship education is assessed in your school?

IN CITIZENSHIP EDUCATION, TO WHAT EXTENT DO ...	NEVER	SOMETIMES	ALWAYS
You share learning objectives with students?			
You build time in to lessons for students to reflect on learning?			
You plan opportunities for self-assessment?			
You plan opportunities for peer assessment?			
You discuss targets with students?			
You model assessment and evaluation?			
Students understand learning objectives?			
Students understand that mistakes are a way of improving?			
Students understand standards of achievement?			
Students improve their work after it has been marked?			

Adapted from www.aaia.org.uk (The Association of Achievement and Improvement through Assessment)

3 Assessing persuasive writing

The following three pieces of work were written by Year 9 students in response to a task asking them to draft a letter to their MP for or against a proposed curfew for young people in their town.

The pieces of work were assessed by their teacher to be, respectively, 'working towards', 'working at' and 'working beyond' the level prescribed in the end of key stage 3 description for citizenship.

1 **Do you agree with the teacher's assessment? Why or why not?**

2 **Which of the following criteria do you think are most important in assessing a piece of work like this? Why?**
   - length
   - amount of detail
   - clarity
   - consistency
   - number of different ideas and arguments
   - quality of ideas and arguments
   - anticipation/defusing of counter-arguments
   - range of interests/perspectives considered
   - quality of social/political/legal/economic understanding
   - quality of moral thinking – e.g. recognition of consequences, application of principles, such as rights and responsibilities, etc.

3 **Are there other criteria which you think should be taken into account? If so, which?**

Example 1 – 'working towards'

Sir/Madam,

I am writing to inform you about my opinion on the Wigton Curfew. I think the Wigton Curfew is clearly a good idea, I think having a curfew will definitely decrease street crime. Now trouble makers will be safe at home after the curfew time. Crimes such as theft, fighting, vandalism or any sort of violence will be decreased by a big number. Least now children at Wigton will be in their homes and not playing in the streets causing trouble.

Yours faithfully,

Example 2 – 'working at'

Dear MP,

I am writing to express my opinion on the recent curfew that took place in Wigton. In my opinion, the Wigton Curfew was a good idea. It was good for a couple of reasons. Firstly, it stopped youths causing trouble on the streets of Wigton. The youths were easy to control until 9 pm then went home sensibly at the time they were told to. The curfew would have had many advantages such as less vandalism caused and more peace in the minds of other people. Youths should already know that it is sensible to not walk around the streets at that time of night as of safety. Another reason the curfew was a good reason was it is less likely for gangs to form and less fighting. When all the youth crime was stopped by the curfew, older people felt safer to go out and felt less intimidated. No youths would be able to get into alcohol and drugs if they had to be in 9 pm as they would be at home. Finally another reason the curfew was good was the fact that it went well and was kept under control. Although there were many good advantages to come from the curfew there were a couple of disadvantages to come from it. One bad thing was it stopped children socialising with their friends. Another bad thing was that only a few people were causing trouble but the curfew stopped all youths going out which wasn't their fault.

Overall, I think the curfew was a good thing to stop antisocial behaviour and went well as planned.

Yours sincerely

Example 3 – 'working beyond'

Dear Eric Matthew

I am writing to inform you of my views on the issue of the Wigton Curfew, and the problems surrounding it. In my opinion the curfew's problems far outweigh the benefits for the few residents and the other children in the area.

Wigton is notorious for its antisocial youths and street gangs but behind the stereotypical mask is an area in which [there are] large numbers of decent, friendly children and people. The many are being punished for the behaviour of the few.

The 17 day trial ban of under 16s being on the streets of Wigton after 9 pm was reported to help as there was no report of any street crime for the first six days, but seeing as though this is just a third of the total time of the curfew this result is disappointing and low. It is increasingly obvious that the gangs simply moved to somewhere else, and the nature of the crimes committed before the curfew was enforced suggest it was youth over 16 that were responsible for these street crimes.

This curfew gives children a reason to rebel and it also takes away basic human rights. Only a few children commit these crimes and simply because of the area that the children did not choose to live in are they being punished and imprisoned.

In contrast to this, if you honestly think that by placing curfews on innocent children and on children who if they commit a crime are blatantly obvious not going to abide by this curfew, and you are willing to fund this program and personally back it up then go ahead but may I say, if I was a tax payer Carlisle resident and a parent then I would seriously reconsider my trust and vote in you as my local MP.

There is few solutions to this problem, but instead of punishing the whole of the youth population of Wigton, why not use your sources and police record to target the few main offenders. To be honest, I don't want the future of Wigton's children to be decided by a bunch of guys in suits.

Thank you for your time,

4 Year 7 report

Study the example of a Year 7 (students aged 11 to 12) Student Citizenship Education Report on the opposite page.

1 **What sources of information does this report draw on?**

2 **What does the report tell you about the school's system for recording student progress and achievements in citizenship education?**

3 **How successfully has the student been involved in the report-writing process? How has this been achieved?**

4 **Think of ways in which this report could help:**

   a) Jane's parents
   b) Jane herself as she moves into Year 8
   c) Jane's citizenship teacher in Year 8.

5 **How could Jane and her Year 8 citizenship teacher use this report in terms of continuity and progression (if at all)?**

6 **How does this example compare with the way:**

   a) you write citizenship reports?
   b) citizenship reports are written generally in your school?
   c) your school involves students in the report-writing process?

7 **How could this example be used to review and improve practice in your school?**

Year 7 Report
Citizenship Education

PUPIL: **CLASS:**

COURSE DETAILS

Citizenship education in Year 7 is provided through a combination of:
- separately timetabled lessons comprising 3 half-term modules on Children's Rights, Youth Crime and Local Government
- a Crime and Safety Awareness Day
- an anti-bullying project
- a whole-year 'Charity Week'
- an opportunity to participate in the school council
- a visit to the Galleries of Justice.

PUPIL COMMENT

I understand a lot more than I did about the rights and responsibilities that citizens have. I'm more confident at expressing my opinions in class and I know more about what the law can do to help me and my family. I really enjoyed the charities week, especially meeting the charity workers and talking to them. I'm still a bit mixed up about what the government does, but I hope to learn more about this next year.

TEACHER COMMENT

Jane has made very good progress in her understanding of citizenship education this year. She has a good grasp of children's rights, how the law affects young people and the role of the police in enforcing the law. She made a valuable contribution to organisation of the charities week, by helping to plan a workshop on fair trade with a local charity worker. It showed just how much more confident she has become on public occasions and how easily she now takes part in group activities. She has also become a well respected class representative for the school council. Her performance on the three pieces of assessed written work was about average for her year. Next year she intends to ask for more advice on written assignments and hopes to play a part in organising the Human Rights Day.

ATTAINMENT GRADE

Jane is currently working slightly above the level expected of the majority of young people of her age.

Signed

Student _____

Teacher _____

Adapted from QCA, **Citizenship at Key Stages 1–4: guidance on assessment, recording and reporting,** 2002

5 Citizenship logbook

Study the example page from a citizenship logbook below.

1   **What are the advantages and disadvantages of students using a logbook like this in citizenship education?**
2   **What training would students need in order to be able use the logbook effectively? Who should give this training?**
3   **How could this logbook be used by teachers to assess students' progress and achievements in citizenship education?**

Activity title: ....
Date of activity: ....

What did we do in this activity?
We ....
....
....

What did I do?
I ....
....
....

What did I learn during this activity?
I learnt ....
....
....
....

What did I enjoy?
I enjoyed ....
....
....
....

What do I think could have been improved in this activity?
It would have been better if ....
....
....
....

What new things do I know, understand and do as a result of this activity?
I ....
....
....

QCA, 2003

Chapter 10:
Citizenship 16–19

Introduction

> " Preparation for, and participation in, citizenship must form an important part of the development of all young adults through training and education for life and the challenges it brings. "
>
> Advisory Group on Citizenship for
> 16–19 year olds in Education and Training

The provision of opportunities for citizenship education becomes, if anything, even more important as young people gain greater freedoms and responsibilities, and take on new roles in the community, for example as workers, voters, parents, tax payers.

This chapter considers citizenship education for post-16 learners in different settings and its implications for professional development.

It is relevant to all those interested in developing citizenship education programmes for post-16 learners – including voluntary organisations, the youth service, training providers, employers, schools and colleges.

Contents include:

Citizenship beyond 16
Planning a programme
Developing effective practice
Learning and teaching
Leadership, management and co-ordination
Assessing and recording progress
Recognising achievement
Youth and community work
Case studies:
    1) Post-16 citizenship projects in Oldham
    2) DAFBY – Democratic Action for Bath and North East Somerset Youth
    3) Sixth form conference at Hounslow Manor School

The chapter should be read alongside the QCA Framework for Post-16 Learning (Appendix 6 on page 225) and guidance pack for providers of post-16 citizenship programmes *Play Your Part: post-16 citizenship*, and the LSDA video resource pack, *Make It Happen: effective practice in post-16 citizenship*.

Citizenship beyond 16

Why is citizenship important beyond 16?

Citizenship education is a lifelong process. Young people's citizenship experiences need to be connected and built on as they gain greater freedoms and take on wider roles and responsibilities in the community.

The provision of opportunities for citizenship education beyond 16 has become, if anything, even more important since the subject was made statutory in secondary schools in 2002.

How does post-16 citizenship differ from citizenship pre-16?

Post-16 citizenship education has the same basic aims and purposes as citizenship pre-16, and employs the same principles of learning and teaching.

Given the increased maturity of the young people involved and the range and types of courses they are following, however, it tends to need a more flexible approach and a greater emphasis on active involvement in the life of the community and the wider world.

How does it benefit young people?

Citizenship education gives young people a voice and helps them to develop confidence to feel they can act with others to make a difference to their communities and the wider world.

> " Citizenship has exposed me to the feeling of wanting to get up and make a change in society and the wider world – it's invigorating. "
>
> Student, Richmond College

Who else does it benefit?

Citizenship education benefits employers, training providers, schools and colleges by helping to improve attendance and retention as well as encouraging a more positive attitude towards work and learning.

In the longer run, it benefits society as whole, by helping to create an active, informed and responsible citizenry.

> " The benefits of citizenship to our training agency have been immeasurable. I can tell you that due to the opportunities for personal development, our retention rates have improved significantly. "
>
> Richard Jackson, Chief Executive, Camden Jobtrain, in **Citizenship News**, October 2003

Is it the same as volunteering?

Citizenship education is not the same as volunteering. However, by building in opportunities for young people to reflect upon and review their experience as volunteers, voluntary work can become a stimulus for citizenship learning.

How far does it overlap with personal development programmes?

As with programmes such as life skills, E2E (Entry to Employment) or PSHE (Personal, Social and Health Education), citizenship education aims to empower young people to act effectively and with self-confidence. However, it can be distinguished from these in at least three ways:

1 Focus
   Citizenship education focuses on issues that concern young people as citizens rather than as private individuals – e.g. public transport, policing, the environment – whether at a local, national, European or international level.

2 Content
   Citizenship education involves areas of learning not normally included in personal development programmes – e.g. consumer law, political literacy, workers' rights and responsibilities.

3 Approach
   Citizenship education is learned through active involvement – e.g. discussions/debates, community action, youth forums.

IMPROVING PRACTICE

1 **Look at the National Curriculum programmes of study for citizenship at key stage 4 (Appendix 4 on page 223). Which aspects of these are still relevant beyond 16? Is it just the knowledge component? What, if anything, needs to be added to meet the specific needs of post-16 learners?**

2 **What opportunities are there for your post-16 learners to negotiate and lead citizenship programmes and activities for themselves?**

3 **What 'greater freedoms' and 'wider roles and responsibilities' do young people have after 16? How do these affect the types of citizenship education programmes that should be offered at this stage?**

4 **What aspects of citizenship do you think can be learned through volunteering? How can you ensure that these kinds of learning actually take place?**

Planning a programme

KEY ISSUES

How can post-16 citizenship be organised?

Which is the best approach?

How can you achieve a balanced programme?

REMEMBER

Most approaches to citizenship education can also be used as vehicles for the delivery and evidencing of Key Skills.

How can post-16 citizenship be organised?

Post-16 citizenship education can be organised in different ways, including:

- taught courses – either 'in-house' or externally accredited, e.g. Entry Level or GCSE Citizenship Studies, AS Social Science: Citizenship
- components within other courses – e.g. within E2E, the ASDAN Award Scheme, Modern Apprenticeships, A levels
- special events – e.g. mock elections, human rights days, fair trade weeks
- research projects/investigations – e.g. local surveys, internet research
- representative structures – e.g. school and college councils, student unions, workers forums
- peer education/mentoring – e.g. organising conferences for younger students, reading schemes
- community involvement – e.g. campaigns, community newsletters, environmental or regeneration projects
- pastoral/tutorial activities – e.g. equal opportunities training, fundraising, student consultations.

Which is the best approach?

No one approach can cover all aspects of citizenship education. The most effective citizenship programmes combine different approaches, selected to reflect the needs of learners and their organisations.

How can you achieve a balanced programme?

Typically, a balanced programme will include opportunities for learners to:
- discuss topical and sensitive issues
- study citizenship issues raised in their other courses
- participate in the life of the organisation
- take part in wider community-based activities
- reflect on and share their citizenship learning.

WWW

For practical guidance on setting up and running programmes of citizenship education for post-16 learners, see:
- **Play Your Part: post-16 citizenship** – a guidance pack from QCA containing detailed cases studies on all the approaches outlined here – available at **www.qca.org.uk/post16index.html.**

- **Make It Happen: effective practice in post-16 citizenship** – a video resource pack from the LSDA, which describes the key features of learning and teaching in post-16 citizenship education – details can be found at **www.post16citizenship.org/**

- Organisations with learners who are working below level 1 on the national qualifications framework should take account of QCA guidance, **Designing a Learner-centred Curriculum for 16–24 year-olds** – available at: **www.qca.org.uk/ages14-19/inclusion**

FOCUS

The citizenship programme for sixth-form students at Gosforth High School includes:
- a student union, with representatives elected by sixth-form tutor groups
- a volunteering scheme for after-school citizenship-related events
- a student magazine
- a 'mood' board where students can express their views on citizenship
- a sports coaching and training programme with the local community
- a 'listeners' programme with the Samaritans
- fundraising and charity events, organised by the students union
- visits, e.g. Adam Smith Institute
- annual citizenship awards for those who have made an outstanding contribution.

IMPROVING PRACTICE

1. What are the advantages and disadvantages of the different approaches to post-16 citizenship education listed here? Which approaches are most suited to your organisation? What implications do they have for staff development?

2. Choose one of these approaches and suggest how you could make it into a vehicle for Key Skills.

3. What opportunities are currently provided in your organisation to ensure an entitlement to post-16 citizenship education for all young people? What are the obstacles to establishing such an entitlement and how can they be overcome?

4. How can you ensure that young people following a citizenship education programme involving activities such as student consultations or equal opportunities training know they are 'doing' citizenship?

Developing effective practice

What counts as effective practice in post-16 citizenship?

Effective citizenship education for post-16 learners is:
- topical – concerned with current political and public policy issues
- relevant – to the interests and daily experiences of young people
- active – involves young people in their own learning
- challenging – pushes back the boundaries
- participatory – engages young people as equal partners
- enjoyable – encourages young people to want to learn and engage more.

Features of successful post-16 citizenship programmes evaluated by the National Foundation for Educational Research (NFER) included:
- a focus on practical action rather than on simply acquiring political knowledge
- the active involvement of young people in decisions about their education and the fostering of a 'student voice'
- dedicated and enthusiastic staff – citizenship 'champions'
- a clear definition of what citizenship means.

See **www.nfer.ac.uk/research-areas/citizenship/**

Case studies showing effective post-16 citizenship programmes in action

TYPE OF PROGRAMME	CASE STUDY
Taught course (in-house)	**HYA Training Limited** Entry level students attend fortnightly sessions over a 10-week programme, on themes such as 'What is citizenship?', 'Rights and responsibilities' and 'Human rights', including discussions on fox hunting, racism, child slavery, forced marriages, ID cards, voting age and the work of organisations like Amnesty International.
Taught course (externally accredited)	**Exmouth Community College** GCSE (short course) Citizenship Studies for all students studying one-year intermediate level courses. Others have the option of taking a one-year course in AS Social Science: Citizenship, or – if studying sociology, politics or law – having extra classes to meet the requirements.
Citizenship component within another course	**Oldham Sixth Form College** Students combined IT with citizenship by developing a website as a gateway to sites which focus on live issues, such as conservation or community action, as a resource for everyone in Oldham.
Special event	**Merton College** AVCE Travel and Tourism students organised a Student Citizenship Conference in connection with their borough's community plan, to inform students about plans to improve the borough, enable them to voice their opinions on these and to help them identify ways in which they could participate in the improvements.

TYPE OF PROGRAMME	CASE STUDY
Research project/ investigation	**Hospitality Plus** Hospitality Plus, a training provider, used citizenship investigations to collect evidence for key skills. Donna Knight, who, elected to do a project on racism, says: 'My project has a link with my work. The hotel, which has a clear policy on racism, employs people from many cultures and this has broadened my horizons on diversity issues.'
Council/union/forum	**B6 Sixth Form College, Hackney** Students established a student union with two representatives from each tutor group. Union officers were elected and a constitution drawn up by students. The student union is represented on a range of committees and on the college governing body. One of its first tasks was to help plan an extension building.
Peer education/mentoring	**Training for Life, Oval Centre** Peer mentoring is a key element in the delivery of a Community Sports Leader's Award. Young people who have successfully completed the award act as mentors to the next intake, devising and implementing most of the learning activities themselves.
Community involvement	**The City of Bristol College** Students worked with young people across Bristol on a local transport policy. They took part in a question-and-answer session with local experts, researched the issues involved and presented proposals to Bristol City Council.
Pastoral/tutorial activities	**Whalley Range High School** Weekly, 50-minute long, tutorial sessions for Year 12 students are taught by sixth-form tutors. The sessions focus on issues of democracy and cultural diversity, and are divided into units of 5–6 weeks in length – supported by tutor and student packs produced by the citizenship co-ordinator.

IMPROVING PRACTICE

Which of the examples listed here could in principle be replicated in your organisation? What implications would this have for:

a) **timetabling/time management?**
b) **resources?**
c) **staffing?**
d) **staff development?**
e) **student training/ development?**

Learning and teaching

KEY ISSUES

What kinds of learning and teaching are most effective in post-16 citizenship?

What sorts of learning are aimed at?

Why is time for reflection important?

FOCUS

HYA Training Limited

Young people at HYA Training Limited spend a day in wheelchairs rating local shops for disability access. Linda Ryan, who runs the citizenship programme, says: 'Giving them this direct experience of life for the disabled has meant disability issues can be raised across a range of activities.'

REMEMBER

Where citizenship education is delivered through other courses or programmes – such as key skills – it is important to structure learning in terms of **citizenship** objectives as well as in terms of the objectives of the programme through which it is taught. Examples of specifically citizenship learning objectives can be found in the QCA guidance, **Play Your Part: post-16 citizenship** – available at **www.qca.org.uk/post 16index.html**

What kinds of learning and teaching are most effective in post-16 citizenship?

The kinds of learning and teaching that are most effective in post-16 citizenship are:
- issues-based – focus on real, everyday problems of concern to young people
- active – draw on first-hand experience of citizenship in action
- youth-led – chosen and implemented by young people themselves
- interactive – use discussion and debate
- collaborative – involve working with others
- participatory – involve action in the organisation and/or the wider community.

> Taking part in the process of social change, working with others, making decisions and taking action – should be at the centre of all post-16 citizenship activities.
>
> QCA, 2004

What sorts of learning are aimed at?

The sorts of learning aimed at are those that help young people to become active, informed and responsible citizens, including:
- extending and deepening their citizenship knowledge and understanding – e.g. about how the law works, who runs the country, global interdependence
- acquiring citizenship skills – e.g. how to argue a case, lobby a politician, organise a campaign
- developing citizenship values and dispositions – e.g. tolerance, respect, listening to others.

Why is time for reflection important?

Time for reflection is important in order for young people to identify and review the citizenship skills, knowledge and understanding they are developing.

It is especially important when citizenship learning is acquired through active involvement in the life of the community or organisation. This means building in time for young people to:
- **prepare their citizenship activities carefully**
- **share, reflect on and consolidate what they have learned**
- **record their achievements, e.g. in a citizenship portfolio, diary or logbook.**

IMPROVING PRACTICE

1   What sorts of citizenship issue do you think young people in your organisation are most concerned about? How are these issues likely to influence your approach to learning and teaching in citizenship education?

2   Devise a 'baseline' activity you could use to establish young people's citizenship learning on joining your organisation for the first time. There are some examples on the LSDA website to get you started – see: www.post16citizenship.org/

Leadership, management and co-ordination

KEY ISSUES

What are the main factors underlying successful post-16 citizenship programmes/activities?

How important is support from senior management? Who should co-ordinate the citizenship programme/activities?

What are the main factors underlying successful post-16 citizenship programmes/activities?

The NFER's (National Foundation for Educational Research) three-year evaluation of the Post-16 Citizenship Development Programme classified the main factors underlying successful citizenship education programmes/activities into three types:

1 **Management:**
   - a flexible framework recognising that citizenship programmes can be developed in a range of ways according to local needs/circumstances
   - sufficient funding for local management of projects to be effective
   - encouragement of local networking/dialogue between those developing citizenship programmes.

2 **Institution-level:**
   - a clear definition of the aims of the programme and what citizenship means
   - senior management support plus a supportive organisational ethos
   - sufficient time and funding for staff to develop aims and objectives, teaching and learning strategies, assessment approaches and preferred outcomes
   - dedicated and enthusiastic staff – citizenship 'champions'
   - appropriate and sufficient staff development/training opportunities
   - tailoring citizenship to the needs, skills, interests and experiences of young people.

3 **Learning context-level:**
   - dedicated and enthusiastic staff, with skills to facilitate as well as teach
   - dedicated time for citizenship (whether as a discrete course, a module, or a specific project); integrating citizenship into a wider tutorial scheme was generally regarded to have been less effective
   - combining skills, knowledge and understanding with practical action – 'political literacy in action' as opposed to a narrower political knowledge approach
   - involvement of young people in decisions about their learning, and the development of a student voice
   - using a variety of experiential learning approaches and resources – e.g. project work, drama, role play, art, photography and exhibitions
   - links with the wider community through off-site visits, external speakers and opportunities for young people to negotiate and work with external partners
   - realistic and effective assessment strategies, based upon the needs, skills and capabilities of young people.

The full evaluation report is available at **www.nfer.ac.uk/research-areas/citizenship/**

How important is support from senior management?

Senior management support is crucial in promoting a vision of citizenship education that is central to the life and work of the organisation, and overseeing the policy development needed to make this vision a reality. Senior management is responsible for:

- appointing someone to co-ordinate, lead and champion citizenship
- fostering an organisational culture that encourages citizenship learning
- committing money for staffing and resources
- providing opportunities for staff development
- raising the profile of citizenship education, e.g. in promotional material or at open days.

Who should co-ordinate the citizenship programme/activities?

The person co-ordinating the citizenship programme/activities should be someone with sufficient authority and experience to lead citizenship work across the organisation – someone able to:

- take an overview of citizenship provision across the organisation
- manage the relationship between its different elements
- identify opportunities for citizenship learning wherever they occur
- contribute to policy and the drawing up of a development plan
- support and motivate colleagues
- develop partnerships both within and beyond the organisation
- co-ordinate assessment, record-keeping and the recognition of achievement
- monitor and evaluate progress.

Where possible, it is helpful to identify a small number of enthusiastic staff and others to form a dedicated citizenship team, responsible for policy development and review, and the delivery of the citizenship programme/activities across the organisation.

> ### REMEMBER
>
> The more everyone in your organisation is able to feel they can play a genuine part in developing citizenship policy and provision, the more effective your citizenship programme/activities is likely to be.

IMPROVING PRACTICE

1 What elements do you think a citizenship education policy should contain? Draw up a list of the headings you would include.

2 How could you encourage other staff – teaching and non-teaching – to become more involved in a citizenship programme/activity?

3 Rate any citizenship programme/activity you are currently running against the success factors listed here.

Assessing and recording progress

Why assess citizenship?

Assessment is important in citizenship education because it helps young people to recognise and value what they have learnt, find out how they are progressing and set targets for the future.

It also helps staff to evaluate their citizenship programmes and make employers aware of what young people have achieved in further and higher education.

> " Being realistic, unless there is some link to the assessment framework, citizenship development may have limited currency and become marginalised. "
>
> FEFC (Further Education Funding Council),
> **Citizenship for 16–19 Year Olds in Education and Training**

What form should the assessment take?

Assessment takes two basic forms, both of which have a part to play in citizenship education:

- formative assessment – providing young people with on-going feedback on their progress
- summative assessment – making a judgement about overall performance at the end of an activity, course, unit or year.

What about self and peer assessment?

Self and peer assessment are important in citizenship education because they give students a greater say in and more responsibility for their own learning.

They can also provide staff with insights into aspects of citizenship education that are otherwise difficult to assess, for example, group work and community involvement.

On what are young people assessed?

In citizenship education, young people are assessed on what they have learnt – what they know, understand and are able to do – not on how 'good' a citizen they are.

How can you assess this?

There are a number of methods for assessing learning in citizenship education, including:

- observation
- discussion – including one-to-ones
- targeted oral questioning
- self and peer assessment tasks
- written tasks – e.g. multiple-choice tests, persuasive writing exercises
- products or artefacts – e.g. videos, displays, campaign material, presentations, web pages, newsletters.

Methods used vary with the situation, for example, a short question-and-answer session is probably sufficient to assess learning following a visit from a community police officer, but a range of techniques is likely to be needed to assess learning during the course of a six-week group investigation into young people's attitudes towards the police, such as weekly small-group discussions, student presentations and a final written report with conclusions and recommendations.

> " We could explore citizenship through a variety of experiences, and use media such as video, art and tape recordings to assess the students' progress. For this group, traditional methods of assessment would not have done justice to their achievements. "
>
> Glenn Harvey, Course Leader,
> Entry Level Citizenship Studies, Aylesbury College

How should you record progress?

Though not everything needs to be recorded, recording students' progress and achievements is an important aspect of citizenship education. Progress can be recorded using existing methods, such as the Progress File or Records of Achievement. Alternatively, you can use citizenship-specific methods, such as:

- citizenship diaries/logbooks – containing details of citizenship activities undertaken, personal reflections, staff comments, etc.
- citizenship portfolios – samples of documentary and other evidence relating to individuals' work in citizenship collected by them throughout the year, such as pieces of writing, formal assessments, letters, photographs, etc.

> **REMEMBER**
>
> The most effective forms of assessment and recording progress involve young people as partners in the process.

IMPROVING PRACTICE

1   What methods could you use to assess young people's citizenship learning from:

   a) a peer education project in a local nursery school?
   b) a campaign against gun crime?
   c) an enrichment course on political literacy?
   d) a citizenship component in an E2E course?
   e) a voluntary placement in a care home?

2   What are the advantages and disadvantages of citizenship portfolios?

3   How could you respond to the view that assessing citizenship is wrong because it brands some young people as 'failing citizens'?

Recognising achievement

KEY ISSUES

Why is it important to recognise young people's achievement in citizenship?

What is the best way to do this?

What about formal qualifications and awards?

FOCUS

Camden Jobtrain

At Camden Jobtrain a celebration day is held each summer in the local town hall for everyone who has taken part in the programme. Two young people from each skill area are invited to join a planning group to decide on activities, speakers, inputs, guest list and refreshments. Typically, the day begins with a formal debate, making use of the council chambers. Later there are speeches by the mayor and other guests and an exhibition of young people's work is unveiled.

Why is it important to recognise young people's achievement in citizenship?

Recognising achievement in citizenship education plays a vital role in motivating young people and helping them to value what they have learnt. It also provides employers, further and higher education institutions and others with information about what young people know, understand and are able to do.

What is the best way to do this?

There are many different ways of recognising and celebrating young people's achievement in citizenship education – including:

- special events – e.g. open days, parents evenings, community events and celebrations, awards ceremonies, school assemblies
- exhibitions and performances – e.g. artwork, photography, drama
- in-house certificates and awards – e.g. for inclusion in Records of Achievement or the Progress File
- learner presentations – e.g. to peers, local politicians, community leaders
- reports – e.g. to parents, prospective employers, further and higher education.

What about formal qualifications and awards?

A wide range of citizenship-related qualifications and awards are available, from local awards offered in connection with local authorities, community organisations, businesses to nationally-accredited qualifications. Citizenship examinations currently accredited by QCA include:

- GCSE Citizenship Studies – a short course assessed by a combination of coursework and final examination
- Entry Level Citizenship Studies – for students likely to find the GCSE short course too challenging, or as accreditation for short projects (Level 1 and 2 qualifications to be available in due course)
- GCSE Integrated Humanities – modules in citizenship combined with other modules in related subjects and curriculum initiatives, e.g. education for sustainable development and enterprise education
- AS Social Science: Citizenship – a more academic course of study addressing citizenship issues through sociology
- International Baccalaureate – includes a requirement for students to record a specified number of hours in CAS activities (Creativity, Action and Service).

Full A-levels and GCSEs in Citizenship Studies are due to be introduced in 2008.

Other qualifications, awards and schemes that may contribute to aspects of post-16 citizenship include:

- Key Skills
- AS and A2 General Studies
- ASDAN Award Scheme
- National Open College Network (NOCN)
- Duke of Edinburgh Award Scheme
- Millennium Volunteers.

FOCUS

City of Bristol College

Students at City of Bristol College asked for formal recognition of citizenship learning through external accreditation, in line with other enrichment opportunities offered by the college. They chose the ASDAN active citizenship award because it offered a youth-led approach. ASDAN offers a set of challenges linked to the college's key skills programme.

IMPROVING PRACTICE

1   What do you think are the advantages and disadvantages of formal qualifications in post-16 citizenship education?

2   How would you respond to the view that 'citizenship should be its own reward', i.e. that involvement in citizenship activities and programmes is sufficient reward and needs no further validation?

3   Write an entry for an examinations booklet explaining what young people can expect to gain from:

a) GCSE Citizenship Studies
b) AS Social Science: Citizenship.

Youth and community work

What can youth and community work contribute to citizenship?

Youth and community work is an important source of citizenship education for young people. It allows for a flexibility of approach and a level of youth involvement in community life that are simply not possible in formal education or training.

> I firmly believe, as an experienced youth worker, that all young people can be motivated to take an active part in their communities and have the confidence to stand up and be counted.
>
> Kate Scully, DAFBY Programme Leader

How does this relate to the 'youth work curriculum'?

The DfES report, *Transforming Youth Work*, calls for the development of a 'youth work curriculum' which seeks to promote the learning of citizenship skills by encouraging young people, among other things, to:

- participate in the specification, governance, management, delivery and quality assurance of youth services
- deliver services to their peers through youth councils and peer education projects
- engage in local democracy
- become involved in local authority review systems through such mechanisms as Ofsted.

> The Government expects local authorities ... [to] involve young people in the governance of relevant services and encourage young people's preparation for the responsibilities, opportunities and expectations of adulthood and citizenship.
>
> DfES, **Transforming Youth Work**

How does citizenship differ from other kinds of youth work?

Citizenship education differs from other kinds of youth work in terms of its focus on issues that concern young people as citizens, rather than just as private individuals, for example public services, local democracy, globalisation and the environment. It emphasises areas of learning not normally covered in personal development programmes, such as legal understanding and political literacy.

What kind of activities does it involve?

Citizenship education in informal settings involves a wide range of activities, from youth forums and councils to community arts projects and campaigns on local, national or international issues.

How does it relate to citizenship in formal education?

It is important for youth organisations to be able to work alongside schools and colleges in a mutually supportive way, so that young people see their different citizenship experiences as connected rather than distinct. This can be achieved in a number of different ways, such as:

- joint youth conferences and forums
- peer education projects
- shared training events for youth workers and teachers.

FOCUS

DAFBY (Democratic Action for Bath and North East Somerset), centred on a village youth club, has sponsored a range of citizenship-related activities, including:

- a local youth action group reporting to the parish council
- a drop-in centre
- a young person's consultation on issues relating to sexual health
- a parliamentary lobby
- a fair trade project
- a consultation day on human rights
- electing an MYP (member of UK Youth Parliament)
- advising Connexions on the design of their offices and marketing their services.

IMPROVING PRACTICE

1   What opportunities for citizenship learning can the youth and community sector provide that are unlikely to arise in formal education or training? What can be done to maximise these opportunities?

2   What kinds of skills do youth and voluntary workers possess that could benefit citizenship teachers in schools and vice versa? What can be done to help them share their expertise with one another?

3   How could you respond to a youth worker who is dubious about the value of citizenship education in formal education on the grounds that 'schools are to blame for many of the problems that young people face in society today'?

1 Post-16 citizenship projects in Oldham

Projecting a citizenship vision

The commitment of both Oldham College and Oldham Sixth Form College to a transformative vision of citizenship is apparent to the visitor immediately on arrival. In their respective reception areas, the former displays prize-winning sculptures created by engineering GNVQ students addressing the theme of celebrating diversity. The latter contains posters and artwork designed by students supporting initiatives such as the Oldham Against Crime partnership and a blood donation day. Most powerful is a collage bearing the caption, 'The problem isn't black and white – it's ignorance and intolerance. The solution is simple … Mix'.

Celebrating diversity at Oldham College

At Oldham College students study mainly vocational courses, for example, in construction, engineering, ICT, hair and beauty therapy, and performing and visual arts. Support for citizenship has come mainly through the college's Learning Mentor team. The injection of a stronger citizenship dimension into the work of the college has come partly through expanding support for a 'Celebrating Diversity' competition each year. Entries are encouraged which build upon the students' interests and areas of study. There were 106 entries in 2003 involving 263 students. Among the winning entries, assessed by a mix of community representatives, performing arts students created a 'Diversity in Music' multi-media PowerPoint presentation. Hair and beauty students created and modelled fashion and make-up designs on the theme of 'Gods and Goddesses of the Past'. Pre-degree art and design students created an ID card montage. Finally, a pre-16 manufacturing group created a sculpture consisting of underwater creatures – different kinds of fish and turtles – with the explanation 'all in different strokes but glad to be in the swim'.

Planning for citizenship

Additional training has been provided for tutors to support an equal opportunities unit of work undertaken by all students in their first term at the college. The college makes use of the *Massive Training* resources, produced by a coalition of trades unions within the Manchester area and focusing on young people's rights and responsibilities. Recently, 50 students participated in a Warwick University focus group exploring community cohesion. Student Union representatives have provided strong support for the initiative. In the future, the college is planning to pilot a ten-week political literacy course with art and design and legal studies students, and may accredit this through AQA's Unit Award Scheme. It is also looking to involve students in organising a Citizenship Week on themes such as voting, fair trade, employment rights, the media, the college and the community, and making a difference.

Citizenship at Oldham Sixth Form College

At Oldham Sixth Form College the focus has been more upon extending curricular aspects of citizenship. It is significant, however, that the first strategic aim of the college is to make a valuable and critical contribution to 'social regeneration in Oldham', and the College Principal has commented recently that 'racial integration and harmony is the key to the on-going success of the college'. Money from the LSDA's Post-16 Citizenship Development Programme has helped to support the development of citizenship resources as well as activities and lesson plans within general studies tutorial programmes. The college has also piloted the GCSE Citizenship Studies short course to extend and enrich the curriculum for around 40 IT and business studies intermediate GNVQ students. Students planned and implemented a range of projects to raise money for Children in Need as an element of their coursework. A further 50 Year 13 students opted to take the AS Level Social Science: Citizenship course – often to complement other social science options such as sociology, law and politics.

Positive student responses

Students' representatives in both institutions have spoken positively about what they have gained from involvement in citizenship projects and learning activities. Some have commented upon how they felt better equipped to engage with political processes and structures – others have emphasised the confidence they have gained from working with others to organise events and effect change.

2 DAFBY – Democratic Action For Bath And North East Somerset Youth

About DAFBY

DAFBY (Democratic Action For Bath and North East Somerset Youth) is a local authority-funded youth democracy project. It is open to all young people aged 13–19 in the B&NES (Bath and North East Somerset) local authority area. Its members come from six local schools, two training providers and two FE colleges. They meet every week on Tuesday and Thursday evening at a local youth centre.

The DAFBY citizenship programme

Local authority services and the local community citizenship programme provide the context for the activities carried out by DAFBY members. The young people themselves decide which issues they want to focus on. To date, activities have included:

- Working for equality
  DAFBY members received training to consult with disabled young people on service provision, and disabled DAFBY members have joined the B&NES disabled equality forum.

- Working for education
  Members of the group have taken part in an LA consultation on plans for post-16 education. They have facilitated citizenship workshops at a sixth form conference and a Year 7 Citizenship Day at a local school. They have also worked closely with Connexions, helping to ensure the local Connexions shop is 'young-person friendly', sitting on interview panels to select personal advisers and participating in the Connexions development group.

- Campaigning for better public transport
  DAFBY took the issue of the cost and availability of public transport for young people to the UK Youth Parliament.

- Reducing youth crime
  Members have had meetings with the police to look at ways in which young people might liaise more closely with them on issues of youth crime.

- Working with the local council
  The local council asked DAFBY to carry out a 'best value' consultation with young people on tourism, culture and leisure. DAFBY members have worked with the corporate projects manager on the community plan and produced induction training for new councillors on consulting young people.

- Identifying economic priorities
  Together with B&NES economic development workers, DAFBY have held workshops on economic development in the area. This work has been incorporated into the community strategy.

- Democracy, representation and voting
  DAFBY members have established a new B&NES youth council. They have run an election workshop, including training on how to stand as a candidate for the UK Youth Parliament, which involved six local schools and a youth centre. Photographs of candidates and their manifestos were put on a special youth elections page of the B&NES website and hard copies were sent to all participating schools. Under the guidance of the Council's electoral services department, polling stations were set in six schools, staffed by DAFBY members and youth and community workers.

" I joined DAFBY because I was getting into trouble at school. They handed loads of leaflets out in school and my mate said there was a conference so I went along and liked it. You've got to get more interested in other things and get involved. Democracy is not just about voting, it's about getting voices heard for young people and adults ... I think the team-building skills I have learnt in DAFBY will help me get into the Army but it will help me do better at any job I go for. "

A 16-year-old not attending school

" I have learnt a lot about democracy and how the process can take a long time through voting and how difficult it is because you have to represent people and have to think about other people's ideas as well as your own. "

A 17-year-old AVCE student

DAFBY was one of the first projects to take part in the LSDA's Post-16 Citizenship Development Programme. Further case studies from this programme can be found in the QCA guidance document, *Play Your Part: post-16 citizenship.*

3 Sixth form conference at Hounslow Manor School

Nervous and worried

'When we were asked to organise and run a morning conference for sixth formers from Hounslow schools, we were worried. As Year 12 students, we had no experience of doing anything on that sort of scale before. We were also nervous about inviting other schools to ours in such a public and high-profile situation.'

Forming a committee

'We formed a small committee group that met each week to try to get together a programme for the day. We settled on topics that we felt would be of interest to most young adults – we wanted the day to be for people like us as well as being run by people like us!'

The day of the conference

'The morning saw each of us leading simultaneous sessions on our chosen topics, which were: youth crime, homelessness, sexual health, youth rights and racism. This took a lot of bottle because it's not easy to talk to a large group of peers (especially if most of them are complete strangers to you) and make sense of complicated and controversial ideas. The participants went from session to session in a carousel so that they were able to take part in everything that was organised. Not only were the issues debated and discussed at length and in a passionate, lively and informed way, but also action points were agreed and resolutions arrived at.'

A boost to our confidence

'When we read the evaluations at the end of the day we were pleasantly surprised by the positive comments we received from everyone. We reflected on the day and considered that it had been worthwhile and had given a tremendous boost to our confidence and self-esteem. There was no way at the start that we thought we could have achieved such a thing, and having done it we felt that our credentials as powerful citizens had been proven.'

Year 12 students, Hounslow Manor School

Section 5:
Continuity and Progression

Chapter 11:
Building on Learning

> " Progression needs to be planned for. "
>
> QCA

Introduction

Continuity of learning and achievement both within and between the different phases of education is a major factor in the effectiveness of citizenship education.

This chapter considers how continuity and progression can be built into the citizenship curriculum, from the foundation stage through to post-16 learning.

It is relevant to anyone involved in teaching, leading or promoting citizenship education to children and young people.

Contents include:
   Curriculum continuity
   Progression
   Training exercise: Transfer to secondary school

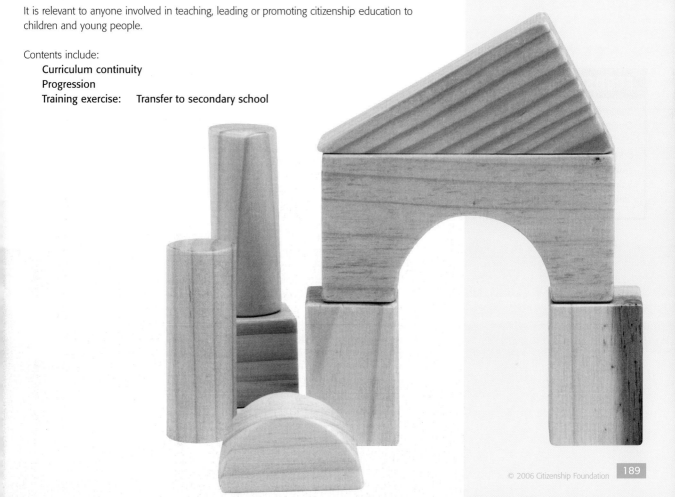

Curriculum continuity

KEY ISSUES

Why is curriculum continuity important in citizenship?

What can you do to prepare primary students for secondary citizenship?

How can you ensure continuity pre- and post-16?

Why is curriculum continuity important in citizenship?

Curriculum continuity is important in citizenship education because citizenship learning is a lifelong process and does not begin or end with any one phase of education.
Fostering continuity within and between phases helps to raise standards by ensuring that citizenship teaching builds on and extends students' existing learning. Failure to do so can leave students feeling either out of their depth or bored and demotivated.

> There is a need for improved continuity and progression to prevent repetition or inappropriately low expectations.
>
> QCA, 2004

What can you do to prepare primary pupils for secondary citizenship?

Year 6 students can have a wealth of citizenship experience. It is important to make sure that this is not lost in the transfer to secondary school.

> At the teacher focus group, the issue of transition from key stage 2 to 3 was raised. Those present felt that secondary schools are not always aware of what has been learnt at key stages 1 and 2.
>
> QCA, 2004

There are a number of ways to foster continuity between key stages 2 and 3, including:
- **primary teachers familiarising themselves with the secondary citizenship curriculum and vice versa**
- **cross-phase liaison meetings/working groups**
- **bridging projects – e.g. a Year 6 project set in collaboration with the secondary school, so students from feeder schools all arrive with a commonly shared task**
- **joint Year 6/7 projects**
- **cross-phase peer education or mediation**
- **teacher visits and observations**
- **consulting students during their Year 7 induction**
- **activities assessing base-line learning**
- **joint in-service training for primary and secondary teachers – based on common themes rather than phase of education**
- **citizenship diaries/logbooks or portfolios**
- **short and accessible summative assessments of primary pupils – both teacher-assessment and self assessment – which they take with them to Year 7.**

One way of transferring information that is effective and not too demanding on teacher time is to create a **class citizenship book**. At the end of each year in key stages 1 and 2, children choose the achievement of which they are most proud and record it in the book. At the end of Year 6, a copy of the book is presented to each child when they leave and to their secondary school. For additional ideas, see *Effective Transition KS2–KS3* at: www.citized.info

FOCUS

Supported by the Letchworth Community Education Trust, students in Letchworth primary schools begin a citizenship workbook in Year 6 and complete it in Year 7 at their new secondary school.

How can you ensure continuity pre- and post-16?

Many of the strategies for fostering continuity between key stages 2 and 3 can also be applied to citizenship at key stages 3 and 4 and at post-16.

In schools with sixth forms, it is important that pre- and post-16 citizenship co-ordinators liaise regularly – or, preferably, are one and the same person. Peer education can also make an important contribution to curriculum continuity at this level.

IMPROVING PRACTICE

1   In the area of transfer with which you are most familiar, what do you think are the main problems in trying to establish continuity in citizenship education? How can these problems be overcome?

2   Devise an activity to assess base-line learning in citizenship education for use when students transfer either from Year 6 to Year 7 or from key stage 4 to post-16 education or training. The activity should be accessible and enjoyable as well as effective.

Progression

KEY ISSUES

Why is progression important in citizenship?

How does citizenship learning progress?

How can you build progression into a citizenship programme?

Why is progression important in citizenship?

Progression is important in citizenship education for children and young people to:
- understand where they are in their learning
- set themselves targets for the future.

It is important for teachers to:
- establish and build on students' prior learning
- pitch learning and teaching at an appropriate level
- devise increasingly challenging activities
- foster continuity within and between the phases of education.

How does citizenship learning progress?

Citizenship learning progresses alongside and is intimately connected to the development of:
- political awareness – knowledge and understanding about how society is organised and governed
- social and moral reasoning – understanding of concepts such as fairness, rights and responsibilities
- emotional development – self-confidence and the ability to relate to and empathise with others.

Years 7 to 9 (students aged 11 to 14) are particularly significant for progression in citizenship learning. It is during this period that many young people first begin to develop the ability to think of society as an entity in its own right – rather than simply as a collection of individuals. They begin to be able to understand how individual and societal interests can conflict, and how the claims of one need to be balanced against the claims of the other.

How can you build progression into a citizenship programme?

The main way to build progression into a citizenship programme is through the principle of the **'spiral' curriculum**.

This involves identifying the different areas of learning that make up citizenship education – its distinctive types of skill, knowledge and understanding – and revisiting them at different levels of complexity and challenge in successive phases of education.

Example of progression in understanding the law

LEARNING ACTIVITY KEY STAGE 1 (AGE 5 TO 7)	LEARNING ACTIVITY KEY STAGE 2 (AGE 7 TO 11)	LEARNING ACTIVITY KEY STAGE 3 (AGE 11 TO 14)	LEARNING ACTIVITY KEY STAGE 4 (AGE 14 TO 16)	LEARNING ACTIVITY POST-16 (AGE 16 TO 19)
Learn about **school rules** and why they exist – by discussing particular examples	Learn about **what makes a good law** – by discussing whether it would be good to have a law banning fireworks	Learn about **youth justice** – by discussing the fairness of different types of punishment	Learn about the **causes of crime in society** – by discussing the implications of crime figures	Learn about the **underlying causes and costs of crime in society** – by discussing trends in crime figures over time

Building in such progression means familiarising yourself with the requirements for citizenship education across the different phases of education, from foundation stage to post-16 learning.

For summaries of what children and young people can be expected to have achieved at the end of each key stage in citizenship education, see:
- for the foundation stage, the **early learning goals**
- for key stages 1 and 2, the **key stage statements**
- for key stages 3 and 4, the **end of key stage descriptions**
- for 16–19, the **framework for citizenship learning**.

See Appendices 5 and 6 on pages 224–225.

IMPROVING PRACTICE

1   Which aspects of citizenship education are common to all phases of education, from foundation stage to post-16 learning? What are the implications for building progression?

2   Consider how the following topics might be dealt with differently at two or more different stages of education:

   a) identity and belonging
   b) money
   c) democracy and rules.

   Think of some learning activities that could be used in each case.

3   At what stage of education do you think it is appropriate for students to take part in:

   a) a mock election?
   b) a project on gun crime?
   c) a visit from an MP or local councillor?
   d) a twinning scheme with a school overseas?
   e) a re-cycling project?
   f) a discussion about the causes and consequences of terrorism?

Training exercise

Transfer to secondary school

Study the grid below. It is designed to collect PSHE/citizenship information to go with a Year 6 pupil to secondary school.

1   **In the primary school:**

   a) who do you think should fill in the grid?
   b) how should the process of completing the grid be managed?
   c) who should ensure that the secondary school receives the completed grid - the pupil, the Year 6 teacher, the head teacher, or all of them?

2   **In the secondary school:**

   a) who do you think should receive the grid and when?
   b) how could it be used to ensure continuity and progression of citizenship learning for the Year 6 pupil?

3   **How would you use the grid – if at all – as a Year 7 teacher/tutor?**

NAME: COMMENTS FROM PUPIL	COMMENTS FROM TEACHER/OTHER ADULT
Positions of responsibility held:	
Involvement in the school and wider community (e.g. paired reading, people I help, clubs I'm involved in):	
PSHE programmes covered (e.g. bullying, drugs education, sex education):	
Citizenship education covered (e.g. work on human rights, fair trade, democracy, organisations working for change):	
Personal reflections on my ability to contribute to whole-school changes, make choices, stand up for what I think is right and cope with challenges:	
Any issues that I feel strongly about (e.g. things happening locally or globally):	

Hilary Claire and Cathie Holden, **Effective Transition KS2 to KS3** (www.citized.info)

Introduction

> Although it is still early days in the development of the subject, it is clear that training and support for teachers needs strengthening to sustain this important addition to the curriculum.
>
> Peter Hayes, CSV

Access to up-to-date and relevant resources is essential for effective citizenship education.

This chapter considers the kinds of resources appropriate for citizenship education, where they can be obtained and how they can be used.

It is relevant to anyone involved in teaching, leading or promoting citizenship education with children and young people.

Contents include:
- Citizenship resources
- Resources for topical and controversial issues
- People as a resource
- ICT and citizenship learning
- Case study: Using an ICT package

Citizenship resources

What kinds of resources are available for citizenship?

There is a wide range of resources available for citizenship education, including:
- text-based – e.g. textbooks, schemes of work, advice packs
- ICT-based – e.g. websites, CD-ROMs, databases, video-conferencing
- media-based – e.g. TV, radio, newspapers, video
- community-based – e.g. external speakers, voluntary organisations, trainers.

Where can they be obtained?

Citizenship education resources can be obtained from a number of different sources, including:
- citizenship and other non-governmental organisations (NGOs)
- government organisations – e.g. DfES, QCA, LSDA
- commercial publishers and organisations
- charities and voluntary agencies
- LAs.

For advice on the quality of resources, you can contact:
- ACT (Association for Citizenship Teaching) – see www.teachingcitizenship.org.uk
- a mainstream citizenship organisation
- your LEA adviser or – if you have one – Citizenship AST.

Information is also available on the DfES Standards, LSDA and QCA websites respectively, **www.standards.dfes.gov.uk**, **www.lsda.org.uk** and **www.qca.org.uk** – by entering 'citizenship' in the search facility.

Written reviews of citizenship resources can be found in:
- *Teaching Citizenship*
- *Citizenship News*
- *The Times Educational Supplement (TES)*.

Why do you need a variety of resources?

A variety of resources, not just text-based materials such as worksheets, is needed to:
- take account of different learning styles
- stimulate student interest and motivation.
- provide a range of perspectives on issues
- develop skills of research and enquiry
- cover the whole curriculum – citizenship both in and beyond the classroom.

Why is it important to use 'authentic' materials?

'Authentic' materials – for example, party manifestos, letters to the press, newspaper articles, campaign documents, posters, TV interviews – bring citizenship topics 'to life' and help children and young people to gain a richer understanding of the issues they get involved in.

What about story and drama?

Resources that rely upon the use of the imagination – such as story, drama, film, art and photography – can help children and young people to see issues from the point of view of other people in society. They can also help you to address potentially controversial or sensitive issues with the safety of 'distance', to present in a simple manner issues which in real life are often complicated and hard to understand.

Do you need a core textbook?

A good textbook can act as a guide to the main areas of the citizenship curriculum and is a resource-bank in its own right.

However, it is only one tool among many. Do not allow a single textbook to dictate your entire programme – it should always be supplemented by other citizenship materials and resources. In choosing a textbook, important things to look for are:
- curriculum coverage
- approach to citizenship
- visual appeal and readability
- quality of learning activities and tasks
- accessibility for the non-specialist teacher.

You can also consult your students. Ask them how accessible, interesting or relevant they think the textbook is.

> Weaker resources focus on the knowledge components of the citizenship curriculum and ask a lot of comprehension-style questions […] Stronger texts […] provide a springboard for whole-class discussion and debate, project work and wider activities in the school and local community.
>
> Peter Brett, St Martin's College, Lancaster

IMPROVING PRACTICE

1   Using the criteria offered here, select two or three different textbooks and evaluate their usefulness as citizenship resources. Then ask your students for their opinions.

2   Think of types of 'authentic' material that could be used to explore issues relating to:

a) GM crops
b) youth crime
c) fair trade
d) elections and campaigning
e) local government/councils.

Resources for topical and controversial issues

What kinds of resources are needed for teaching topical and controversial issues?

Teaching topical and controversial issues requires resources that are up-to-date, accurate and that represent a range of perspectives.

How can newspapers help?

Local and national newspapers provide excellent source material for topical and controversial, issues. Free newspapers can usually be obtained in bulk, and local newspapers will often provide class sets of recent editions. Alternatively, set up a collection-point where staff can donate their own newspapers when they have finished with them.

Students can collect cuttings on specific themes, such as crime or European issues, and compare the way a story is covered in different newspapers. Headlines and images crystallise the issues involved and make good stimulus material for discussion work.

> Newspapers can also provide the immediate and topical resource, ensuring that citizenship can react to spur of the moment events. The way newspaper stories and images were used by teachers to support activities after the 2004 tsunami in Asia was a good example of this.
>
> Chris Waller, ACT

What have TV and radio to offer?

News and current affairs programmes are powerful and accessible sources of information on current affairs, including those specially designed for children and young people, such as *Newsround*.

TV 'soaps' raise topical and controversial issues in familiar, easy to understand contexts and can serve as a valuable starting-point for citizenship work.

There are also specially commissioned educational programmes on topical issues. See Channel 4 (www.4learning.co.uk) and Teachers TV (www.teacherstv.com).

> Television is seen by young people as more trustworthy than radio, internet or newspapers, with newspapers being seen as the least trustworthy form of communication of all.
>
> NFER, **Citizenship Education Longitudinal Study Annual Report 2005**

How can you use websites?

Websites can provide:

- up-to-date news stories – e.g. from the BBC: (www.news.bbc.co.uk), Children's Express (www.childrens-express.org), 10x10 (www.tenbyten.org/10x10.html)
- background information – e.g. BBC *Newsround* (www.news.bbc.co.uk/cbbcnews/hi/teachers/citizenship) or Oxfam's 'Cool Planet' (www.oxfam.org.uk/coolplanet)
- ideas and activities for classroom use – e.g. on events in the world news (www.dep.org.uk/globalexpress), online lesson plans/resources linked to the *Guardian* and *Observer* (www.learn.co.uk) and controversial issues (www.citizenshipfoundation.org.uk)
- opportunities for students participation in current debates – e.g. on charity issues (www.g-nation.co.uk) and politics (www.headsup.org.uk)
- authentic material – e.g. websites of government departments, political parties, campaign and pressure groups.

There are also commercial programmes that provide materials, ideas and activities for citizenship education, for example Espresso (www.espresso.co.uk) and ProQuest, a large newspaper database (www.proquest.co.uk).

What about the library?

Reference libraries often keep back copies of local newspapers or press cuttings files on matters of local interest and official documents relating to local activities, for example, minutes of council meetings, consultation papers, planning applications, electoral registers.

They also keep government publications, such as *Social Trends* and *Regional Trends*, dealing with topics like employment, education, health, social services, wealth, the environment and law enforcement.

REMEMBER

You should always try to ensure you offer a balanced presentation of opposing views on topics that are sensitive or controversial, using a range of sources that are broadly equivalent both in force and standard of argumentation.

IMPROVING PRACTICE

1   Pick a citizenship topic that is in the news and consider the kinds of resources you would need to present the issues involved to children or young people in a balanced way.

2   Identify some citizenship issues raised in TV 'soaps' recently. Choose one and decide how it might be used as the basis for a group discussion.

3   Think of three citizenship issues – one of local, one of national and one of European or international interest. What are the difficulties in offering a balanced perspective at the different levels of interest and how can they be overcome?

People as a resource

KEY ISSUES

How can external contributors support citizenship learning?

Who can be involved?

What kind of preparation is needed?

What about visitors?

How can external contributors support citizenship learning?

External contributors can help children and young people to find out about and become more involved in their communities and the world beyond their school, for example by acting as visiting speakers, making arrangements for visits and trips, organising community placements and local partnerships.

They have distinctive insights and experience that can help to bring citizenship issues 'to life' and interest children and young people in aspects of citizenship education that might otherwise seem dry and uninteresting.

Who can be involved?

A range of different individuals and organisations can be involved, including:
- local councillors, government officers, MPs, MEPs
- magistrates, police, lawyers, victim support
- trades unions
- voluntary, religious, community and charitable organisations
- businesses, financial institutions and media companies/organisations
- social services, drug and alcohol teams, primary care trusts
- drama and theatre groups
- university undergraduates, PGCE Citizenship students
- youth groups
- citizenship organisations
- other children and young people
- school/college governors and parents.

What kind of preparation is needed?

It is essential at the outset to establish which aspect(s) of your citizenship programme you want the external contributor to deliver.

You should establish whether the liaison will raise any issues relating to political or commercial interests, or if it will have implications for health and safety or child protection – you should refer to official policies where they exist. This is particularly important when inviting visitors to discuss matters that may be controversial or sensitive.

You should brief the contributors carefully beforehand, explaining what they are expected to do and how their contribution will be evaluated. Ideally, they should have an opportunity to meet with the other adults involved before any work with children or young people takes place.

> WWW
>
> For information on issues such as child protection, see the QCA guidance document, **Citizenship and PSHE: working with external contributors** at: **www.qca.org.uk/citizenship**

What about visitors?

In the case of visitors, students should be prepared in advance so they can get the most out of the experience, for example, by drawing up a list of questions to ask or carrying out a survey of issues to discuss.

In preparing for a visit from an MP or local politician, for example, it is a good idea to prepare a fact sheet beforehand and allow the students to choose which issues they would most like to talk about, such as women or ethnic minority MPs, councillors' expenses, etc. If the visit is going to be used as a media opportunity, this should also be planned beforehand and permission sought from the visitor(s) and students involved.

Children and young people should be involved in as many aspects of a visit as possible, including:
- writing invitations
- meeting, welcoming and introducing guests
- asking questions
- making presentations
- saying 'thank you' afterwards
- writing a press or media release.

IMPROVING PRACTICE

1 Consider how you could prepare a group of children or young people for a visit from one of the following:

   a) a trades union official
   b) the Mayor or a local council leader
   c) a representative from Age Concern
   d) a magistrate or police officer
   e) the Chair of Governors.

   How would you follow up the visit?

2 If you were setting up a mock election with actual candidates from your local constituency, how would you deal with an enquiry from a BNP (British National Party) candidate who wished to participate?

3 Think of some local or national issues that are controversial or sensitive in your community. What preparations would you make before allowing an external contributor to raise them with your students?

ICT and citizenship learning

KEY ISSUES

How does ICT support citizenship learning?

How does it help children and young people extend their knowledge and understanding of citizenship issues?

What sort of citizenship skills does it help to develop?

How does it help children and young people to communicate their ideas and opinions?

FOCUS

Operation Superhighway is a series of internet problem-solving activities developed by Actis, an online curriculum service provider, and the Northamptonshire LA. In one of these, primary and secondary students work directly with the Northampton police on hypothetical situations set in the local area, e.g. vandalism and bullying, or news about two children gone missing on the way to school. Students email police headquarters for information, clarification and advice, and have a community beat officer in the classroom to answer their questions.

How does ICT support citizenship learning?

ICT supports citizenship learning by helping children and young people to:
- extend their knowledge and understanding of citizenship issues
- develop and apply citizenship skills
- communicate their ideas and opinions
- record their achievements
- provide a focus for discussion and debate.

It also helps you to research citizenship topics and create more stimulating teaching material.

How does it help children and young people extend their knowledge and understanding of citizenship issues?

Ways in which ICT helps children and young people extend their knowledge and understanding of citizenship issues include:
- internet searches for data and information sources – e.g. news sites, government/official websites, websites of political/campaigning organisations
- virtual 'field trips' and simulations – e.g. Rizer on youth crime (www.rizer.co.uk)
- international school linking through global gateway – www.globalgateway.org.uk
- multi-media CD-ROM presentations – e.g. on topical and sensitive issues, such as the Holocaust and genocide.

What sort of citizenship skills does it help to develop?

ICT is particularly helpful for developing skills of research and enquiry, including how to find, collate and combine information on citizenship issues, and to organise and present findings. It is also helpful for developing skills of analysis, for example about the use and abuse of statistics in areas of social policy, such as crime, health and education.

How does it help children and young people to communicate their ideas and opinions?

ICT enables children and young people to communicate their ideas and opinions in a variety of ways, including through:

- e-mails – e.g. to local/national politicians and organisations, or other young people in this country or overseas
- word-processing – e.g. letters, press releases, campaign material, surveys, reports
- public presentations – e.g. Powerpoint
- video-conferencing – e.g. linking with other schools or youth groups, or with politicians or community partners
- setting up websites – e.g. for a school or youth forum.

It also enables them to enter into discussion and debate with other children and young people or with adults on issues that are current in society, for example, through online discussion forums and message boards. Organised in the right way, this can provide opportunities for citizenship learning through active participation in real issues where, by persuading others, students feel they are making a difference to society.

FOCUS

Students at South Dartmoor Community College run their own online discussion forum. The forum ranges over different topics, including racism, fox hunting, communism and genetic engineering. Students use aliases online. The forum is more secure than an open chat room and has a section where teachers can set homework and offer web links for projects and assignments.

IMPROVING PRACTICE

1 What do you consider to be the main problems in using ICT to support citizenship education with your students? How can these problems be overcome?

2 How could you use ICT to enhance citizenship learning that comes from:

   a) a campaign to save a local playing field?
   b) a project about global warming?
   d) a study of the UK's relationship with the European Union?
   e) participation in a school council or youth forum?

Using an ICT package

Southfields Technology College, Workington

Supporting learning across the range of themes

At Southfields Technology College, the 'Espresso' package of learning resources has been thoroughly embedded into the schemes of work for citizenship at key stage 3 and 4, including citizenship units on:

- Year 7
  'Belonging to a community'
- Year 8
  'Youth crime' and 'The criminal justice system'
- Year 9
  'Human rights' and 'Government and Democracy'
- Year 10
  'Crime and responsibility'
- Year 11
  'Global citizenship issues'.

Espresso is also drawn upon in citizenship-related units in PSHE and RE. The school finances this resource from within its specialist school budget, but other schools pay for Espresso through E-Learning Credits.

Enhancing learning

Teachers at the college are very enthusiastic about the ways in which Espresso can enhance learning and teaching in citizenship lessons: on account of its wide range of engaging starter and plenary activities on core citizenship topics; useful interactive matching and sorting activities, for example Inside a Magistrates' Court; built-in video clips; and adaptable worksheet materials.

Student feedback was also positive. They said that Espresso made lessons 'colourful', 'active' and 'more fun'.

Sample classroom activity

As part of a Year 9 lesson in the 'Government and democracy' unit, the teacher used Espresso to look at the House of Commons on the Parliamentary Education Unit website, show a video clip on the work of MPs and carry out a matching activity on the work of parliament. The students then undertook two activities provided by Espresso:

- a small-group discussion in which they prioritised parliamentary bills they felt were most important
- a whole-class debate, using the ICT element to share ideas visually, attempting to reach a consensus.

Throughout the lesson, the teacher reinforced key words such as 'bill', 'committee', House of Commons/Lords' and 'whips' and, at the end, used a writing frame to help students set out the reasoning behind their choice of bill. See: www.espresso.co.uk

Chapter 13: Continuing Professional Development

Introduction

A systematic approach to continuing professional development (CPD) is essential to establish high standards for citizenship education that are comparable with standards in other subjects and to ensure that all children and young people are given the opportunity to acquire the skills, knowledge and understanding that will enable them to become active, informed and responsible citizens.

This chapter considers priorities for professional development in citizenship education, the sorts of training available and how you can develop a CPD programme for citizenship education that reflects the needs both of individuals and of your institution as a whole.

It is primarily intended for citizenship co-ordinators and senior managers with responsibility for CPD, but may also have application for anyone responsible for teaching, leading or promoting citizenship education in primary and secondary schools and in post-16 education and training.

Contents include:
> **Planning CPD in citizenship**
> **Assessing training and development needs in schools and colleges**
> **Whole-school/college INSET**
> **Staff development in post-16 citizenship**
> **Sources of CPD for citizenship**

In working with this chapter, you may find it helpful to revisit some of the numerous stimuli for citizenship CPD included in other chapters in the Handbook, including the cases studies, training exercises and 'Improving practice' features at the end of each topic.

Planning CPD in citizenship

Why is professional development important in citizenship?

CPD is important to establish high standards for citizenship education that are comparable with standards in other subjects and to ensure that all children and young people are given the opportunity to acquire the skills, knowledge and understanding that will enable them to become active, informed and responsible citizens.

It is particularly important because of the relatively recent appearance of citizenship education – as a non-statutory element in primary schools, a statutory subject in the National Curriculum in secondary schools and a component in post-16 education and training.

It is also important because of the breadth of learning opportunities citizenship education encompasses – in the classroom, in the life of the institution and in its links with the wider community.

Who needs training?

Since citizenship education relates to every aspect of the work of an educational institution, CPD is relevant to everyone involved, including:
- senior managers
- citizenship co-ordinators
- citizenship teachers
- subject leaders and teachers
- form tutors
- governors
- support staff
- community partners.

What kinds of training?

Training and development needs are likely to relate to one or more of six basic areas:
- understanding citizenship – what the subject is all about
- skills of organisation, management and co-ordination
- subject knowledge
- skills relating to learning and teaching skills
- developing citizenship in the life of the institution
- developing citizenship in the wider community.

Where do you begin?

To be effective, a CPD programme has to be planned systematically, in a step-by-step way. This involves:

1 **Identifying needs**
   CPD begins with an audit of the institution's citizenship training needs – consulting colleagues on what they may be able to offer to the training process as well as identifying areas in need of development. The School Self-Evaluation Tool provides a useful framework for this (available at: www.teachingcitizenship.org.uk/resources/downloads and www.matrix.ncsl.org.uk). See also Appendix 7 on page 226.

2 **Setting priorities**
   On the basis of your assessment of the institution's training and development needs, you should then set your priorities for professional development for the coming year. These should be developed in co-ordination with your CPD manager and linked to your citizenship education development plan and your institution's overall development plan.

3 **Implementing training and development**
   To convert your priorities into action, you need to plan how to implement them in terms of concrete targets, tasks and action plans and including costs, both in terms of resources and staff time.

4 **Review and evaluation**
   Finally, it is important to have in place some mechanism for reviewing and evaluating the success of the training that has been given, not only to reflect on the training programme to date but also to be able to set new training priorities in the future.

WWW

A good way to identify staff training needs is to ask young people for their experiences and perceptions of citizenship education, and their views on any courses they have experienced. The NFER report, **Listening to Young People: the citizenship education longitudinal study – the views of young people**, details the views of 6,400 young people about citizenship education in their schools and communities. It is available at: **www.nfer.ac.uk/research-areas/citizenship/.**

IMPROVING PRACTICE

1 **Look at your institution's present development plan. What opportunities does it present for developing CPD in citizenship education?**

2 **Think of some ways in which pupil or student consultation or research might be used to identify training needs in citizenship.**

3 **Consider different ways in which you might review and evaluate the effectiveness of a CPD programme in citizenship education. How could you involve children or young people in the process?**

Assessing training and development needs in schools and colleges

What are the main training and development needs in schools and colleges?

Staff training and development programmes need to reflect the fact that not only is citizenship education a relatively recent subject in schools and colleges, but also that it involves a wide range of learning contexts – both within and beyond the classroom.

A framework for assessing training and development needs in citizenship

PERSONNEL	AREA OF CITIZENSHIP TRAINING	
Senior managers	• Understanding citizenship in a whole-school/college context • Implementing citizenship in the curriculum • Links to other school/college policies, e.g. behaviour policy • Creating a citizenship ethos • Citizenship in school/college life • Setting up and maintaining a school/college council	• Links with parents and the community • Development planning • Monitoring and evaluation • Recording and reporting on pupil/student progress • Continuity with primary, secondary and post-16 sectors • Self-evaluation/preparing for Ofsted inspection
Citizenship co-ordinator	• Understanding citizenship • Citizenship in the curriculum • Subject knowledge • Appropriate teaching and learning skills • Curriculum construction • Assessment, reporting and recording • Links with other subjects • GCSE Citizenship Studies • Suspended timetable events and activities • Citizenship in school/college life	• Links with parents and the community • Setting up and maintaining a school/college council • Management and leadership • Running citizenship INSET • Mentoring colleagues • Special needs • Reviewing/upgrading resources • Self-evaluation/preparing for Ofsted inspection
Citizenship teachers	• Understanding citizenship • Citizenship in the curriculum • Subject knowledge • Appropriate teaching and learning skills • Schemes of work • Assessment, recording and reporting • GCSE Citizenship Studies	• Suspended timetable events and activities • Citizenship in school/college life • Links with parents and the community • Differentiation and learning styles • Self-evaluation/preparing for Ofsted inspection
Teachers of other subjects	• Understanding citizenship • Citizenship in the curriculum • Citizenship through other subjects • Appropriate teaching and learning skills • Schemes of work • Assessment, recording and reporting	

PERSONNEL	AREA OF CITIZENSHIP TRAINING	
Form tutors	• Understanding citizenship • Citizenship in the curriculum • Recording and reporting on student progress	• Class councils/school or college council/circle time • Community involvement
Whole staff	• Understanding citizenship • Citizenship in the curriculum • Citizenship in school/college life	• Pupil and student consultation • Links with parents and the community
Governors and community partners	• Citizenship in the curriculum • Understanding citizenship • Citizenship in school/college life • Pupil/student consultation	• Links with parents and the community • Self-evaluation/preparation for Ofsted inspection

What sorts of training and development needs do pupils and students have?

Pupils and students have training and development needs arising out of their citizenship learning, including:
• understanding citizenship
• citizenship in the curriculum
• recording and reporting on progress
• appropriate learning skills, e.g. discussion and debate, enquiry and communication
• participation in school/college life, e.g. class/school councils
• pupil/student consultation
• links with parents and the community
• peer education/mediation.

IMPROVING PRACTICE

Using the framework given here, undertake a training and development needs assessment for your school/ college – preferably in co-ordination with your CPD manager and in the light of your school/college's overall development plan. Consider the following:

1 What citizenship strengths does your school/college already have? How can they be shared?

2 What are the key priority areas for short- and medium-term development?

3 How do these needs fit in with wider training needs of all staff and the school/college's development plan?

4 How could they be prioritised over the next two to three years?

5 Should the training needs of pupils/students be included in the assessment? If so, how?

Whole-school/college INSET

KEY ISSUES

Why is **CPD** in citizenship a whole-school/college issue?

How can whole-school/college **INSET** be used?

Where do you begin?

Why is **CPD** in citizenship a whole-school/college issue?

CPD in citizenship education is an issue for the whole school/college because although citizenship learning takes place largely through the taught curriculum, that learning is reinforced through the ethos, values and culture of the school/college and its links with the wider community.

This means that all school/college staff, teaching and non-teaching, are potential contributors to citizenship learning and should be able to benefit from professional development in citizenship education.

How can whole-school/college **INSET** be used?

Whole-school/college INSET in citizenship education can be used to:
- **raise awareness and understanding of the subject amongst staff**
- **audit existing provision**
- **assess training and development needs**
- **develop a whole-school/college policy**
- **raise the status of citizenship education in the school/college**
- **facilitate self-evaluation/preparation for Ofsted inspection.**

Where do you begin?

The kind of training needed depends on the way in which the citizenship curriculum is delivered in your school or college and how advanced this is.

The NFER Citizenship Education Longitudinal Study identified four approaches that schools were taking when they first began to address citizenship education, as show below.

Four approaches to citizenship education

Progressing schools – developing citizenship education in the curriculum, school and wider community; the most advanced type of provision

Implicit schools – not yet focusing on citizenship education in the curriculum, but with a range of active citizenship opportunities

citizenship in the curriculum

active citizenship in the school and wider community

Focused schools – concentrating on citizenship education in the curriculum, with few opportunities for active citizenship in the school and wider community

Minimalist schools – at an early stage of development, with a limited range of delivery approaches and few extra-curricular activities on offer

Where citizenship education is only just beginning to develop in a school or college, the most effective starting-point for CPD is with school/college leaders and managers. It is important to have a CPD policy that has the full commitment and support of the senior management team and is linked to your overall school/college development plan.

A good way to start, therefore, is with an INSET session for the senior management team, ideally including subject heads and staff responsible for managing the pastoral programme, such as year heads and assistant year heads.

A follow-up session might involve the staff as a whole, introducing the broad aims of citizenship education and making links with the social aims and values of the National Curriculum as set out at the beginning of the National Curriculum Handbook. Working towards a whole-school/college event, such as a Human Rights Day, can provide a useful focus for this. Staff could be asked to prioritise their own responses to a prepared list of possible aims for citizenship including, for example, 'promote responsible behaviour', 'increase voting rates', 'increase tolerance and social cohesion', 'encourage participation in community activities'. They could go on to consider how their individual subjects can be thought of as contributing to the social development of students and the well-being of society. A third INSET activity might be working in year groups to consider ways in which the pastoral programme can contribute to the development of students as citizens.

Future sessions might involve working more intensively with subject staff whose subjects have been identified as 'carrier' subjects for citizenship education in the school/college.

IMPROVING PRACTICE

1 Which of the four approaches to citizenship education identified in the **NFER** study do you see as matching most closely your own school's/college's approach? Why?

2 What are the respective advantages and disadvantages of using outside experts and in-house volunteers for whole-school **INSET** in citizenship education?

3 Prepare a Powerpoint display to introduce support staff to the aims, objectives and values of citizenship education in your school/college – no more than 10 slides.

Staff development in post-16 citizenship

Why is staff development important in post-16 citizenship?

Staff development is important because citizenship education is a relatively recent development in post-16 education and training, and is, as yet, not always well understood. It is particularly important because of the breadth of learning programmes and activities that citizenship education encompasses at the post-16 level – from taught courses in the classroom to special events, student participation, peer education and community involvement.

Who needs training?

Given that citizenship education and its values can touch on every aspect of an organisation's work, staff development is relevant for any member of staff – teaching or non-teaching.

What kinds of training?

The precise nature of the training that is required depends upon the kind of citizenship education programme you wish to implement. In practice, however, it is likely to relate to one or more of the following areas:
- understanding citizenship – what it is all about
- approaches to post-16 citizenship education
- subject knowledge – such as law, politics, economics
- learning and teaching styles – especially participatory approaches
- organising and managing a citizenship education programme
- developing citizenship education through the life of the organisation
- developing citizenship education through the wider community
- assessment, recording and recognising achievement
- working with topical, controversial and sensitive issues
- linking citizenship education with other courses and activities.

Where do you begin?

Whether they are aware of it or not, most staff will already have some of the skills and experience needed for post-16 citizenship education. When assessing staff training and development needs, therefore, it is helpful to start by identifying what your staff already know and understand, then to build on this in any training programme you develop.

A good way to start is with an audit of what colleagues have to offer – both as individuals and as teams – as well as areas they would wish to develop. This could be followed up by a session involving the staff as a whole, introducing the broad aims of citizenship education and making links with the more general aims of education as staff see them. Basing staff training and development around the planning and staging of a special event, such as a Human Rights Day, can provide a useful context for this.

WWW

Although originally intended for secondary schools, the **School Self-Evaluation Tool** provides a useful framework for staff development in citizenship education across the 16–19 sector. An online version is available for registered users at: **www.matrix.ncsl.org.uk/curriculum** – see Appendix 7 on page 226.

Staff development events, case studies and materials to help organisations identify needs and run in-house training activities are available from the Learning and Skills Development Agency (LSDA) at: **www.post16citizenship.org**

Details of **Make It Happen**, a video resource pack for post-16 citizenship education are available at: **www.post16citizenship.org/materials**

Other sources of CPD in citizenship education and a list of helpful organisations can be found in Appendices 8 and 9 on pages 227 and 230.

Who can you turn to for advice?

For advice on CPD in citizenship education, consult:
- the Association for Citizenship Teaching (ACT)
- the DfES Citizenship Team
- the Qualifications and Curriculum Authority (QCA)
- the Teacher Development Agency (TDA; formerly TTA)
- your LA adviser and Advanced Skills Teacher for Citizenship (if you have one)
- the Learning and Skills Development Agency for post-16 learners (LSDA)
- citizenship organisations and NGOs
- higher education institutions, particularly those involved in the Citized network
- your citizenship co-ordinator/team leader or other citizenship colleagues.

IMPROVING PRACTICE

1 Of the areas listed here, what do you consider to be the greatest area of need for staff training and development in citizenship education in your organisation? Why?

2 Design a questionnaire that could be used by your organisation to:

   a) audit existing staff interest and expertise in citizenship education
   b) assess the need for training and development.

3 How important do you think it is for all staff to have a common understanding of citizenship education? What can be done to achieve this?

Sources of CPD for citizenship

KEY ISSUES

Where can you find training and support for citizenship?

Where can you find training and support for citizenship?

There are a number of different sources of training and support in citizenship. They include:

1 **School/college-based**
   The most basic form of CPD in citizenship consists of the sharing of expertise that already exists among colleagues in your school or college. Training opportunities can be expanded by linking citizenship to official initiatives and strategies, such as *Literacy and Citizenship, Assessment for Learning, the National Healthy Schools Standard, Post-16 Citizenship Development Programme*, or to school policies such as equal opportunities or behaviour and attendance policy. Shared training sessions with cluster or pyramid groups of local schools and colleges are particularly useful for developing expertise in areas such as primary/secondary and secondary/post-16 transition, community links, and planning larger scale events, such as inter-school conferences or student forums.

2 **LA**
   LA advisory teams provide training programmes where there is a clear demand from teachers and schools in their area. The LA may have an adviser or consultant with responsibility for citizenship – to whom requests for help should be addressed. The LA may also have one or more Advanced Skills Teachers (ASTs) of citizenship, offering CPD in local schools as well as a teaching commitment in their own school. LAs should be able to help you develop networks of citizenship co-ordinators, and arrange regular meetings or intranet connections. They can also help you to establish cross-school structures and initiatives, such as LA-specific accreditation for citizenship achievement.

3 **DfES/QCA**
   The DfES publishes free guidance material which can be used in training sessions, including case studies and *The School Self-Evaluation Tool*. These are available at www.dfes.gov.uk/citizenship along with links to the useful www.teachernet.gov.uk site. Schemes of work and guides for teachers and managers are available at www.standards.dfes.gov.uk. Regular newsletters are available on the QCA website at www.qca.gov.uk and its linked site www.ncaction.org.uk/subjects/citizen provides exemplar student materials.

   The DfES, along with QCA, Ofsted, ACT, and the Citizenship Foundation has published a short video, *Making a Success of Citizenship Education,* plus supporting leaflets which can be shown to governors and parents as an introduction to citizenship or to enlist their support. These have been distributed to schools and further copies of the leaflets are downloadable from the DfES website at www.dfes.gov.uk/citizenship.

4 **Ofsted**
   Ofsted publishes annual subject reports and regular updates for inspectors, highlighting areas for development and suggesting training priorities. They are available online at: www.ofsted.gov.uk.

5 **Professional bodies**
   The Association for Citizenship Teaching (ACT) provides advice and training in citizenship education at www.teachingcitizenship.org.uk. Other professional bodies that can provide support for CPD in citizenship are the Association for Teachers of Social Science (ATSS), the Humanities Association and the Development Education Association (DEA).

6 Citizenship organisations

Specialist citizenship organisations are an important source of CPD, for example, the Citizenship Foundation, Institute for Citizenship, Community Service Volunteers (CSV), School Councils UK (SCUK), Changemakers and ContinYou. Many of these produce training materials freely available on their websites.

7 Higher education

Universities and colleges are able to provide a range of CPD services in citizenship, from mentoring Initial Teacher Training students and beginning citizenship teachers to MA-level qualifications and distance learning packages. For details of courses and online materials useful for CPD at school level as well as HE, visit: www.citized.info.

8 Charities and campaigning organisations

Charities and campaigning organisations often offer training and/or publish educational materials useful for CPD, for example, Oxfam, Unicef, Amnesty International, World Wildlife Fund for Nature, RSPCA, and Ecoschools. It is worth remembering that materials produced by single issue organisations, however 'worthy', may need to be scrutinised for balance.

9 Examination boards

Examiners' reports published by AQA, Edexcel and OCR identify areas for development in exam work. Examination boards often provide training for schools considering following their courses.

10 Printed and online materials

A number of publications can be useful for CPD in citizenship, such as:

- Jerome, L., et al., *The Citizenship Co-ordinator's Handbook*, Nelson Thornes, 2003.
- Gearon, L. (ed), *Learning to Teach Citizenship in the Secondary School*, RoutledgeFalmer, 2003.
- *Teaching Citizenship* – the ACT journal, published quarterly.

11 Training videos

Channel 4 has produced three INSET programmes, under the series title *Teaching Citizens*, which introduce whole-school issues in citizenship, and a more in-depth programme on Teaching Controversial Issues. The Citizenship Foundation has produced a training video for key stages 3 and 4, called *Raising the Standard: identifying good practice in secondary citizenship*, which comes with detailed suggestions and back-up notes for trainers, published by Connect publications. CPD programmes are also available on Teachers TV – at www.teachers.tv.

Sources of CPD for citizenship

FOCUS

Certificated or accredited courses

Certificated or accredited professional development courses can help you with general professional development, threshold validation, advancement as an AST or in progress along leadership routes through the National College of School Leadership programmes. Many such courses are also accredited with CATs transfer points and can be counted towards MA-level courses.

At the time of writing, the DfES is piloting a certificated course for citizenship teachers in three regions (the North-West, the West Midlands and the South-East). Besides these face-to-face courses, a distance learning certificated course is also under development. The certification framework is set by DfES and parallels that of the PSHE Certificate, though methods of delivery will differ from region to region. The courses are principally aimed at subject leaders and teachers and are relevant to primary, secondary and post-16 settings. In each region the pilot courses include:

- taught elements covering the main issues facing subject leaders, teachers and managers
- opportunities to build portfolios evidencing a range of teaching and management skills
- opportunities to develop school-based practice such as curriculum planning and delivery with the support of experienced citizenship trainers
- opportunities to develop local networks of colleagues committed to professional advancement and self-improvement
- accreditation from DfES, and local HE institutions through MA level CATS points, providing routes into further M-level qualifications.

The pilot year will be independently evaluated, and also reviewed by Ofsted.

WWW

Further information will be available in due course online at: **www.dfes.gov.uk** and **www.tda.gov.uk**

Appendices

Appendix 1

Knowledge, skills and understanding

Developing confidence and responsibility and making the most of their abilities

Pupils should be taught:

- to recognise what they like and dislike, what is fair and unfair, and what is right and wrong
- to share their opinions on things that matter to them and explain their views
- to recognise, name and deal with their feelings in a positive way
- to think about themselves, learn from their experiences and recognise what they are good at
- how to set simple goals.

Preparing to play an active role as citizens

Pupils should be taught:

- to take part in discussions with one other person and the whole class
- to take part in a simple debate about topical issues
- to recognise choices they can make, and recognise the difference between right and wrong
- to agree and follow rules for their group and classroom, and understand how rules help them
- to realise that people and other living things have needs, and that they have responsibilities to meet them
- that they belong to various groups and communities, such as family and school
- what improves and harms their local, natural and built environments and about some of the ways people look after them
- to contribute to the life of the class and school
- to realise that money comes from different sources and can be used for different purposes.

Developing a healthy, safer lifestyle

Pupils should be taught:
- how to make simple choices that will improve their health and well-being
- to maintain personal hygiene
- how some diseases spread and can be controlled
- about the process of growing from young to old and how people's needs change
- the names of the main parts of the body
- that all household products, including medicines, can be harmful if not used properly
- rules for and ways of keeping safe, including basic road safety, and about people who can help them stay safe.

Developing good relationships and respecting the differences between people

Pupils should be taught:
- to recognise how their behaviour affects other people
- to listen to other people, and play and work cooperatively
- to identify and respect the differences and similarities between people
- that family and friends should care for each other
- that there are different types of teasing and bullying, that bullying is wrong, and how to get help to deal with bullying.

Breadth of study

During the key stage, pupils should be taught the knowledge, skills and understanding through opportunities to:
- take and share responsibility (e.g. for their own behaviour, by helping to make classroom rules and following them, by looking after pets well)
- feel positive about themselves (e.g. by having their achievements recognised and by being given positive feedback about themselves)
- take part in discussions (e.g. talking about topics of school, local, national, European, Commonwealth and global concern, such as 'where our food and raw materials for industry come from')
- make real choices (e.g. between healthy options in school meals, what to watch on television, what games to play, how to spend and save money sensibly)
- meet and talk with people (e.g. with outside visitors such as religious leaders, police officers, the school nurse)
- develop relationships through work and play (e.g. by sharing equipment with other pupils or their friends in a group task)
- consider social and moral dilemmas that they come across in everyday life (e.g. aggressive behaviour, questions of fairness, right and wrong, simple political issues, use of money, simple environmental issues)
- ask for help (e.g. from family and friends, midday supervisors, older pupils, the police).

Framework for personal, social and health education and citizenship at key stage 2 (pupils aged 7 to 11)

Knowledge, skills and understanding

Developing confidence and responsibility and making the most of their abilities
Pupils should be taught:
- to talk and write about their opinions and explain their views on issues that affect themselves and society
- to recognise their worth as individuals by identifying positive things about themselves and their achievements, seeing their mistakes, making amends and setting personal goals
- to face new challenges positively by collecting information, looking for help, making responsible choices and taking action
- to recognise, as they approach puberty, how people's emotions change at that time and how to deal with their feelings towards themselves, their families and others in a positive way
- about the range of jobs carried out by people they know, and to understand how they can develop skills to make their own contribution in the future
- to look after their money and realise that future wants and needs may be met through saving.

Preparing to play an active role as citizens
Pupils should be taught:
- to research, discuss and debate topical issues, problems and events
- why and how rules and laws are made and enforced, why different rules are needed in different situations and how to take part in making and changing rules
- to realise the consequences of anti-social and aggressive behaviours, such as bullying and racism, on individuals as well as communities
- that there are different kinds of responsibilities, rights and duties at home, at school and in the community, and that these can sometimes conflict with each other
- to reflect on spiritual, moral, social, and cultural issues, using the imagination to understand other people's experiences
- to resolve differences by looking at alternatives, making decisions and explaining choices
- what democracy is, and about the basic institutions that support it locally and nationally
- to recognise the role of voluntary, community and pressure groups
- to appreciate the range of national, regional, religious and ethnic identities in the United Kingdom
- that resources can be allocated in different ways and that these economic choices affect individuals, communities and the sustainability of the environment
- to observe how the media present information.

Developing a healthy, safer lifestyle
Pupils should be taught:
- what makes a healthy lifestyle, including the benefits of exercise and healthy eating, what affects mental health and how to make informed choices
- that bacteria and viruses can affect health and that following simple, safe routines can reduce their spread
- about how their body changes as they approach puberty

- which commonly available substances and drugs are legal and illegal, their effects and risks
- to recognise the different risks in different situations and then decide how to behave responsibly, including sensible road use, and judging what kind of physical contact is acceptable or unacceptable
- that pressure to behave in an unacceptable or risky way can come from a variety of sources, including people they know, and how to ask for help and use basic techniques for resisting pressure to do wrong
- school rules about health and safety, basic emergency aid procedures and where to get help.

Developing good relationships and respecting the differences between people
Pupils should be taught:
- that their actions affect themselves and others, to care about other people's feelings and to try to see things from their points of view
- to think about the lives of people living in other places and times, and people with different values and customs
- to be aware of different types of relationship, including marriage and those between friends and families, and to develop the skills to be effective in relationships
- to realise the nature and consequences of racism, teasing, bullying and aggressive behaviours, and how to respond to them and ask for help
- to recognise and challenge stereotypes
- that differences and similarities between people arise from a number of factors, including cultural, ethnic, racial and religious diversity, gender and disability
- where individuals, families and groups can get help and support.

Breadth of study

During the key stage, pupils should be taught knowledge, skills and understanding through opportunities to:
- take responsibility (e.g. for planning and looking after the school environment; for the needs of others, such as by acting as a peer supporter, as a befriender, or as a playground mediator for younger pupils; for looking after animals properly; for identifying safe, healthy and sustainable means of travel when planning their journey to school)
- feel positive about themselves (e.g. by producing personal diaries, profiles and portfolios of achievements; by having opportunities to show what they can do and how much responsibility they can take)
- participate (e.g. in the school's decision-making process, relating it to democratic structures and processes such as councils, parliaments, government and voting)
- make real choices and decisions (e.g. about issues affecting their health and well-being such as smoking; on the use of scarce resources; how to spend money, including pocket money and contributions to charities)
- meet and talk with people (e.g. people who contribute to society through environmental pressure groups or international aid organisations; people who work in the school and the neighbourhood, such as religious leaders, community police officers)
- develop relationships through work and play (e.g. taking part in activities with groups that have particular needs, such as children with special needs and the elderly; communicating with children in other countries by satellite, e-mail or letters)

- consider social and moral dilemmas that they come across in life (e.g. encouraging respect and understanding between different races and dealing with harassment)
- find information and advice (e.g. through helplines, by understanding about welfare systems in society)
- prepare for change (e.g. transferring to secondary school).

Programme of study for citizenship at key stage 3
(students aged 11 to 14)

Knowledge, skills and understanding

Teaching should ensure that 'knowledge and understanding about becoming informed citizens' are acquired and applied when 'developing skills of enquiry and communication', and 'participation and responsible action'.

Knowledge and understanding about becoming informed citizens
Pupils should be taught about:
- the legal and human rights underpinning society, basic aspects of the criminal justice system, and how both relate to young people
- the diversity of national, regional, religious and ethnic identities in the United Kingdom and the need for mutual respect and understanding
- central and local government, the public services they offer, how they are financed and the opportunities to contribute
- the key characteristics of parliamentary and other forms of government
- the electoral system and the importance of voting
- the work of community-based, national and international voluntary groups
- the importance of resolving conflict fairly
- the significance of the media in society
- the world as a global community, the political, economic, environmental and social implications of this, and the role of the European Union, the Commonwealth and the United Nations.

Developing skills of enquiry and communication
Pupils should be taught to:
- think about topical political, spiritual, moral, social and cultural issues, problems and events by analysing information and its sources, including ICT-based sources
- justify orally and in writing a personal opinion about such issues, problems or events
- contribute to group and exploratory class discussions and take parting debates.

Developing skills of participation and responsible action
Pupils should be taught to:
- use their imagination to consider other people's experiences and be able to think about, express and explain views that are not their own
- negotiate, decide and take part responsibly in both school and community-based activities
- reflect on the process of participating.

Knowledge, skills and understanding

Knowledge and understanding about becoming informed citizens
Pupils should be taught about:
- the legal and human rights and responsibilities underpinning society and how they relate to citizens, including the role and operation of the criminal and civil justice systems
- the origins and implications of the diverse national, regional, religious and ethnic identities in the United Kingdom and the need for mutual respect and understanding
- the work of parliament, the government and the courts in making and shaping the law
- the importance of playing an active part in democratic and electoral processes
- how the economy functions, including the role of business and financial services
- the opportunities for individuals and voluntary groups to bring about social change locally, nationally, in Europe and internationally
- the importance of a free press and the media's role in society, including the internet, in providing information and affecting opinion
- the rights and responsibilities of consumers, employers and employees
- the United Kingdom's relations in Europe, including the European Union, and relations with the Commonwealth and the United Nations
- the wider issues and challenges of global interdependence and responsibility, including sustainable development and Local Agenda 21.

Developing skills of enquiry and communication
Pupils should be taught to:
- research a topical political, moral, social or cultural issue, problem or event by analysing information from different sources, including ICT-based sources, showing an awareness of the use and abuse of statistics
- express, justify and defend orally and in writing a personal opinion about such issues, problems or events
- contribute to group and exploratory class discussions and take part in formal debates.

Developing skills of participation and responsible action
Pupils should be taught to:
- use their imagination to consider other people's experiences and be able to think about, express, explain and critically evaluate views that are not their own
- negotiate, decide and take part responsibly in school and community-based activities
- reflect on the process of participating.

Key stage statements for key stages 1 and 2 (pupils aged 5 to 11)

During key stage 1, pupils learn about themselves as developing individuals and as members of their communities, building on their own experiences and on the early learning goals for personal, social and emotional development. They learn the basic rules and skills for keeping themselves healthy and safe and for behaving well. They have opportunities to show they can take some responsibility for themselves and their environment. They begin to learn about their own and other people's feelings and become aware of the views, needs and rights of other children and older people. As members of a class and school community, they learn social skills such as how to share, take turns, play, help others, resolve simple arguments and resist bullying. They begin to take an active part in the life of their school and its neighbourhood.

During key stage 2, pupils learn about themselves as growing and changing individuals with their own experiences and ideas, and as members of their communities. They become more mature, independent and self-confident. They learn about the wider world and the interdependence of communities within it. They develop their sense of social justice and moral responsibility and begin to understand that their own choices and behaviour can affect local, national or global issues and political and social institutions. They learn how to take part more fully in school and community activities. As they begin to develop into young adults, they face the changes of puberty and transfer to secondary school with support and encouragement from their school. They learn how to make more confident and informed choices about their health and environment; to take more responsibility, individually and as a group, for their own learning; and to resist bullying.

Attainment target and end of key stage descriptions for key stages 3 and 4 (students aged 11 to 16)

The following descriptions describe the types and range of performance that the majority of pupils should characteristically demonstrate by the end of the key stage, having been taught the relevant programme of study. The descriptions are designed to help teachers judge the extent to which their pupils' attainment relates to this expectation. The expectation at the end of key stage 3 matches the level of demand in other subjects and is broadly equivalent to levels 5 and 6.

Key stage 3

Pupils have a broad knowledge and understanding of the topical events they study; the rights, responsibilities and duties of citizens; the role of the voluntary sector; forms of government; provision of public services; and the criminal and legal systems. They show understanding of how the public gets information and how opinion is formed and expressed, including through the media. They show understanding of how and why changes take place in society. Pupils take part in school and community-based activities, demonstrating personal and group responsibility in their attitudes to themselves and others.

Key stage 4

Students have a comprehensive knowledge and understanding of the topical events they study; the rights, responsibilities and duties of citizens; the role of the voluntary sector; forms of government; and the criminal and civil justice, legal and economic systems. They obtain and use different kinds of information, including the media, to form and express an opinion. They evaluate the effectiveness of different ways of bringing about change at different levels of society. Students take part effectively in school- and community based activities, showing a willingness and commitment to evaluate such activities critically. They demonstrate personal and group responsibility in their attitudes to themselves and others.

Framework for post-16 citizenship learning

ESSENTIAL OPPORTUNITIES	CITIZENSHIP LEARNING OBJECTIVES	EXAMPLES OF CITIZENSHIP ACTIONS	EXAMPLES OF CITIZENSHIP ACTIVITIES
Post-16 citizenship should give young people opportunities to: • identify, investigate and think critically about citizenship issues, problems or events of concern to them and • decide on and take part in follow-up action, where appropriate and • reflect on, recognise and review their citizenship learning.	**Citizenship learning increases young people's knowledge, skills and understanding so they are able to:** • demonstrate knowledge and understanding about citizenship issues • show understanding of key citizenship concepts (for example rights and responsibilities, government and democracy, identities and communities) • consider the social, moral and ethical issues applying to a particular situation • analyse sources of information, identify bias and draw conclusions • demonstrate understanding of and respect for diversity and challenge prejudice and discrimination • discuss and debate citizenship issues • express and justify a personal opinion to others • represent a point of view on behalf of others • demonstrate skills of negotiation and participation in community-based activities • exercise responsible actions towards and on behalf of others.	**Citizenship actions involve young people using skills of enquiry, communication, participation and responsible action to:** • discuss and debate citizenship issues • make a change • challenge an injustice • lobby representatives • increase representation • provide a service or benefit to others • empower self or others • resist unwanted change • make informed choices and follow up decisions and/or actions • take part in democratic processes to influence decisions.	**Citizenship activities involve young people working with others on issues such as:** • writing and/or presenting a case to others about a concern or issue • conducting a consultation, vote or election • organising a meeting, conference, forum, debate or vote • representing others' views (for example in an organisation, at a meeting or event) • creating, reviewing and revising an organisational policy • contributing to local/community policy • communicating and expressing views publicly via a newsletter, website or other media • organising and undertaking an exhibition, campaign or display • setting up and developing an action group or network • organising a community event (for example drama, celebration, open day) • training others (for example, in citizenship skills and knowledge, democratic processes).

QCA, **Play Your Part: post-16 citizenship**, 2004

Appendix 7

Revised school self-evaluation matrix for citizenship education

The matrix below can be used by subject departments or by the whole staff to evaluate the implementation and progress of citizenship education in a school, to set priorities for carrying forward the citizenship agenda and to identify areas of need for continuing professional development. It is a revised version of *The School Self-Evaluation Tool for Citizenship Education*, described in chapter 8.

	FOCUSING	DEVELOPING	ESTABLISHED	ADVANCED
1 Vision and policy into practice				
2 Resources and their management				
3 Teaching and learning				
4 Staff development				
5 Student participation				
6 Parental and community involvement				

Organisations that help

There is a range of specialist organisations that can provide help with training and development in citizenship education, including:

- Association for Citizenship Teaching
  www.teachingcitizenship.org.uk
  A member organisation for anyone involved in citizenship education; publishes the journal *Teaching Citizenship* once a term, offers advice, training and support, and a website with a forums facility for debate and the exchange of ideas, as well as annual conferences.

- Centre for Citizenship and Human Rights Education
  www.education.leeds.ac.uk/research/cchre/
  Based at the University of Leeds; focuses on research, consultancy and postgraduate studies relating to citizenship and human rights education, with an emphasis on issues of ethnic diversity, race equality and children's rights; welcomes the involvement of institutions and professionals.

- Centre for Citizenship Studies in Education
  www.le.ac.uk/education/centres/citizenship/
  Based at the University of Leicester; focuses on teaching, research and curriculum development relating to citizenship education and social inclusion; continual professional development is a special area of interest.

- Centre for Global Education
  www.yorksj.ac.uk
  Based at York St John College; supports teachers in the introduction of global issues into the school curriculum; runs a resource centre with free access for local students and teachers.

- Changemakers
  www.changemakers.org.uk
  Dedicated to the promotion of young person-led community action; offers advice, consultancy and training on empowering young people to run community action projects; runs the Active Citizenship in Schools Award (ACiS) with ContinYou, supported by the DfES; currently developing a model to link active citizenship with enterprise education.

- Citizenship Foundation
  www.citizenshipfoundation.org.uk
  Publishes classroom materials for primary and secondary schools and for young people with particular needs such as students in PRUs (Pupil Referral Units) and in the youth justice system; undertakes research and development in citizenship education; runs competitions for schools – e.g. mock trials, youth parliament, political journalism – and action projects such as Youth Act and Giving Nation; provides training materials and programmes for primary and secondary teachers and others, including bespoke training on request; website contains general information on citizenship education, teaching resources and many links.

- Community Service Volunteers (CSV)
  www.csv.org.uk
  Promotes volunteering across all age groups and supports high-quality active citizenship projects in schools, including peer mentoring and buddying schemes; publishes teaching and training materials and offers bespoke training on request.

- Hansard Society
  www.hansardsociety.org.uk
  Dedicated to promoting effective parliamentary democracy; runs the youth participation websites Being Heard and HeadsUp; provides teacher resource packs and in-depth courses and study days for organisations and individuals who want to know more about politics and parliament.

- Institute for Citizenship
  www.citizen.org
  Publishes teaching and training materials, particularly on democratic participation, economic and European citizenship; runs a strong active citizenship programme of training for young people; provides bespoke training for teachers on request.

- Institute for Global Ethics
  www.globalethics.org
  Dedicated to raising the quality of ethical decision-making in private and public domains; supports citizenship in schools through teaching materials on moral decision-making and training teachers in appropriate methodologies; with the Citizenship Foundation, runs the Impetus Award, which recognises the achievement of young people promoting human rights values in schools and communities.

- National Centre for Citizenship and the Law
  www.nccl.org.uk
  Provides interactive citizenship activities for young people, supported by resource packs; arranges special programmes for PGCE students and other adults.

- Parliamentary Education Unit
  www.parliament.uk/directories/educationunity.cfm
  Provides resources about the work of parliament; answers enquiries from teachers and students; will visit schools and conferences.

- School Councils UK (SCUK)
  www.schoolcouncils.org
  Provides training on many aspects of running school councils in both primary and secondary schools; trains students as well as teachers – runs a 'train the trainers' programme.

Key publications

Official

DfES/QCA (1999) *National Curriculum Citizenship*, London: DfES

DfES (2004) *Every Child Matters: change for children*, London: DfES

DfES (2004) *Every Child Matters: change for children in schools*, London: DfES

DfES (2004) *Making Citizenship Education Real* (Citizenship Education Longitudinal Study: Second Annual Report), London: NFER

DfES (2004) *The School Self-Evaluation Tool for Citizenship Education*, London: DfES

DfES (2004) *Working Together – giving children and young people a say*, London: DfES

DfES (2005) *Listening to Young People: Citizenship Education in England* (Citizenship Education Longitudinal Study: Second Cross-Sectional Survey), London: NFER

Further Education Funding Council (2000) *Citizenship For 16–19 Year-Olds In Education And Training* (Report of the Advisory Group to the Secretary of State for Education and Employment), Coventry: The Further Education Funding Council

Learning and Skills Development Agency (2005) *Make It Happen: effective practice in post-16 citizenship* (video resource pack), London: LSDA

QCA (1998) *Education for Citizenship and the Teaching of Democracy in Schools* (The Crick Report), London: QCA

QCA (2000) *Curriculum guidance for the foundation stage*, London: QCA

QCA (2001) *Citizenship: a scheme of work for key stage 3*, London: QCA

QCA: (2001) *Citizenship at Key Stage 3: getting involved – extending opportunities for pupil participation*, London: QCA

QCA (2002) *Citizenship: a scheme of work for key stages 1 and 2*, London: QCA

QCA (2002) *Citizenship: a scheme of work for key stage 4*, London: QCA

QCA (2002) *Citizenship at Key Stages 1–4: guidance on assessment, recording and reporting*, London: QCA

QCA (2002) *Citizenship at Key Stages 1 and 2: taking part – developing opportunities for children to participate*, London: QCA

QCA: (2002) *Citizenship at Key Stage 4: staying involved – extending opportunities for pupil participation*, London: QCA

QCA (2004) *Play Your Part: post-16 citizenship*, London: QCA

Other

Claire, H., Tanner, J. & Whitworth, L. (eds.) (2004) *Teaching Citizenship in Primary Schools*, Exeter: Learning Matters

Gearon, L. (ed.) (2003) *Learning to Teach Citizenship in the Secondary School*, London: RoutledgeFalmer

Jerome, L., Hayward, J., Easy, J., Turner, A.N. (2003) *The Citizenship Co-ordinator's Handbook*, Institute for Citizenship/Nelson Thornes

Rowe, D. (2001) *Introducing Citizenship* (video and manual for primary schools), London: A&C Black

Rowe, D. (2005) *Citizenship – Raising the Standard: identifying good practice in secondary citizenship education* (DVD and manual), London: Citizenship Foundation/Connect Publications

Teaching Citizenship – official magazine of the Association for Citizenship Teaching, Questions Publishing

Acknowledgements

p.i Professor Sir Bernard Crick, *The Crick Report*, 1998; **p.1** Professor Sir Bernard Crick, *National Curriculum Citizenship*, 1999; **p.4** Lord Chancellor, 1998; **p.4** David, Youthcomm, *Citizenship News*; **p.5** Stephen Twigg, Former Education Minister; **p.12** David Bell, Chief Inspector of Schools, 2005; **p.15** Emma Valerio, *Advice to a Primary School*, London Metropolitan University, 2004; **p.16** Unicef and Save the Children, *Time for Rights*, 2002; **p.18** Hampshire County Council, *Citizenship Education: A planning framework for citizenship in schools*, 1998; **p.21** Ofsted, 2002; **p.22** Dame Mavis Grant, Headteacher, Canning School, Newcastle-upon-Tyne; **p.27** Lorna Reed, Headteacher, Wroxham School, *TES* (*Times Educational Supplement*), 14 March 2003; **p.31** Susan Barker, Headteacher, St Peter's CE Primary School, Wallsend; **p.33** Framework for PSHE and citizenship at Key Stage 2; **p.38** Case study of Wroxham Primary School, **p.38** Case study of St Peter's CE Primary School, Wallsend; **p.40** and **194** Hilary Claire and Cathie Holden, *Effective Transition KS2 to KS3* (www.citized.info); **p.41** adapted from the QCA booklet, *Citizenship at Key Stages 1-4: guidance on assessment, recording and reporting*, 2002; **p.42** from an idea by Roy Honeybone, editor, *Teaching Citizenship*; **p.43** Peter Brett, St. Martin's College, Lancaster, *Teaching Citizenship*, 2004; **p.44** DfES, 2003; **p.45** from the DfES and QCA key stage 3 strategy document, *Designing the Key Stage 3 Curriculum*; **p.50** Ofsted, 2004; **p.51**, **53, 122, 124, 126** and **142** Ofsted, 2003; **p.58** Penketh High School, Warrington, Culcheth High School, Warrington, Trinity High School, Redditch; **p.59** Swanshurst School, Birmingham; **p.62** QCA Key Stage 3 scheme of work for citizenship, 2003 (from an original idea by Chris Waller); **p.75** and **203** South Dartmoor Community College, Devon; **p.80** Hazel Grove High School, Stockport; **p.82** David Bell, Chief Inspector of Schools, 2005; **p.82** Torney-Purta et al., *Citizenship and Education in Twenty-Eight Countries: civic knowledge and engagement at age fourteen*, 2002; **p.84** UN Convention of the Rights of the Child; **p.87** Lawrence Sheriff School, Warwickshire; **p.88** DfES 2004; **p.90** Sarah Purtil, Kingsbury High School, in *TES* (*Times Educational Supplement*), 14 February 2003; **p.90** Pete Pattison, Citizenship Co-ordinator, Deptford Green School, London; **p.92** St Christopher's Special School, Wrexham; **p.93** Frederick Gough School, Bottesford; **p.94** Hastingsbury Upper School, Bedford; **p.98** Community Service Volunteers; **p.99** www.dfes.gov.uk/citizenship; **p.101** Solway Community School, Cumbria; **p.102** Altrincham Girls Grammar School; **p.114** Deptford Green School, London; **p.119, 160** and **166** QCA, 2003; **p.120** Kevin Newman, St Andrews Boys School, West Sussex; **p.123** DfES, *Citizenship Education in Your School: an update for school governors*, 2005; **p.124** Citizenship Education Longitudinal Study Report, NFER, 2004; **p.140** Royton and Crompton School, Oldham; **p.151** *Working Inside the Blackbox: Assessment for learning in the classroom*, 2002, London: DEPS; **p.161** adapted from www.aaia.org.uk (The Association of Achievement and Improvement through Assessment); **pp162-3** David Coulson-Lawes, Caldew School, Cumbria; **p.165** adapted from QCA, *Citizenship at Key Stages 1-4: guidance on assessment, recording and reporting*, 2002; **p.167** Advisory Group on Citizenship for 16-19 year olds in Education and Training; **p.168** Richmond College; **p.168** Richard Jackson, Chief Executive, Camden Jobtrain, in *Citizenship News*, October 2003; **p.171** Gosforth High School, Newcastle-upon-Tyne; **p.172** HYA Training Limited, Exmouth Community College, Oldham Sixth Form College, Merton College; **p.173** Hospitality Plus, B6 Sixth Form College, Hackney, Training for Life, Oval Centre, The City of Bristol College, Whalley Range High School, Manchester; **p.174, 190** QCA, 2004; **p.175** Richmond upon Thames College, London; **p.178** FEFC (Further Education Funding Council), Citizenship for 16-19 Year Olds in Education and Training; **p.179** Glenn Harvey, Course Leader, Entry Level Citizenship Studies, Aylesbury College; **p.181** City of Bristol College; **p.182** Kate Scully, DAFBY Programme Leader; **p.182** DfES, *Transforming Youth Work*; **p.184-5** Oldham College and Oldham Sixth Form College; **p.186-7** DAFBY – Democratic Action for Bath and North East Somerset Youth; **p.188** Hounslow Manor School; **p.190** Letchworth Community Education Trust; **p.191** Aylesbury High School, Buckinghamshire; **p.195** Peter Hayes, CSV; **p.197** Peter Brett, St Martin's College, Lancaster; **p.198** Chris Waller, ACT, **p.198** NFER, Citizenship Education Longitudinal Study Annual Report 2005; **p.204** Southfields Technology College, Workington; **p.225** QCA, *Play Your Part: post-16 citizenship*, 2004.